English Leadership

ENGLISH LEADERSHIP

ENGLISH LEADINGS IN MODERN HISTORY

AN ESSAY BY

JOSEPHUS NELSON LARNED

WITH AN INTRODUCTION BY

WILLIAM HOWARD TAFT

The Geographic Factor in English History

BY DONALD E. SMITH

English Contributions to Scientific Thought

AND

The English Gift to World Literature

BY GRACE F. CALDWELL

Essay Index Reprint Series

BOOKS FOR LIBRARIES PRESS
FREEPORT, NEW YORK

First Published 1918
Reprinted 1969

STANDARD BOOK NUMBER:
8369-1416-3

LIBRARY OF CONGRESS CATALOG CARD NUMBER:
70-93353

PRINTED IN THE UNITED STATES OF AMERICA

FOREWORD

In these days, when peace has appeared in the offing of the harbor of our hopes, when the day of judgment for nations and institutions is imminent, in days when the great alliance of all English-speaking peoples in a common cause, for a common ideal, has brought to them as never before a realization of their common inheritance and of their common effort toward the same social end,—at such a time it seems peculiarly fitting to bring to light a manuscript on "English Leadings in Modern History," written before the war by the late J. N. Larned, presenting the claims of the English peoples to the gratitude of a democratic world.

The incomplete form in which the manuscript was left at Mr. Larned's death necessitated a careful revision and the addition of some new material. For this editorial work the publishers obtained the services of Grace F. Caldwell. The editor has taken all possible care to preserve Mr. Larned's meaning intact; all corrections or changes have been made solely for the purpose of clarifying and enforcing the meaning which the author himself intended to convey. The additional material inserted by the editor is distinguished from the original text by inclosure in brackets. The footnotes citing other works in support of, or in contrast with, the opinions of the author show to what a remarkable degree his scholarship stands the test of comparison with later authorities.

The purpose of the author is best expressed in his own words: "I do not intend to speak boastfully of the English peoples (under which racial name I include the English-speaking peoples of America as well as the English of Great Britain), although I shall uphold large claims for them, of preëminent leadership in most of the modern movements of human advance. Such claims are indisputable, but I find them to be grounded as much, at least, on the influence of helpful circumstances in history as on the working of qualities that are peculiar to the English race. Hence a boastful account of English leadings in modern history would be inconsistent with my views. . . . This may all have been done before, in an equally concise way, but I have no knowledge of a similar tracing of the facts on their several lines, and I have thought them too interesting, at least, to be left in neglect. I will put no interpretation upon them,—attempt to give them no meaning, but leave them to bear to those who read this essay whatever significance they may."

In Mr. Larned's "English Leadings in Modern History," the theme of English leadership along one line, the political, is very carefully and broadly worked out; but the suddenness of his death in 1913 prevented him from carrying out what was obviously his purpose,—to trace out not only one but several lines of English leadership. In order that this end might be attained, the publishers have included in this volume an introductory essay on "English Political Genius" by William Howard Taft, and three other essays grouped about Mr. Larned's—one by Donald E. Smith on "The Geographic Factor in English History," the other two by Grace F. Caldwell on "English Contributions to Scientific Thought" and "The English Gift to World Literature." In the selection and arrangement of this material the publishers have attempted to secure unity by keeping close to the fundamental idea in Mr. Larned's work, "English Leadings in Modern History."

THE PUBLISHERS.

1918

CONTENTS

Introduction

ENGLISH POLITICAL GENIUS

William Howard Taft

INTRODUCTION

ENGLISH POLITICAL GENIUS

REPRESENTATIVE popular government and civil liberty are the benefits which England has conferred upon the world. A study of their growth is full of interest. It began in the forests of Germany, with the Angles and Saxons before they invaded England, and has continued, for many centuries, down to the present world struggle for their successful maintenance and supremacy. For a time in this war the cause of free institutions seemed to hang in the balance. Now, although there is much of the battle yet to fight, its ultimate victory is assured. It is well always, but now more than ever, to tell, chapter by chapter, the wonderful story of the hammering out by Englishmen, in more than a thousand years, of the links of the chain that now hold government subject to the will of the people, and the purpose of government to the maintenance of individual freedom and equality of opportunity.

Mr. Larned, one-time Librarian of the Buffalo

Library, gave his life to the study of history, and has left works of far greater volume and scope than the treatise to which this is the introduction. But while a detailed account of the various eras in England's history is most important for the serious students who have the time and inclination to master the events, and to fit them into the mosaic of each century's progress, it may be questioned whether for the mass of men he does not serve a more useful purpose who reduces to a brief survey the course of the great events in the making of civil liberty and representative government so that the busy man may read it, and by reason of its trenchant description and its emphasis in proper proportion, he can carry the summary in his mind permanently for constant use. This is what Mr. Larned has done in the essay entitled "English Leadings in Modern History."

Instead of reviewing the admirable and interesting essay in which Mr. Larned has traced from their Teutonic home the work of the English people in hammering out a government of the people, by the people and for the people, I commend to every lover of liberty regulated by law a reading of the essay itself. Its perspicuous style, its happy arrangement, and its sense of proportion will fix in his mind permanently the main and retainable steps in the most remarkable story in secular history of the growth of a germinal idea through a bitter, hard and discouraging struggle of twelve centuries to the rule of the people by representative institutions, which secure to them individual liberty, and equality of opportunity in the pursuit of happiness.

Mr. Larned has pointed out that Montesquieu wrote his book on the "Spirit of the Laws" in the 18th century while the transfer of the executive power from the King to a responsible Cabinet was going on. His admiration and approval of the English form of government were based on its division into three branches,—the executive in the King, the legislative in Parliament, and the judicial in the courts. It was under the influence of Montesquieu, too, and of the framework of the British constitution at that time that our own Federal Constitution was framed and adopted, in which the executive power, independent of Congress in most respects, was vested in an elected President, and his power separated with much care from that of the legislative branch, and from that of the judiciary. Since then, as we have seen, the legislative and executive branches are united under one control. This introduction is not the place to discuss the advantages and disadvantages of the two systems. Many have claimed that the English system makes the administration of the government more responsive to the people's will because a majority in the House of Commons may turn out a government at any time, whereas a President holds office for four years, no matter how popular opinion may change in the meantime. But this argument is not quite fair. The change of executive in England is not necessarily responsive to the will of the people and the electorate. It is responsive to the change of opinion of the existing members of the Parliament who have been elected on issues involving bitter partisanship and who are quite likely to continue their support of the Cabinet they established long after the people may wish them out of office.

A Parliament may last five years, should the majority therein desire it. Our Congress must be renewed in the House of Representatives and in one-third of the Senate every two years. It is, therefore, open to argument which form of government is more quickly responsive to the ultimate wish of the people, but both, practically and in the long run, accord with their rule.

Mr. Larned does not deal specifically, however, with the growth of English civil liberty and individual freedom, except as that is effected by free representative institutions and the rule of the people in government. Side by side with the development of such institutions and indeed as a part of it, was the growth of a bill of rights. The four important fundamental instruments in which it is found are the Magna Carta, the Petition of Right, the *Habeas Corpus* Act and the Bill of Rights of 1688. It is most interesting to note that the bills of right in modern constitutions derived from British precedent are not confined to mere declarations of the value of individual liberty; they are not mere formal monitions to those responsible for government, directing that they be just and fair and impartial in the protection of individual rights; they are usually not declarations of substantive law. They, most of them, relate to procedure—they are adjective law. They grew in English history out of the necessities of actual abuses of power. They are the machinery by which the self-reliant and independent individual is offered the opportunity to vindicate his right and to secure it by invoking the action of an independent and courageous judiciary sworn to carry out the guaranteed procedure to determine whether the rights of the individual are being violated, and, if so, to cure the wrong. It will be observed that the great principle of Magna Carta that "no man shall be deprived of life, liberty or property without due process of law," is not a declaration that he shall not be unjustly deprived of either—it is only a direction that he shall have his hearing and due procedure before losing anything which he claims either as property, liberty or life. This is no covenant insuring him justice. It only gives to him the machinery by which he will probably secure justice. He is to have his day in court, and he is to have a judgment by an impartial tribunal. Take the *Habeas Corpus* Act of 1679, enacted by Parliament even under the Stuart, "who never said a foolish thing and never did a wise one." That act made it the sworn duty of a judge appealed to to look into the legality of the detention of any subject of the King, to issue a writ, called the writ of *Habeas Corpus,* and bring the person of the prisoner into court and there investigate the legality of his custody. Either the prisoner or a friend might invoke the action of the court. It was a writ of high privilege, and a Judge who refused to issue it when his action was properly sought by a petition, was subject to heavy penalty. Other guaranties of liberty were the hearing before the Grand Jury before a man could be indicted for infamous crimes, and the trial before a petit jury before a man could be convicted. In the course of softening the cruel severities of the common law of crimes, the judges threw around the defendant the protection of many rules of procedure calculated to save him from unjust convictions which have now been embodied in our Federal Constitution as a part of our modern bills of rights.

As our Federal bill of rights is embodied in a written constitution which it is the function of the Courts to interpret and enforce in cases brought before it, even as against an act of Congress, it has had more judicial exposition by our Supreme Court than these same guarantees had in English Courts. In England Parliament is omnipotent and can violate the Bill of Rights at will. Not so Congress whose lawmaking is limited by the Constitution. This circumstance has given at least one of our guarantees a wider effect than it had at common law. The declaration that "no man shall be deprived of life, liberty or property without due process of law" meant in the Magna Carta and means in English Courts that the process must be one sanctioned by custom, i. e., by the common law or by act of Parliament. It is directed only against executive abuses of individual right. In our Constitution, in its 5th and 14th amendments, it means more than this. It is directed against both executive and legislative abuses of individual right, against abuses by Congress and state legislatures as well as against those of a President or a Governor. Therefore, the Supreme Court has not hesitated to ignore as invalid any law of Congress or a state which does not secure to an individual the procedure in defending his rights which shall prevent his deprivation of them arbitrarily and without a full hearing by some kind of a tribunal.

These guaranties of civil liberty in the English constitution are a part of the common law and were formulated as part of it. They were not framed by a theorist in government. They are not part of a magnificent system of law, admirably arranged, comprehensively stated and logically framed, like the civil law. The civil law is a beautiful system. It has come down from the Roman law, and has been worked over and over until in modern times it finds its most beautiful expression in the Code Napoleon and the kindred codes of other civil law countries. As a scientific exposition of law, the civil law is superior to the common law. The common law is not a code—it has been worked out by special instances through decisions of courts in thousands and hundreds of thousands of cases. It has been established by custom of the realm and interpreted by courts and finally formulated by them.

Tennyson's characterization of it, where he speaks of

> "the lawless science of our law,—
> That codeless myriad of precedent,
> That wilderness of single instances,"

has much of truth in it.

And yet for many centuries it has served the purpose of the English people and of those who have derived their civilization from the English people, and it has done so because it has reflected the practical character of those peoples and the practical way in which they have made the rules of action to be enforced as law.

Mr. Larned makes reference to the independence of the judiciary established at the end of the 17th century, but he does not dwell upon it. That was a most important step in making good the guaranties of the Bill of Rights. Under the Stuarts, and indeed in all previous reigns, judges had been appointed to serve during the pleasure of the King. Under the influence of the revolution of 1688, and by the acts of settlement soon thereafter passed, judges ceased to hold office during the pleasure of the King, and were given a tenure during their good behavior. At first this tenure was only during the life of the King whose commission they held, but by a subsequent legislation in one of the Georges, the tenure was made independent of the King appointing, and they served, as they now do, for life. The effect of this independent tenure upon the judiciary of England can hardly be overestimated. There is nothing more greatly to the honor of English civilization than the high character of England's courts and the confidence that the English people have in the ability, learning and impartiality of their judges. The jury system gives to the people the certainty that in issues of life and liberty an impartial panel of the countrymen of the accused will be summoned to take part in the decision of his case, and in England the jury system, with the assistance of the judges of the court, has had wonderful success. Justice is not delayed, the criminal laws are enforced with admirable dispatch and the results command the confidence of the nation. Of course this has not always been so. Even in England the administration of justice came to be laden with abuses of delay and heavy costs so that when Queen Victoria came to the throne one could not speak of the working of the English administration of justice in any such terms as I have used. If one would see how deplorable was the condition of the courts upon the accession of Victoria, he should read Lord Bowen's description of the improvement in the administration of justice during the half century celebrated in the Queen's Jubilee. The reforms were effected by the leaders of the bar and the judiciary, and now there is no system of courts in the world so admirably conducted as that we find in England. She continues to set a model before the world in this regard.

One of the lessons that must be taught, however, in respect to English liberty, English representative institutions, and English administration of justice, is that the success of them all must rest on the political capacity of the individuals of the English people to understand their institutions, to realize their responsibility for the successful working of them, and to feel that the Government under which they are living is their government and entails upon them the duty of keeping it pure and clean and effective. Those of us who are properly enthusiastic and grateful for the inestimable boon of civil liberty of English origin that we enjoy are apt to assume that it is a benefit which can be conferred upon any people and enjoyed by them to their very great advantage, no matter what their history, their education and their previous experience in government. This is a fundamental error. Self-government is a boon which people must properly prepare themselves to carry on. As President Wilson has said in his book on "Constitutional Government," self-government is character and can only be acquired after hard experience in attempting it. Take the peculiar institution of English liberty—the petit jury. It is exceedingly hard to inject that into the judicial system of a country brought up under Spanish antecedents and traditions, and especially in a community like the Philippines conducted as a Spanish colony. Were intelligent Filipinos summoned to a jury to sit in a case, they would doubtless understand the evidence and possibly reach a sound conclusion as to the bearing of the evidence, but what they would fail to bring into the jury box would be the feeling of responsibility with which they should approach the decision of the question. They would not appreciate that the proceeding was part of their government, that they were of the government, and that the proper administration of justice was something for which they were individually responsible. They would look upon the government as something different from themselves, something antagonistic to themselves, something which must look out for itself in achieving results in its administration. A law-breaker escaping in such a country would never be apprehended by the unofficial members of the community. They would regard that as the business of the sheriff or of a police officer. They could not understand the obligation of the hue and cry for the capture of an escaping thief or murderer. They would look upon the contest with indifference. Such an attitude toward government deeply ingrained by its history and treatment of its people must be overcome before the people may successfully take part in the administration of justice through a jury system and before indeed they can hope successfully to make a representative government useful to the people. Therefore, when we speak of a Republic in China or a Republic in Russia, we must be patient with its faults, with its deficiencies, with its failures, and must realize that only by the hardest kinds of knocks can a people learn the character needed to make self-government a success. This is not an argument against their beginning. This is not an argument for the maintenance of tyranny anywhere, but it is an appeal to reason and common sense in our optimistic expectations as to working of a popular representative government by a people who are utterly ignorant of self-restraint and sense of responsibility. These the great body of a people must have before the benefits of self-government can be really manifested and enjoyed.

A characteristic of the growth of English liberty and of free representative institutions was its conservative character. When a reform was to be brought about, when an evil presented itself so acutely that something had to be done to remedy it, Englishmen did not break down the whole system of their government and rebuild it. They merely added something to the structure to supply the need or repair the defect. That is the reason why their statutes are nothing but patchwork. That is the reason why such written laws do not commend themselves to any lawgiver trained under the civil law system; but that is also the reason why they work. The changes have been based on the existing structure and system and the variation is as slight as the purpose of it requires. The resulting edifice is like an old house added to as the needs of the family require it, as the attacks of the elements show its weaknesses, as modern necessities develop its needed changes. The lines of such a house do not satisfy the eye of the trained architect, but for living purposes the association between the past and the present strengthens the affection of the owner for the house and gives to his living therein the ineffable comfort and loyalty of tradition and association. The House of Lords has been an excrescence on the body democratic of the English Government. It has at times furnished what our written constitution interpreted by the Supreme Courts gives to us. The House of Lords has taken under its own control the maintenance of the British constitution. Its hereditary and Tory proclivities have made it a certain refuge where popular storms have threatened a breach. But by reason of its reactionary opposition to reform bills, to home rule, to the continued expression of popular will in House of Commons majorities, the people of England finally became convinced that a change was necessary. Now in France, or in other countries where popular changes are possible, the House of Lords would have been abolished—not so in England. In 1911 a change was made, and possibly more radical changes were foreshadowed. But the House of Lords was retained. It must act upon money bills within a month after their reception or they become law, and if after two years and three sessions of Parliament the Lords fail to pass a bill which has passed the Commons three times, it becomes a law upon the royal signature. The royal signature is another instance of the way in which old forms are retained which have lost their substantial significance. A bill which passes both Houses of Parliament needs the royal signature to make it law. It has not been withheld for 200 years, although the letter of English law seems to give the sovereign the right to sign or not as he chooses. Should he fail to sign to-day, however, it would deprive him of his throne.

The government of England was united with that of Scotland and with that of Ireland into the government of Great Britain. The union with Scotland has been completely successful. Scotland has retained her courts, her religion and her local community governments, and has found it possible to live contentedly under a Parliament in which it has had its proportionate representation of members. The relations between England and Ireland, however, up to the last half century were one of the great blots upon English history. The difference in race and the difference in religion united to create a misgovernment of Ireland by England down to recent times, so unlike England's treatment of her colonies since the American Revolution as to call down upon her statesmen the severest criticism. The natural economic disadvantages of Ireland were greatly increased by restrictive trade legislation in favor of English manufactures and agriculture impoverished the Irish tenant farmer and limited Irish manufactures to such a degree that the desertion of Ireland by all her people who could migrate was the only logical result. In the last half century, however, English statesmen have sought to reverse this policy and to encourage Irish agriculture and Irish industries by governmental aid. In no country has such governmental aid been as successful as it has been in Ireland, and it is noteworthy that during this war, from an economic standpoint, the Irish farmer is more prosperous than the English farmer. But meantime, through the stubbornness and unreasonable attitude of a comparatively small part of the Irish people, the Home Rule and local self-government which the Irish people have demanded, and which the English people have been willing to grant, has been halted, and even in this great war, which should awaken in Irishmen the patriotic support of the English and the world cause, a feeling of bitterness has again grown up against the British Government, which adds another grievous burden to its already many burdens in fighting this war. The Irish question has been like the shirt of Nessus for England, and she is paying now in the bitterest form the penalty for her injustice of the past.

In her colonial governments, England stands

unrivaled in her success in the world. They are of two kinds. One is of those communities settled by the British in Canada, in Australia, in New Zealand, South Africa—self-governing dominions that have not severed their relation to the mother country and have enjoyed in the arrangement of their own affairs an independence wisely granted by the home government, so that as the tie between them has grown lighter, the mutual affection has been strengthened. No higher or better evidence could be given of this than the wonderful sacrifices that Canada, Australia, New Zealand and South Africa have made in this world war in defense of their mother country. It is one of the most inspiring features of the war to note how strong this bond between England and her daughters has been, and how nobly they have responded to their filial obligation.

England began her colonial enterprises with the same spirit as that of other nations, for the purpose of extending her trade and exploiting the colonies, which she created either by conquest or settlement. We of the United States may claim to have taught England a wiser and a more altruistic policy in dealing with her dependencies. When she attempted to circumscribe the activities, energies and enterprise of her own children on this continent, and sought to tax them, without a voice in their government, she found the same stuff in them of which her own people had given so many evidences in times past. The colonies loved the mother country, were really attached to it, and only made their declaration of independence after a year of revolt. The English people were themselves divided in respect to the wisdom of their policy, and it is the truth to say that the Americans were forced to revolution through the tyrannical narrowness and blind obstinacy of George III, who, exercising his control of Parliament by corruption and patronage, was able to carry this fatal policy through to its logical conclusion. Chatham, Fox and Burke and other far-sighted British statesmen saw the blunder, but could not avert it. There has been a discussion as to whether England did change her colonial policy as a result of the American Revolution. It seems to me that in this case the argument *post hoc procter hoc* is a legitimate one, and that no matter what the detailed study of the local currents of politics may indicate, the lesson in the severance of the United States from Great Britain manifested itself in all the action of England thereafter toward her colonies. Her consideration for the French Canadians, her very liberal treatment of Canada in its growth to its present national proportions, and her generous support of the somewhat radical political development of Australia and New Zealand, are illustrations. Her not altogether consistent policy in South Africa has finally flowered into one of wisdom and generosity after a grievous war in respect to which her motives were misrepresented, and into which she was plunged by the unjust and oppressive policy of the Boer Government toward many of her own subjects engaged in the development of all that territory. A study of the British North America Act, the Australian constitution, and the act constituting the British South African Government, and a comparison of these fundamental instruments with the Constitution of the United States, is interesting to show the influence of the British Constitution and of the Federal Constitution upon these young Republics, and to demonstrate the wise absence on the part of the Home British Government of any effort to restrain the political proposals of a majority of the people in each Dominion. The actual governmental connection between these Dominions and the Home Government has been diminished to small proportions. The Home Government sends to each a representative, who is the nominal chief executive, and under whom the local Premier and Cabinet, selected by the legislative body, actually administer affairs. There is usually an appeal as of course from the decision of the highest courts in the Dominions to the Judicial Committee of the Privy Council in England, but even this in some cases, as in Australia, is left in an important class of cases to the discretion of the court to be appealed from. The Home Government retains, of course, control in foreign affairs, but wherever the separate or local interests of the Dominion are affected, the custom now has grown to be to give representation in the negotiation to the Dominion concerned, and rarely, if ever, to conclude negotiations without the consent of that Dominion. The dream of many British statesmen is Imperial Federation, which shall increase in Imperial matters the direct participation of the Dominions. This is in the process of formation, and the Dominions have given such an earnest, by their great and patriotic sacrifices in this war, of their interest in the English Empire and their contribution to its strength, that we may expect the settlement of the war to be followed by some important changes—changes which will give them a more direct voice in the British Empire than they now have by statutory or constitutional provision. In the construction of the government of these Dominions by the people themselves, with the consent of the home country, the principles of free representative institutions and the guarantees of British civil liberty have been made part of the web and woof of the life of these subjects of the British King. And even as in French Canada, where the civil law obtained and such guarantees were unknown under the French home government, they were fully extended under the ægis of the British constitution.

The French and Spanish and German colonies were governed from the colonial office in Paris, Madrid or Berlin, and have always been so, though the French colonial policy, far more successful than that of the others, has been liberalized of late years greatly to the advantage of her colonies.

In addition to these great republican dominions still acknowledging allegiance to Great Britain, she has a large number of Crown colonies, of which India is the greatest. In these colonies she is engaged in the business of governing native and backward peoples. The 300,000,000 of India, divided among Mohammedan, Buddhist and other eastern religions, have made a problem of government most difficult of solution. When England wrested control of India from France, in the Seven Years' War, under Pitt, she found kingdoms and peoples in a constant state of war. Under her East India Company much wrong was done, and much plundering in the name of that company. Gradually she restored peace, gradually with the transfer from the East India Company to the Crown, the spirit of government in India improved, and so, with a comparatively small military force, England has maintained, for now 150 years, her power in India. The antagonisms between the followers of Mohammed and Buddha have doubtless contributed to the solution of the problem, because each prefers the rule of Christian Great Britain to the rule of either. England has been charged with exploiting India for her own trade and benefit. That this was so in the past is probably true, but that her policy for years past has been one of great care of Indian interests, the fair commentator must admit. England has maintained her power in India, and maintains it to-day because of the confidence of those governed in her administration of justice. The Oriental peoples under her rule in India would not trust a system of justice administered wholly by their own people, but they have been taught by a century of experience that in an English court, and with an English judge, justice is not a mere theory and an empty declaration, but a real purpose and a real result.

The good that England has conferred on the world by her government of India cannot be overestimated. The extending of civilized life and its maintenance throughout that great empire is largely due to her and her statesmen. She has successfully maintained there a League to Enforce Peace. She has dealt liberally and tactfully with the customs and prejudices and religions of the people. Never until recently, however, have her statesmen thought it wise to extend any measure of self-government to the Indian people. They have been slow to offer the means of education to these hundreds of millions under them. Now they are setting out on a different policy, slowly and conservatively, as Englishmen move in political matters, but with more wisdom perhaps in this regard than we.

The effect of the American policy in the Philippines has been marked in India and has had an influence upon the liberal English Government in that country. In the Philippines we took over the Government with the avowed purpose of educating the Filipinos and fitting them for self-government, and there was, in my judgment, every augury of ultimate success, provided we did not force matters, provided we did not extend power to the Filipino politician too rapidly, and provided we retained in the government of the Philippines the body of trained American civil servants than whom there were no better anywhere. It is impossible to train for complete self-government the generation of Filipinos which lived under and felt the influence of Spanish social and political views and Spanish political methods. Time was needed to teach the Filipinos the English language that they might, through that as their speaking and reading tongue, acquire from American literature and newspapers a knowledge of free institutions. To do this doubtless two generations would be required. But America has given the Filipinos not more than half a generation for this purpose, and with the surrender of power it has, in my opinion, parted forever with the opportunity to make successful one of the most interesting experiments in preparation of an Oriental people for self-government that world history has ever presented. We may be sure that the far-seeing statesmen of Great Britain will profit by our blunder in this regard, and that in their extension of self-government to the East Indians they will go forward slowly and with a due regard to the actual progress of the people and their slowly growing capacity.

Mr. Larned, while he admits the strong qualities of the Teuton nature in the early English, and attributes to these traits something of the wonderful results, the causes of which he has been tracing, is disposed to minimize their influence upon the development of free representative institutions and civil liberty in England in comparison with the fortunate circumstances which he so luminously arrays and describes. I don't know that it is of any particular value or moment to attempt an apportionment of credit for results in a period of twelve centuries to human purpose and character on the one side, and to fortuitous circumstances, on the other. Be that as it may, the original rude strength of the Teutonic peoples, with the environment of the English, has made them a people leading the world in the cause of civil liberty and popular institutions of government, and these have in turn given to the English people a strength of national character and a sense of world responsibility which have prompted them in two great crises in the world's history to take over the burden of saving it from military tyranny and all the ills that would follow. No one can study the history of the French Revolution, the permanent benefits of which every student of history must recognize, without realizing that the rescue of the world from the military tyranny to which its excess by reaction led on was ultimately defeated by English pluck and English determination. The younger Pitt died in the dreadful shadow of the battle of Austerlitz, when the sun of that day seemed to crown the permanent glory of a military dictatorship of the world. But Pitt's purpose was taken up by his successors, by Canning and others, and through the military skill and sturdy high sense of duty of Nelson and Wellington, the greatest military leader of the world was brought to end his days in miserable captivity on an isolated rock in the Atlantic. Not that England did all this, but it was the constancy of England's purpose, the willingness of the English people to sacrifice men and treasure, and their intelligent sense of responsibility that made the formation of the various alliances before whom Napoleon had ultimately to bow the knee, possible. And so to-day, while every one admires the calm courage and the inspiring gallantry with which the French people have met the onslaught of the brutal military autocracy of Germany in its quest for the overlordship of the world, no one can justly deny to Great Britain her great agency in gathering together the forces making for the defeat of Germany. The load she has had to carry can hardly be overstated. She has not been subject to the dreadful devastation of an important part of her rich and industrial territory, as France has, but she has, as France has, offered up the flower of her youth in this war. With her great navy she has put an insuperable obstacle to German ambitions. She was as unprepared for land war as the United States was when it came into the struggle, and she has in England and in Scotland raised an army so large that if we in the United States were to make equal effort, it would give us a military force of 15,000,000 of men. She has carried on this war with Ireland refusing its proportionate support and requiring something of British strength to restrain revolt. For nearly four years she had to bear with the neutrality of the United States, though realizing that she was fighting the battles of that former daughter of hers. And she has done these things with a modesty in respect to her effort that is noteworthy. To France, to the people of her dominions, to the people of the United States, to the Navy of the United States, to the soldiers of the United States, she accords all praise; only once in a while, as in the wonderful speech of her Premier, Lloyd George, of August 7th, does she make clear in a moderate statement what she has done. That brilliant leader set out her sacrifices and her achievements without boasting, but in such a way as to give a due sense of proportion to the great and controlling part that she is playing in the war.

It is true that we of the United States are to win this war, but we are to win it only in the sense that a great military reserve, withheld from the battle and ultimately brought in fresh and strong, and unaffected by previous strain and loss, may carry the enemy's defenses and put him to flight. In the measure of credit for such a victory, he who would ignore the debt of gratitude due to the forces who during the heat and burden of the day have maintained the battle and created the situation in which the reserves can win, would indeed be an unjust historian. In view, therefore, of what Britain has done and is doing for the world in the cause of freedom and popular representative institutions, not only by making governments which work and preserve a consistency between efficiency and justice in government and the real rule of the people, but also in striking hard the blow needed to subdue abhorrent tyranny prompted by the lust of universal power, Britain has vindicated the beneficent influence of free institutions upon the spirit and usefulness of her people. But for them she could not and would not have done for the world what she has done in the cause of human civilization.

ENGLISH LEADINGS IN MODERN HISTORY

J. N. Larned

ENGLISH LEADINGS IN MODERN HISTORY

Conspicuously, before everything else, the English have been leaders in the political civilization of the world. Every notable feature of difference between the modern and the ancient organizations and institutions of government bears the stamp of an English origin or an English shaping into its practicable form. All civilized nations, to-day, have accepted or are accepting English solutions of the problem of government by the will or with the consent of the governed. Popular government by representation, deputized democracy, constitutionalized authority,—these are almost universal in the social order of the present day, because Englishmen found the way to success in them and showed it to the rest of mankind. Why have they been the people to do these things? They are not of a distinct race. They hold no gifts of faculty or power that are peculiar to their blood. Their near kinsfolk, of the great Teutonic family, are all around them in western Europe;

they have shared the same historic life of mediæval and modern times; and many of those kinsfolk were long before the English in turning from predatory and barbarizing to industrious and civilizing pursuits. In the general Teutonic character there are, without doubt, some faculties and some moral qualities that account for the development of our modern institutions of representative government somewhere within that family of peoples, rather than in any other racial group. It furnished the necessary stability of feeling and gravity of thinking; it gave the requisite balance between personal impulses and rational perceptions of social need. But, so far as can be known, this preparation of character for a new political evolution of society was originally just as ready in the tribes of the Franks when they entered Gaul, and in the tribes of the Alamanni when they settled on the opposite side of the Rhine, as it was in the Angles and the Saxons when their conquest of Britain was made. More surely still, it must have been ready among the Saxon tribes that stayed upon the Elbe, not less than among those that went colonizing across the North Sea. Why was it, then, that representative institutions of government grew up, from shire-moot to parliament, in the new home and not in the old home of Saxons, Angles and

Jutes? Why in England and not in the kingdoms of the Franks? Why did the "commons" of England come into partnership with the lords of the realm in the exercise of taxing and law-making powers, while the corresponding third-estate of continental western Europe was almost voiceless and valueless in history till nearly eighteen centuries of the Christian era were passed? I have said that the explanation of this remarkable distinction of the English can be found as much in the circumstances of their history as in capacities or qualities peculiar to themselves; I shall try to make that statement good.

Repeating words which I used once in another place—"The fundamental circumstance, which seems in itself to half explain English history, is, of course, the insularity of the nation.[1] . . . The shelter of the island from foreign interference and from surrounding perturbations was necessary to the evolution of the representative system of government, with supremacy in Parliament, responsibility in administration, security of just independence in courts; and not less necessary to a persisting growth of the industries, the trade, and the

[1] For discussion of the geographic factor in English history, see the essay on this subject by Donald E. Smith, in this volume.—Ed.

resulting wealth, on which the empire of Great Britain depends. In their

> 'fortress, built by Nature for herself,
> Against infection and the hand of war
> . . . set in the silver sea,
> Which serves it in the office of a wall,
> Or as a moat defensive to a house,
> Against the envy of less happier lands,'

the English have rejoiced in many and great advantages over every neighbor, and have used them with a capability that has wasted none. Protection from invasion is not more than half the blessed service their insulating sea has done them. It has also put a happy curb on greedy ambitions in their ministers and kings; kept them for nearly five hundred years from aggressive continental wars; moderated their share in the frictions, jealousies, neighborhood rivalries and dynastic entanglements of European politics, and in consequence has turned the energies of their ambition more profitably to the remoter fields of commerce and colonization. At the same time, by shutting out many distractions, it has held their more careful attention to domestic affairs. It has fostered self-reliance in the national spirit, and unity of belief in one another. If it has fostered, too, some narrow self-sufficiency and unteachable contentment with English ways, even those may have had value to the nation in time past, though losing their value now. By standing a little to one side of the movements of thought and feeling in continental Europe, the English have experienced a more independent development of mind and character, tending sometimes toward narrowness, but oftener to the broadening of lines."

A general and definite tracing, however, of causes to account for the leading agency of the English peoples in modern civilization, especially on its political side, must begin at a time prior to their entrance into the island of Great Britain,—prior, indeed, to their emergence into history as a people distinctly known; it must begin, rather, among obscurely placed ancestral members of the Teutonic family of tribes.

Among these Teutonic tribes as they were known to Tacitus, in the first century after Christ, there seem to have been germs of that remarkable coöperative combination of democracy with aristocracy, which the English have developed, in their political constitution, to its present perfected state. There was everywhere a recognized nobility of birth, derived generally from the fathers of each settlement, who had shared in the original parceling of homesteads, and in the original enjoyment of communal rights to the use of lands and woods which were the property of the tribe as a whole. The families of this social primacy,—the "old families" of each community,—had become an ennobled class, commanding the deference of the simple "freemen" of the tribe, who represented, in their parentage or in themselves, the later-comers, the *parvenus,* whose admission to homesteads and common rights had been an act of grace, so to speak, on the part of their predecessors in each village or mark. But no political superiority attached to this social rank; for freeman and noble, in the tribal elections, cast equal votes. Apparently the elective chieftainships, both civil and military, went generally to men of rank, but often enough otherwise to show that the offices of magistracy and of leadership were all within a freeman's reach.

[This primitive stage was not unique among the Teutons, but one through which many peoples have passed. A recent historian has given a vivid description of this condition among the early Greeks: "By fraud, oppression, unjust seizure of lands, union of families in marriage, and many other influences, the strong man of ability and cleverness was able to enlarge his lands. Thus there arose a class of large landholders and men of wealth. . . . Wealthy enough to buy costly weapons, with leisure for continual exercise in the use of arms, these nobles became also the chief protection of the state in time of war. . . . The country peasant was obliged to divide the family lands with his brothers. His fields were therefore small and he was poor. He went about clad in a goatskin, and his labors never ceased. Hence he had no leisure to learn the use of arms, nor any way to meet the expense of purchasing them. . . . When he attended the Assembly of the people in the city, he found but few of his fellows from the country-side gathered there—a dingy group, clad in their rough goatskins. The powerful Council in beautiful oriental raiment was backed by the whole class of wealthy nobles, all trained in war and splendid in their glittering weapons. Intimidated by the powerful nobles, the meager Assembly, which had once been a muster of all the weapon-bearing men of the tribe, became a feeble gathering of a few peasants and lesser townsmen, who could gain no greater recognition of their old-time right of self-government than the poor privilege of voting to concur in the actions already decided upon by the king and the Council." [1]]

[1] Quoted from Robinson and Breasted's *Outlines of European History,* Vol. I, pp. 130-2. For explanation of the use of brackets, see the Foreword.—Ed.

Whether or not the Teutons of the time of Tacitus had gone far enough in the practice of popular election to arrive at some beginnings of a representative system, the diligent Roman historian did not find out. That great political invention may have had a later origin, within the long period after Tacitus that is dark in Teutonic history, and especially dark in all that touches the internal life of the race. It was a period of tremendous revolutionary ferment and change. Great movements of migration began, with the massing of kindred tribes in powerful confederations, bringing into Teutonic history nation-like names, of Franks, Saxons, Suevi (or Alamanni), Goths, and other wandering hordes. Then came the grand avalanches of more or less barbaric invasion, which overwhelmed the empire of Rome in the West. Of the catastrophes of the time we know something, hardly more. The conditions underneath, the forces at work, the processes of the marvelous evolution of a new historic life, are almost wholly hidden from us, and likely never to be revealed. Till the new masters of Gaul, Spain, and Britain had fairly finished their conquest, and had established for themselves a somewhat fixed and orderly settlement in their new domain, there is, since the writings of Tacitus, next to nothing of record to denote, or even to suggest, their political experiences.

When the light of recorded history began to touch them again, the three tribes and parts of tribes which had crossed the North Sea and became Englishmen caught its earliest faint gleams and were brought most distinctively into view. Their "Anglo-Saxon Chronicle" and some fragmentary relics of their folk-literature are found to be the oldest Teutonic records that had been saved. Of the political organization and of the social state in general of the Anglo-Saxons more is known than of any other division of the great Teutonic race. The framework of their communities in England, as first discoverable, shows divergence from that which Tacitus described, but this divergence is more in details than in substance and form. In the transplantation of Teutonic society and institutions the tokens of a natural evolution appear much more traceable in England than in Italy or Gaul or Spain.

In all cases the Teutonic conquest had given rise to kingship, and kingship had generated new and broader distinctions of rank. In all cases, too, wealth had gained and was gaining power, and the measure of wealth was the ownership of land. Everywhere, in England as well as in Europe, the social tendencies were toward the uplifting of an all-dominant landlord class, and the corresponding depression of a great body of the people into landless and dependent folk. But in England, apparently, those tendencies were held most and longest in check; and the strength of the resistance to them was in the local organizations of society which the English were enabled by good fortune to preserve. Their tunscipes, or townships, their hundreds, or wapentakes, and their shires,—offspring of the ancient Teutonic mark-system,—were original and lasting strongholds of democracy, strongholds which time weakened but never quite broke down.

It was in these that the representative system took form, in these that the political habit of representation became fixed in the English mind. The tunmoot—the old English town-meeting—was not, in itself, a representative moot but an assembly of all the freemen of the township; this township, however, sent its reeve and "four best men" to represent it in the moots of the hundred and the shire. Thus far in the making and administering of law,—for the moots did both,—the people were represented. Here, however, the application of the principle ceased; for the national assembly—the witenagemot (assembly of "the wise")—was not a representative body, but a council of the greater officials surrounding the king,—assumed to be a royal selection of wise and capable men. [1] At what period the inspired device of representation for the people in the hundred and shire moots had been conceived and adopted cannot be known. Probably it antedates the migration to Britain, since representative political assemblies found in existence early on the continent—though later than their known appearance in England—are not likely to have sprung from the borrowing of an English idea. No doubt they were indigenous wherever found in mediæval times; but the origin of a representation of the people in governmental assemblies must have been somewhere within the Teutonic race. [Nor could the principle have been copied from the Greeks whose ancient institutions were unknown to the early Teutons.] It is one of the priceless gifts from that race to mankind; the gift of an invention which answered to profounder needs of humanity than any ever fashioned out of pistons and wheels. That the English people became the special keepers and perfecters of this great gift is accounted for sufficiently, as I have said, by the circumstances of their history, and cannot with reason be ascribed

[1] Cf. Haskins, *The Normans in European History*, p. 102, for similar opinion.—Ed.

to anything of character or genius that was peculiar to themselves. It was the English, rather than any of their kinsmen, who kept the sap of democratic life in the whole primitive Teutonic polity, because in Britain it was protected in a degree from some of the destructive influences which on the Continent had withered it, root and branch.

The tribes of the English conquest had experienced no foreign disturbance of that primitive polity before they went to Britain, and they submitted to no such disturbance of it there. No influence from the imperialized civilization of Rome had ever touched them in their far-northern home on the Continent, and whatever in Roman Britain might have exercised such an influence upon them was destroyed by their ruthless swords. In their own social fabric they had the germ of a civilization better than the Roman, but it was only in the germ. They were barbaric, predatory, unsparingly destructive in the warfare they waged. So far as they subjugated and occupied the Romanized island of Britain, they seem to have reduced it, as nearly as might be, to the condition of the country they had left. Its Romano-British population was mostly driven out after stubborn resistance, taking refuge in Brittany across the Channel, or in the mountains and moors of Scotland,

Cornwall and Wales. The Roman cities were destroyed or abandoned to decay. In their tribal-minded ignorance and egotism, the conquerors found little use for anything in the arts or ideals or modes and manners of life that the Romans had left behind. Since Christianity meant nothing to them but an insulting hostility to the gods of their own mythology, they trampled it out. Substantially, we may say, on taking possession of their British dwelling place, they cleared it of its former furnishings, scrubbed out all removable traces of the tenants they had evicted, and settled themselves to reproduce and continue, as identically as they could, the life they had lived in the Danish peninsula and on the Elbe.

In the continental provinces of Rome the Teutonic conquest was attended by no such sweeping expulsion of former inhabitants and destruction of Roman institutions and Roman work,—for this reason: The invasions on the Continent were, most of them, a gradual and peaceful occupation of the soil by large numbers, for the most part unresisted, consequently not provocative of a savage temper in the invaders. ["There was no sharp line[1] of demarcation between the hetero-

[1] Cf. Robinson's essay, "The Fall of Rome," in his *The New History*, pp. 175-194.—Ed.

geneous inhabitants of the Roman Empire and the Germans, or even the Huns. . . . They mingled with the Roman citizens in the same manner that aliens mingle to-day with our people, anxious to be reckoned American citizens as speedily as possible. There was no lining up of Roman against barbarian; the barbarian gladly fought for the Roman against his own people and exhibited very few traces of national feeling."] The attack upon Britain was made by comparatively small independent bands who won their several footings in the land by sudden swift strokes, born of desperation and fiercely resisted; such a conquest was sure to be destructive in its methods and results. In Gaul and Italy, again, and largely in Spain, the conquest was accomplished or controlled in the end by half-nationalized combinations of tribes which had been near neighbors of the decaying empire, or admitted to actual settlement within its borders, for a century and more. Sometimes at war with the provincial Romans and sometimes employed to defend them, these Germans of the Rhine and Danube frontier had been, for a number of generations, so much in contact with the people whom they finally subjugated, and with the arts and refinements of Roman life, that they had acquired a certain measure of respect for both.

The antagonizing strangeness of things and people which provoked the Saxon and Angle invaders of Britain could not have been felt by the Franks and Goths. The latter were even professed Christians before they entered the empire, and the Franks became so while their Gallic kingdom was in the making.

The differing influences which came from these differing circumstances of the conquest produced a wide divergence, necessarily, in social results. The Franks, for example, were settled in the midst of a people who must have outnumbered them considerably, and whose superiority to themselves in much useful and desirable knowledge they could not ignore. By force of arms they had made themselves the masters of these people, and had reduced them, as a body, no doubt, to dependence or servitude; but their subjects and servants became their teachers, nevertheless, and influenced them as teachers can. They underwent an imperializing education, which the English invaders of Britain missed, and this circumstance prepared the Teutons on the Continent for an easy abandonment of the democratic birthrights of their race.

As I have said, the changes of social organization, which occurred naturally in all the new settlements of the migrating tribes, tended everywhere toward the creation of a dominant landlord class and the consequent depression of the general body of the people. This went with the rise of monarchy and the parceling of the conquered lands. The same prestige and ascendency which raised the leaders of the conquest to thrones gave them also authority in the division of the territorial spoil. The important warriors of each king's following would secure the lion's share; and, according to the potency of his kingship, the king would improve the opportunity for binding his chief followers to himself, by attaching to his grants of land obligations of homage and of service. They, in their turn, might distribute favors in a subdivision of these royal grants on similar terms. Apparently it was thus that the mediæval system of land-tenure called feudal, with its tie of vassalage, had its beginning; and it grew to perfection first among the Franks, because the primitive Teutonic instincts which resisted it democratically were, without doubt, soonest lost among the Franks. Originally a land-system, it developed a most mischievous political system, planting a territorial aristocracy whose growth in power very soon became destructive alike to royal authority and to popular freedom. Beginning as a system of tenure which affected only large portions of the new kingdoms, it brought a pressure of lordly power to bear against all other land-owning, until little of independent ownership remained. What there was of protective and commanding power in the turbulent society of the time was gathered rapidly into the hands of the territorial lords, and vassalage became the price of the shelter it could give and the grace it could accord. The lesser landowners were driven, one by one, to surrender their independent titles and become tenants and vassals of powerful men, or of strong religious bodies, which also acquired an important place in the feudal scheme.

There appears to have been more or less working of these processes in all the regions of the Teutonic conquest; but nowhere else to the perfection of feudalism that was realized by the Franks. From their domination, more than from local growths, came its ultimate prevalence in Western Europe. By subjugation of the German fatherland they carried it even there, imposing it upon the Saxons of the continent while the Saxons of England were still holding its growth in check.

So far, a quite plain force of circumstances had half saved the English from the feudalizing drift of the time. Centuries of contention for supremacy between the small kingdoms which Jutes, Saxons and Angles had seated separately in the island afforded little gain of prestige to royalty and not much growth of dependent lordships; but quickly after the ending of those conditions they were almost reversed. The West Saxon Egbert and his successors, in the sovereignty of all England, were raised to less importance in their political capacity than as the war-chiefs of a nation that was fighting for its life. Early in the line of these nationalized chieftains and kings came Alfred, the noblest of all crowned men in heroic and kingly character. As a warrior he glorified the crown he wore; as a Christian he sanctified it; as a tireless toiler for the well-being and improvement of his people, he centered their affection upon it. Kingship, after Alfred had represented it, must have commanded new and larger forces of influence in England, but they worked in social developments that were far from wholly good.

In the period which followed, the English were carried more obviously than before in the feudal direction. They were being carried toward much the same results, but more slowly and by a somewhat different way. The relations of dependence among them were not exactly those which the Franks had developed; the true vassalage of Frankish feudalism may not have been introduced; but their lesser landowners were becoming dependent tenants of the greater ones, and landless men who would have been freemen in the olden time were becoming serfs. As yet, the folkmoot of the townships and the representative moots of the hundred and the shire lived on, keeping something of their old function and force; but by the middle of the eleventh century they seem to have been reduced to a feeble state. If nothing had intervened to interrupt and alter the processes that were operating then, one cannot see why the evolution of society in England, during the next half-dozen centuries, should have differed essentially from that of France.

But there *was* an intervention of good fortune, which came calamitously disguised. There seems to be no doubting that the English were saved by their national overthrow in the Norman conquest, from a complete decay and extinction of those old local folk-organisms which were the ultimate seat of life for all that grew up in their government of constitutional freedom and popular power. This could not have been the result if the Norman Duke William had been a conqueror of the common sort, fashioning his stolen kingdom with nothing of skill beyond the carving of the sword. Happily for England and for the world, he was a statesman in brain, as well as an autocrat in will and a soldier of daring and adventurous heart. His ambitions were all selfish, but his selfishness was shrewd, forethoughtful, profoundly wise. He saw that the firm seating of himself on the throne he had taken from the Saxon Harold depended more on the future disposition of the English than on the fealty and valor of his Norman support. He saw that he must not lean on the latter, if he would be a king in fact as well as in name. The Norman barons who had followed him to England with their retainers, and fought for him at Senlac, were as keen in self-seeking ambitions as himself. "The greatest secular figure [1] in the Europe of his day, he is also one of the greatest in the line of English sovereigns, whether we judge him by capacity for rule or by the results of his reign, and none has had a more profound effect on the whole current of English history."] The conquest of England was a speculative undertaking on the part of all who had to do with it, and the sharing of

[1] Cf. Haskins, *The Normans in European History*, pp. 11-15, 53. Cf. also E. A. Freeman, *History of the Norman Conquest* (third edition), Vol. II, pp. 164-67.—Ed.

profits and prizes was sure to be a matter of jealous dispute. It would be necessarily a sharing in the feudal mode. Neither William nor his followers are likely to have been able to conceive the possibility of anything else. At least, nothing else can have been practicable in the situation with which the Conqueror had to deal.

But, to feudalize England in the completeness of the system which the Northmen of Normandy had taken over from the Franks would be to give the Conqueror a merely titular kingship, as empty of real regality as that of the Capetians who wore crowns at Paris in that day. Nobody could understand this fact better than he. He had had experience in his feudal dukedom quite sufficient for the instruction of a political mind like his. He had fought down his turbulent feudatories there and brought them to a respectful submissiveness; but how could he plant the same baronage in a conquered country, over a subjugated population, duplicating its wealth and power, and still rule it, on the feudal footing, as he meant to do? That was the hard problem that he undertook to solve; and he solved it, as few men could have done. To his keen practical sense two things were clear: (1) that the feudalism to be organized in England must have as much as possible of the rebellious aptitudes and opportunities of its French constitution taken out of it; and (2) that the common people of England must be reconciled to his possession of the crown of their kingdom, so far as to stand with him and his house, against the Norman lords he should put over them, on issues that were likely to arise between the latter and himself. His rare soundness of judgment and resolute energy accomplished both. On one hand he pruned down the feudalism that he laid on his new subjects; on the other hand he kept life in their local institutions and in their customary laws, which meant to them infinitely more than anything remote in the government of the land at large.

The feudal system that King William constructed in England was a piece of political architecture very different from that of the Carolingian realms. Great fiefs and territorial jurisdictions which crippled royal authority were in William's system few and far between. Large estates were, in general, a patchwork of pieces, scattered widely apart. The functions and importance of the judicial and administrative officers of the crown were systematically magnified in the whole organization of government. Finally, all the landowners of substance in England, whosesover vassals they were, were summoned before the king, to become "his men," swearing "oaths of allegiance that they would be faithful to him against all others." Thus the conqueror leveled up and leveled down the whole gradation of feudal fealty, putting his subjects, great and small, whatever their secondary vassalage might be, on one plane of primary common vassalage and allegiance to himself. Thus he defeudalized his regal office. Thus he prepared the conditions for a more nationalized kingship than any other people in western Europe would know for centuries to come.

At the same time, his measures on the other line of policy established him and his successors in perfect legitimacy on the English throne. He claimed it, not by right of conquest, but by legal right. King Edward the Confessor, he averred, had promised the succession to him, and Harold, while Earl of Wessex, had sworn fealty to him as Edward's heir. These pretensions had no legality, but they had great popular effect; and William shaped all his proceedings to consistency with them. He secured a formal election to the throne by what might pass for a witenagemot, and a solemn coronation at Westminster by the English Archbishop of York. In return William swore to "hold fast to right law"; what is known of the legislation and jurisprudence of his reign seems to show that he meant the old English law, and that, in letter if not in spirit, his oath was fairly kept. His son Henry, by a charter which became the basis of the Magna Carta of the next century, confirmed or reënacted the laws of Edward the Confessor; and it is certain that the Norman conquest caused very little change in the substance of English law, though its administration was greatly altered and improved.

No doubt the "right law" to which the Conqueror had sworn to hold fast was painfully strained by those cruel proceedings which transferred the great English estates from native to Norman hands; but the whole spoliation was accomplished with a scrupulous respect for legal forms. The rightful king, it was claimed, coming to crown, had found himself resisted, and the penalties of treason had been incurred by all who failed to uphold his right. This was the theory which gave its plausible warrant to what Professor Freeman has described as "a system of legal confiscations and legal grants, harsh no doubt and unrighteous, but still carried out strictly according to the letter of the law," whereby a "legal and orderly transfer of lands and offices from natives to strangers went on, step by step, during the whole of William's reign." At the same time, many of the native English were permitted to redeem their lands from forfeiture, or to receive them as a gracious new grant from the king, and so became tenants-in-chief of the crown. Very soon, if not immediately, all tenants-in-chief,—holders of land, that is, from no intermediate lord, but directly from the king,—acquired a political status which proved to be of extraordinary importance in the constitutional development of the kingdom, as we shall see later on.

Within a decade after his landing in England the Conqueror had convinced the greater body of the English people that they served their interests best by upholding the royal authority which he had established; against the baronage that desired to break it down. "All the troubles of the kingdom after A.D. 1075," says Bishop Stubbs, "proceeded from the insubordination of the Normans, not from attempts of the English to dethrone the king." It was by English support that his sons, both William Rufus and Henry I, won and held the crown, against their elder brother, Robert, whom the Normans in England preferred. Before the death of Henry, the identification of the English nation with its Norman royal dynasty was complete, and the people were more unified in national feeling than ever before. The vigorous, hard, ably selfish government of the first William and the first Henry, oppressive though it was in many ways, had been a tonic, a reviving stimulant, to the English spirit. The very foreignness of its central administration must have endeared the old native institutions of local government anew in English thought and feeling; must have reanimated the participation of the people in the moots or courts of the hundred and the shire, and reawakened something of the democratic instincts of the elder time. How else can we account for the rapid and unique development in England of a representation for the people beyond those moots, and in all public action, both great and small, which began within less than a century after the Normans came in? Certainly there is no sign of progress to that end in the pre-Norman period. Nothing then shows a promise of growth from the ancient roots of the representative system, that would carry it from the shire-moot to the witenagemot, and make it dominant in the political constitution of the realm. On the contrary, everything known of the conditions existing before William of Normandy took the kingdom in hand is indicative, as I have said, of social processes that were working the destruction of popular rights, more slowly, but just as surely as the pure feudalism of the Franks.

The statesmanship of the Conqueror put a check on these processes,—by his effective emasculation of the feudal system which he himself introduced; by his preservation and encouragement of the native local institutions of the kingdom; and by the consequent reanimation of English political life.

But that was not all that William accomplished. He brought to the English a new popular institution, which appears to have borne for their benefit fruits which it never yielded elsewhere. This was the proceeding of "inquest," thought to be traceable to Frankish origins.[1] When royal rights were in question or royal interests concerned, the Carolingian kings commissioned a certain number of men to ascertain and declare the facts involved. In France nothing came from this procedure of inquest; it exercised a royal privilege and died out. But in England it became the germ of the whole system of inquisition and trial by jury. Continuing the work of his Norman predecessors, Henry II gave to English law a dignity, a force and a supremacy which it never lost, and seated it in courts which have been models for the judicature of all the world. Nor was this the sole significance of

[1] Supported by Haskins, *"The Normans in History,"* pp. 109-110, and by Pollock and Maitland, *"History of English Law,"* Vol. I, p. 142.—Ed.

the introduction of inquest. For the selection of juries at the county courts prepared opinion and made ready the procedure for political elections, at the same place, to represent the minor land-owners in the great council which became the Parliament of England. ["A bulwark[1] of individual liberty, the jury also holds an important place in the establishment of representative government, for it was through representative juries that the voice of the countryside first asserted itself in the local courts, for the assessment of taxes as well as for the decision of cases, and it was in negotiations of royal officers with the local juries that we can trace the beginnings of the House of Commons."] Why the simple institution that withered and perished on one side of the Channel became so magnificently fruitful on the other is easy to understand. It was in harmony with the popular constitution and spirit of the English local courts; it fitted naturally into the ancient English system, reënforcing it and being reënforced, while in France nothing that could coöperate with it had survived. ["But for the conquest[2] of England, it

[1] Cf. Haskins, "*The Normans in European History,*" p. 113. —Ed.

[2] Cf. Pollock and Maitland, *History of English Law,* Vol. I, p. 141.—Ed.

would have perished and long ago have become a matter for the antiquary."]

What England owed to the Conqueror's emasculation of her feudal system became apparent when Henry I died. The accession then of a weak king, whose right was disputed by a woman and a child, let loose the inhering anarchy of the system. This anarchy ran riot for nineteen years, a period during which the system was given opportunity to exhibit the rapid spending of its mischievous power. For a little time it afflicted the country with deplorable ruin and suffering; but in the end it had numbered its own days. Its strength and spirit were broken by the strong master, Henry II, who came next to the crown, and the aristocracy of England was never again really feudalistic in constitution or in disposition. It never swaggered in the kingdom; never bullied crown and commons with equal insolence, as the feudal nobility of the Continent was to do for several centuries to come. On the contrary, the English system, in order to secure joint action in withstanding the aggressive growth of royal power, was constrained to seek respectful alliance with the plain people; and that is one of the greatest of the saving events in the English evolution of government by the governed. The political union of lords and commons, in movements to maintain the rights of each and both, and to define the sovereignty of the crown, could have happened nowhere else in the world, either then, in the thirteenth century, or at any later period within the mediæval range of time. For no other monarchy in western Europe had overawed its nobility, and no monarchy in the east was less than absolute and despotic already; furthermore, no country but England had yet, or would have for ages, a rising commonalty of third estate, acquiring any measure of political ability or weight, outside of its thriving commercial and industrial towns. The municipal liberations which began so early in the city-republics of northern Italy and the chartered towns of Spain, France, Germany and the Netherlands, were not accompanied by any coherent development of a *rural* third estate, like that diffused through the counties of England, where it embodied far more of the forces that were working for a fully representative and constitutional government than ever came into action from the towns.

It was there, in the population of the broad agricultural country, outside of city walls and apart from merchant or trade-gilds, that a body of minor landowners had grown up, near enough in social status to the nobility, important enough in weight of property, considerable enough in numbers, and trained to enough activity in local politics, to command some respect from the baronial order and to have a recognizable footing in the body politic of the kingdom. In these minor landowners lay the substantial and efficient political strength of the English commonalty, from the beginning of its acquisition of influence in national affairs, continuously down to times that are within the memory of living men. They who came to be the gentry and yeomanry of the counties were the first to win representation in the national council; were always in the lead of the burgesses of the towns; were always foremost in those popular movements that won success; were always the unifying element that gave solidarity, weight and strength to the general mass; and this unifying element had existence nowhere else.

Without doubt this peculiar and most important feature of English mediæval society had its beginnings in Anglo-Saxon times; but it owed the vigor of its development in part to the Norman Conqueror's skillful hedging of feudalism and still more to the casual and probably unforeseen effects of the change he made in the constitution of the great national council or court. That which had been a witenagemot,—the king's selection of politically wise men as found in the higher offices of state and church,—became, after the Conquest, an assembly of the tenants-in-chief of the crown, roughly representative of the nation through its most representative class.[1] By the time of Henry II, if not before, it had come to be the recognized right of every tenant-in-chief to attend the meetings of the national council. The political status thus given must have gone to many landowners of comparatively small estate, thereby broadening immensely the social basis of that accretion of popular influence in public affairs which began in these times.

And this was only half of the result that followed the Conqueror's reconstitution of the great council of the realm. Both lords and commons were touched in another way, with extraordinary effect. Though every tenant-in-chief had the right to attend the meetings of the national council, the greater barons, nevertheless, were honored in the royal summons to such meetings by a distinguishing form. The summons went to each of that rank in personal letters from the king; whereas the remaining body of tenants-in-chief received it as a general proclamation, delivered through the

[1]Cf. Ogg, *Governments of Europe*, p. 7, for another view.—Ed.

sheriff in each county or shire. It is not conceivable that this courteous distinction was made at the beginning with any political intent; but the consequences were great and strange. Those who received the personal summons came thereby to be marked off by a very distinct line from those who did not. They were marked, in the course of time, as forming what we may call an official order of nobles,—a body of "hereditary counselors of the Crown"; who acquired no nobility of blood, and whose descendants did not form a noble caste. [1] This nobility of a parliamentary office, the peculiar nobility of the English "peerage," descended consequently to one inheritor of each generation in one main line of each baronial family, and the branching families of younger sons were thrown off from the stem of peerage-nobility, to become mixed with the lesser landlord class,—with the knights and gentlemen of English society, —and to be reckoned with them as part of the commons or third estate. This rescue of England from the growth of a mean and mischievous swarm of petty nobles, by the political merging of its minor aristocracy in the mass of the commons,

[1] Cf. Freeman, *The House of Lords and Other Upper Houses*, pp. 1, 7, 13. Stubbs, *Constitutional History of England*, Chap. 13, Sec. 159.—Author.

resulting as it did from a mere procedure of court etiquette which had no such intent, is one of the many singular favors of circumstance with which the political history of the English people is filled.

In the third estate of Continental countries there was nothing, which related and tied them to the aristocracy, unifying all that could act from the people at large with political weight and force. The localized, bourgeois third estate of the French towns or commons, for example, acted on by no mediating social influence, could not be organized into a national oneness of interest and action, as the English commons were. So long as the French monarchy was weak and the feudal aristocracy strong, the communes were natural partisans of the crown, and gave it such help as they could in the long struggle which made royalty supreme. Ultimately they were placed at the mercy of the triumphant kings, and lords and people sank together at the royal feet. Thus circumstances in France forced the commons to an alliance which brought despotism upon them, just as plainly as other circumstances in England led the commons to an alliance which had among its results a future of political freedom.

By favor of circumstances, then, lords and commons in England were brought to an effective union for checking the growth of royal power, and by continued favor of circumstances their union in that effort was crowned with success. No other European monarch of his day held the power which Henry II gathered into his hands. While sovereign of England, more substantially than any king before him, he was the feudal lord, likewise, of half of France. As the King of England, Duke of Normandy, Duke of Aquitaine, Count of Anjou, Count of Maine, Count of Poitou and Count of Touraine, with claims to the lordship of Brittany and Toulouse, he rivaled in rank and prestige, and even exceeded in actual power, the emperor of the Holy Roman Empire. Naturally his eminence as a Continental prince contributed to the support of his authority in England; but he happened to be one of the few monarchs who magnify the powers of their regal office by the strength in themselves. Its domination in his hands was for good; he used it, as has already been said, to establish order and peace through the benignant operation of justice. But there was danger in the dominance he had given the crown. Had his sons, who succeeded him, been as able as they were willing to be despots, the ensuing combination of classes in the nation, to limit and define the royal power, might have had less success. But Richard Cœur de Lion was too hot-headed, and John too mean to be formidable in the encounter with a well-developed will. Richard, an absentee king during all but seven months of the ten years of his reign, attentive to nothing in England but the extortion of money for his crusading adventures and his wars in France, prepared a feeling in the kingdom that was easily worked into revolt by the baseness and malignity of John. "Our evil king came at the moment when an evil king was needed," says Freeman; and that is a simple statement of fact. Coming when he did, King John is to be counted among the most notable of the many gifts of good fortune to the English people. Everything in his character and every circumstance of his reign,—his forfeiture and final loss of Normandy, Anjou, Maine and Touraine, [Brittany, Poitou and other minor provinces], the suspicion of his murder of Prince Arthur, his quarrel with the Church, the defeat of his Continental allies at Bouvines, his many notorious cruelties and crimes,—all combined to unite his subjects against him and to strip him of the power to resist their demands. To these demands, voiced by a united people, the King was forced to accede at Runnymede on June 15, 1215; the Great Charter signed on that memorable day is a document which underlies in its principles and in its influence all that has been most successful from that day to this in the enfranchisement of the peoples of the world. ["The Great Charter is the first great public act of the nation, after it has realized its own identity.[1] . . . The whole of the constitutional history of England is little more than a commentary on Magna Carta." "Although it is not the foundation of English liberty, it is the first, the clearest, the most united, and historically the most important of all the great enunciations of it."[2]]

That the English won the Great Charter when they did,—due largely though it was to a chain of circumstances singularly favoring,—entitles them to distinction as world-leaders in political development; that they preserved it as they did is their yet stronger claim to the grateful admiration of the world. [In this connection it is interesting to note the words of President Wilson spoken at Mount Vernon on July 4, 1918: "From this green hillside[3] we also ought to be able to see with comprehending eyes the world that lies around us and conceive anew the purpose that must set men free. It is significant—significant

[1] Cf. Stubbs, *Constitutional History of England,* Chap. XII, sec. 155.—Ed.

[2] Cf. Stubbs, *The Early Plantagenets,* p. 158.—Ed.

[3] Quoted from the *New York Times* of July 5, 1918.—Ed.

of their own character and purpose and of the influence they were setting afoot—that Washington and his associates, like the barons at Runnymede, spoke and acted, not for a single people only, but for all mankind."] Throughout the next two centuries they were seldom neglectful of any opportunity to secure confirmation of the Charter from successive kings, from many of them repeatedly, by attaching that condition to their fiscal grants; thus before the end of the Middle Ages it stood confirmed no less than thirty-eight times. [1] Political principles evolved in England during this period were the outcome of a constitutional freedom and a sense of popular right far in advance of any national attainment in other parts of the world. On the Continent, two-thirds of a century later than Magna Carta, the cities of Aragon, already represented in the Cortes of that small kingdom, obtained their "Great Privilege," which went even beyond Magna Carta in its affirmation of popular rights; but there was no broadly nationalized, land-owning third estate to support the burghers of the free towns; and this exposed them in the end to an easy suppression

[1] This statement of Mr. Larned's is evidently based upon Gneist, *"History of the English Constitution,"* Vol. I, p. 311. —Ed.

of their political rights. Italy had produced its city-republics, where premature and untrained democracy ran to factions which were already breeding the despots of the following age. The free German cities were rising to an independence which helped to keep up the feudal repression of nationality, and added still more to the political confusions of Europe by concentrating on mere objects of trade a powerful civic spirit and a rare organizing capacity which in English towns had been directed toward national unity. The communes of France were struggling with their seigniorial neighbors and lending a hand to the upbuilding of a monarchy whose absolutism would ultimately crush them. The industrial towns of Flanders were being intoxicated with riches, making much display of a turbulent free spirit, but planting nothing that would ripen fruits of freedom in time to come. Alone, of all peoples, the English had attained a degree of social unity without which no lasting political progress was ever possible, and were enabled thereby to establish the government of their nation on a constitutional basis, substantially fixed and importantly defined.

Magna Carta was not a political constitution according to the conception of the present day;

nor was it a grant of liberties from king to subjects. The texture of it came, with little coloring, from the polity of the Old-English, pre-Norman time, for, while professedly and substantially it was a confirmation of the charter of Henry I, that in turn had been a confirmation and reënactment of the laws of Edward the Confessor. In Henry's charter there was only the voice of a king who made promises to his subjects. In Magna Carta, on the contrary, there was the stern voice of a nation exacting the fulfillment of those promises from all its kings. This is the distinction which has made Magna Carta fundamental in the history of constitutional government.

Although not in its terms a political constitution, the Great Charter did, nevertheless, in its effects, alter the nature of the national council. In providing for the summoning of "archbishops, bishops, earls, and greater barons," and of "all tenants *in capite,*" to meetings of the "Common Council of the Nation," it declares that "the consent of those present on the appointed day shall bind those who, though summoned, shall not have attended." This principle led inevitably to the choosing of deputies for a representative attendance by those who stayed at home; and it would hardly be practicable to confine such an act of election to the king's tenants-in-chief. For, as Freeman says, "There can be no doubt that the king's tenants-in-chief were a much larger body, and took in men of much smaller estates, than we might at first sight be inclined to think; still they did not take in the whole body of freemen, not even the whole body of men holding land by free tenure. But, as soon as the election of definite representatives was fully established, since those representatives could be chosen nowhere but in the ancient county court, every freeholder, at least, if not every freeman, won back his right." [1]

To maintain the Great Charter of the English people, until time should give it the force of established law, required as much unity and energy of public spirit as had gone to the winning of it, —required, in its turn, favoring circumstances quite as much as before. Again a source of such serviceableness to the upbuilding of constitutional government was found in the character of John's successor, Henry III, whose folly and personal weakness made it possible to strip from him even the unquestioned prerogatives of the crown he wore. There were, however, thirty years of sorry

[1] Quoted from Freeman, *History of the Norman Conquest,* Vol. V, p. 477.—Ed.

submissiveness in the nation to plunder and misgovernment at the hands of a swarm of foreign favorites of the king, while a powerful papal court was permitted to practice such extortions as the kingdom had never experienced before. Suffering under these intolerable conditions, the nation waited only for a fit leader to organize its discontent. The man who proved equal to the needs of the time was Simon de Montfort, a noble of French birth, but with English blood in his veins, and thoroughly in sympathy with the national feeling against king and court. On his proposal the national council,—beginning now to be called a "parliament,"—summoned by the extravagant king in 1258 to vote supplies, proceeded instead boldly to take from the king's control many functions of executive government. The first result was an organization of baronial power fully as dangerous as royal absolutism; but Earl Simon, nobly faithful to the popular polity of his adopted country, took the lead in resistance to the feudal uprising which resulted.

After Montfort's victory at Lewes which made him, for a time, master of the situation, his clear comprehension of the logical drift of political conditions in England became evident. When he dictated the call of a parliament to deal with the new state of affairs, he caused writs to be sent out which required the election of four representative knights from each shire. When that parliament had subjected the king to control by a council in which Earl Simon was chief, he caused another to be assembled in the following year (1265) by a summons which brought two representatives from each city and borough, as well as two from each shire. Thus was established by a great earl a signal precedent for the representation of the English commons, first on the side of the land-owning gentry of the counties, and then on the side of the burghers of the towns. It was a precedent too vital to be set aside by Montfort's overthrow and death the following summer; but for the next thirty years the adhesion to it was capricious and imperfect. Then came, in 1295, the fixing of an accepted pattern for the future, by the seating of two representatives from each borough and each shire, in what is known as the "Model Parliament" of Edward I. The agency of that great king in establishing a constitutional and representative government for England was completed two years later, when he reissued the Great Charter, restoring the original provision forbidding taxation without parliamentary consent, which Henry III, in his shifty confirmation of it, had been allowed to omit. Thenceforward, this law of taxation, the potent safeguard of liberty and popular rights, might often be violated, but it stood indisputable as a fundamental law of the land.

[Edward I holds a very prominent place in the growth of English constitutional government, not only as a great constitutional reformer, but also as a great legislator, for his reign was distinguished by a series of laws which stand in the forefront of English statutes. "Edward's task [1] was to resume what Henry had begun; to preserve what was best, and adapt it to new conditions; to accept at the same time the most beneficial and necessary of the reforms which had been forced on the Crown; and to fuse the old and the new into the structure of the Constitution. Although he adapted and supplemented rather than originated, he completed the ground plan of the English government as it exists to-day. Those who came after had only to complete the edifice on the foundations which he had reared. . . . Through the efforts of Edward the common man was placed more securely than ever before under the law of the land as against the feudal lord.

[1] Cf. A. L. Cross, *History of England and Greater Britain*, pp. 167-8.—Ed.

By the close of his reign the three common law courts, the King's Bench, the Common Pleas, and the Exchequer, had taken shape each with its distinct records, and they continued practically unchanged till the close of the nineteenth century. . . . All this and more was brought about largely by a series of laws or statutes so comprehensive and so superior in numbers and importance that the reign of Edward can almost be said to mark the beginning of English legislation."] Thus England, at the close of the thirteenth century, had become a fully organized constitutional monarchy, with a powerful section of its common people,—an independent upper-middle class,—represented, with nobles and clergy, in a national legislature, —a legislature which held recognized authority to control, by just constraints of law, not only the actions of their sovereign but even the filling of his purse.

The nearest approach elsewhere to this political advancement of the people was in the transient and uncertain representation of towns in the Cortes of Castile and Aragon. A few years later, France made her first experiment in the consultation of deputies from the people by their king, which might have led on to the evolution of a representative legislature, if France had been less feudalized; but no such results could be hoped for. It was tried in 1302, when Philip IV, quarreling with the Pope and trying to tax the clergy, summoned deputies from the towns to meet with the barons and prelates, in the hope that he might thus secure the aid of the third estate. A second meeting of the three estates was called in 1314, and a third forty-one years later, in 1355. From that time until 1614 occasional assemblies of what came to be known as the States-General[1] were convened, to meet exigencies that arose, but never with any regularity or on any acknowledged principle that could establish the constitutional existence of the assembly as the law-making body of the government. After 1614 the States-General was suppressed for one hundred and seventy-five years; it reappeared only to inaugurate the great Revolution, in 1789. [The failure of the third estate to secure permanent right of representation is perhaps explained, in large measure, by the great extent of France and the consequent widely

[1] In France, during and after the 13th century, the name *parliament* was applied, not to royal councils or legislative assemblies, but to certain great judicial bodies, in different parts of the kingdom, twelve in all, of which the Parlement of Paris was the superintending head. The king required royal ordinances to be registered by the Parlement of Paris, which sometimes remonstrated against them, and sometimes refused registration, but rarely with success.—Author.

differing local interests; these encouraged sectionalism rather than unity, and thus enabled the crown to play off one faction against another,—a game which resulted in the ultimate subjection of all classes to an overwhelming absolutism.]

Meanwhile, events in the fourteenth century were productive both in England and on the Continent of an uncommon medley of social and political influences, more or less discordant, but tending on the whole toward the strengthening of forces on the side of the common people. Under them all ran the effects of the atrocious Hundred Years' War opened by the claims of Edward III to the crown of France.

The English successes in the early campaigns of the war were intoxicating to national vainglory, making parliament deferential to royal wishes and demands, and careless in the guarding of popular rights. To the lords the war was profitable, in enormous plunder, in personal distinctions and honors, and in gains of importance to their order. Relatively the commons were losers, for a time, from these effects. But geographic advantages, historic accident and time were working in their favor; for, during this war, a great increase in industrial and commercial prosperity was brought to many English towns through

Edward's alliance with the Flemings and the consequent general stimulation of seafaring enterprise; Flemish weavers and dyers came to England, introducing improvements of process and skill which enabled the English very soon to manufacture cloth for themselves from their large production of wool, hitherto exported in the fleece and imported as cloth. Out of these conditions there grew up an organization of English merchants, under the name of Merchant Adventurers, which, entering into competition with the Hanseatic and other trade leagues of the Continent, soon outstripped all its rivals, and laid the foundation for that extraordinary commercial career upon which England now entered. [Thus the Hundred Years' War bore fruits for all time in the impetus it gave to English commercial supremacy. But this is not its ultimate significance; for the local rights granted by Edward III to the rapidly growing towns, in return for their financial support, enabled them to become independent of feudal control, and so laid the foundation for that final overthrow of the feudal aristocracy which was to come a century later in the Wars of the Roses; this overthrow in turn was absolutely necessary before there could be brought about a permanent establishment of that popular constitutional government, in whose development the English have been so continuously leaders.]

The Hundred Years War was a strong impetus toward the establishment of constitutional government not only through the increased freedom which it brought to the great middle class of the English towns, but also through the quickening which it undoubtedly gave to a remarkable movement among the great mute lower classes which formed the understratum of English society,—a movement which brought about nothing less than a social revolution. The political vantage ground which the English people were to gain before the end of the thirteenth century would not, within the next three hundred years, be reached by any other people in the world. Throughout this period their hold upon that ground would not be sure or unbroken, but they would succeed in keeping so strong a semblance of possession that their rights would never be lost.

Till near the end of the thirteenth century, the mass of the agricultural laborers of England, as of other countries, had been held in various forms of bondage to the owners of the soil. Their loss of freedom ranged from that of a few actual slaves, who disappeared early, to that of the villeins, who, in one view, were tenants of the lord they served, since they occupied and cultivated allotments of ground for their own benefit, and their labor was divided between these and the requirements of their manorial lord, but who, in another view, were serfs, since the terms of tenancy were not a matter of free arrangement and could not be changed without the lord's consent. Now, however, at the end of the thirteenth century, the decay of feudal conditions began to relax the rigors of villeinage, which in turn was giving way to systems of hire for labor and of money-rental for land. This great social revolution, far earlier in England than elsewhere, was hastened, at about the middle of the fourteenth century, by the effects of a frightful pestilence called the "Black Death." From one-third to one-half the population of the kingdom is believed to have been swept away, producing a scarcity of labor which forced landowners to let their lands to tenant-farmers, thus strengthening the middle class, and preparing the way for the enfranchisement of the lower classes.

Out of these social changes, helped, no doubt, by other influences, came an extraordinary propagation of the extreme socialistic and democratic ideas of John Ball and other priests. Along with

Wycliffe's religious wakening of the age, it first grew into the Lollard movement, which ran its course in the later years of the fourteenth century and after. The underclasses in England were never again stirred to so open and aggressive an assertion of equality among men, till the French Revolution drew some faint echoing from their ranks. The influences which contributed to this movement in the popular mind arose mainly, without doubt, from various causes of disturbance in religious belief. Throughout the century the Papacy, in the English mind, was sinking low and lower in authority and respect, because of the national antagonism aroused by the removal of its seat from Rome to Avignon, followed by the election of a series of popes who were believed to be under French control, and then by the forty years of "the Great Schism," during which a succession of rival popes, or popes and antipopes, thundered anathemas and excommunications at one another from Avignon and Rome, dividing the whole Christian Church into hostile camps. [English antagonism to papal authority was still further increased by the interference of the popes in English ecclesiastical appointments, by the increasing wealth of the higher clergy, and by the growing idleness and decadence of the monastic orders.] Consequences of demoralization in the religious orders, among the secular clergy, and more or less throughout the hierarchy of the Church, were very grave.

In themselves these causes of disturbance to the religious attitude of the English mind might not, directly, touch anything in close relation to social or political ideas; but the loosening of established habit in some one large arena of thought and feeling, among the minds that are acting on each other in an intimate mass, is quite sure to spread to other habit-formations in the same minds, opening new views on other sides of existence,—giving escape to other ideas. That this had now happened in England seems plain. Out of the new stir of thought, in one direction, came the wonderfully advanced doctrines of theological and ecclesiastical reform, maintained with incredible boldness by Wycliffe, between 1370 and 1382, and made known to the common people by the "poor priests" whom that great precursor of the Protestant Reformation inspired and trained for this missionary work; in the other direction came the socialistic agitation led by John Ball, with its culmination in the Wat Tyler insurrection of 1381. That much of what went into the English Reformation of nearly two centuries later grew from Wycliffe's seed-planting,—in his translation of the Bible and in his arguments against the doctrine of transubstantiation, the worship of saints, the use of images, and the "Judaising" of worship by splendors of accessory and elaborations of ceremony,—may be surmised, though the growth may not be traced. It can be said with safety, however, that his rightful rank among the chiefs who give glory to the history of the English peoples has never been awarded by the common acclaim it should have; for it was he who first attempted to give to the mute millions of the understratum that voice which was, five hundred years later, to make itself heard in the reforms of the nineteenth century.

Hitherto in this rapid survey of progress in England toward a constitutional government under representative institutions, we have been tracing an almost unbroken succession of events and circumstances strangely helpful, on the whole, to such progress, sometimes even inviting the action which secured it. We have come now to a period whose most important event had the primary effect of confirming to Parliament the highest prerogative it could yet think of exercising. When Richard II was confronted by his banished cousin,

Henry of Lancaster, at the head of a successful rebellion, Parliament assumed, for the first time, the right to take the crown from a living sovereign and place it on another head. The English kingship had always been theoretically elective with the choice limited, however, to members of one royal house. As the fact is expressed by Taswell-Langmead, "the Norman Conquest introduced a new dynasty, and a more comprehensive idea of royalty . . . but it effected no legal change in the nature of the succession to the Crown. Election by the National Assembly was still necessary to confer an inchoate right to become King."[1] The Norman Conqueror recognized this, and obtained the election in due form. His successors were invested with the regal office by the same formal expression of a national choice. But the transferring of the choice from one who had already received it to another, who, although not in the most direct line of descent, was nevertheless deemed more worthy, was an assumption by Parliament of an altogether new prerogative, involving the complete custody of the crown. [He (Henry of Lancaster) based his

[1] Quoted from Taswell-Langmead, *English Constitutional History,* p. 194.—Ed.

claim[1] on two grounds, right of descent from Henry III, and right of conquest. . . . In any event, Henry's claim of descent was merely a pretext. His second claim was the decisive one. Parliament chose him because, as the ablest male of the royal house, he had overcome a king who had defied the laws and oppressed the subject. The title of the new Lancastrian house was then a parliamentary one. In the end it had to give way to the older rival line which it had supplanted; but its accession was of the deepest constitutional significance. It confirmed a precedent that kings could be deposed for misrule and established a new one that Parliament could choose a successor not necessarily the next in blood. The fact that, as elective kings, the Lancastrians made a bargain to govern in accord with the will of Parliament was also of the profoundest importance."] Thus was established the precedent for what may be described as a recalled and transferred election.

The effect of the deposition of Richard II and the election of Henry IV was to give the nation a king who treated its representatives—his electors—with extreme respect, and the power of the

[1] Cf. A. L. Cross, *History of England and Greater Britain*, pp. 240-246.—Ed.

Commons rose high. [The powers and privileges of parliament[1] recognized by Henry IV,—powers and privileges so momentous in the development of English constitutional government,—were chiefly these: (1) No new law could be passed without the approval of parliament; (2) Redress of grievances must precede supply of funds, no taxes could be levied or collected without the consent of parliament, and these taxes could be voted only on the last day of the session, after the petitions of the people had been granted; (3) Parliament maintained its right to cut down the king's expenditures, and audit his accounts, to dismiss his ministers and force upon him its advice on the conduct of wars, on the drawing up of treaties and on all other important measures of government; (4) Members were free from arrest while in attendance upon, or on their way to, meetings, and were granted freedom of debate with immunity from punishment for utterances made in the meetings of the parliament.

Even though most of these powers and privileges of parliament were not permanently estab-

[1] Cf. Adams and Stephens, *Select Documents of English Constitutional History,* nos. 103-115; H. D. Traill, *Social England,* Vol. II, p. 279-282; A. L. Cross, *History of England and Greater Britain,* pp. 246-247; Maitland, *Constitutional History of England,* pp. 182-4.—Ed.

lished until centuries afterward, some of them not even yet, nevertheless, the fact that the justice of these claims was *recognized* and *acknowledged* by the sovereign, and their value *appreciated* by the representatives of the people, makes them principles of fundamental importance in the development of constitutional government. "Prematurely[1] Richard had challenged the rights of the nation, and the victory of the nation was premature. The royal position was founded on assumptions that had not even prescription in their favor; the victory of the house of Lancaster was won by the maintenance of rights which were claimed rather than established. The growth of the commons, and of the parliament itself in that constitution of which the commons were becoming the strongest part, must not be estimated by the rights which they had actually secured, but by those which they were strong enough to claim, and wise enough to appreciate. If the course of history had run otherwise, England might possibly have been spared three centuries of political difficulties; for the most superficial reading of history is sufficient to show that the series of events which form the crises of the Great Rebellion and the Revolution might link themselves on to the

[1] Cf. Stubbs, *Constitutional History of England*, Vol. II, pp. 652-653.—Ed.

theory of Richard II as readily as to that of James I. . . . The failure of the house of Lancaster, the tyranny of the house of York, the statecraft of Henry VII, the apparent extinction of the constitution under the dictatorship of Henry VIII, the political resurrection under Elizabeth, were all needed to prepare and equip England to cope successfully with the principles of Richard II, masked under legal, religious, philosophical embellishments in the theory of the Stewarts."] "Never before and never again for more than two hundred years," says Bishop Stubbs, "were the Commons as strong as they were under Henry IV." The resulting good will of the nation at large upheld him on the throne against repeated conspiracies and rebellions. His son, Henry V, maintained himself in equal popularity by renewing, with brilliant temporary success, the Hundred Years' War with France. Then came the lamentable situation produced by the succession to the throne of a child who had no manhood in him to be matured. Struggles for the control of the nominal regality which attached to the name and person of Henry VI were sure to run, as they did, into strife for the possession of the crown he wore. In the resulting civil wars, constitutional government went early to wreck,

—so nearly that only a few occasional forms of an imitative parliamentary procedure were kept, in evidence of suspended popular rights. At the end of the Wars of the Roses nearly all of the old nobility had perished in battle or on the scaffold, or had gone to exile or suffered impoverishment by the confiscation of estates. New families, of less prestige and influence, and less capable of putting restraints on the crown, had risen to the higher ranks and supplied the peerage of the realm. The commons, accustomed to act under baronial leadership, were unprepared to take upon themselves the responsible defense of public interests and rights.

Thus there developed conditions which opened the way to an arbitrary kingship, and the sovereigns of the Tudor family were qualified to make the most of them. For more than a hundred years, from the accession of Henry VII to the death of Queen Elizabeth, the monarchy became, in practice, nearly as absolute as that of France. But occasional parliaments, even though pliant to the royal will, kept the theory of constitutional government in force and the essential spirit of a free people alive, even through the brutal autocracy of Henry VIII. That spirit in the nation, product of long culture under free institutions, might be bullied into dumb stupor or infatuated to foolish adoration, but it never lost its potential energy.

["With the transition [1] from mediæval to modern history, the conditions were altered in England's favor. The geographical expansion of Europe made the outposts of the Old World the *entrepots* for the New; the development of navigation and sea-power changed the ocean from the limit into the link of empires; and the growth of industry and commerce revolutionized the social and financial foundations of power. National states were forming; the state which could best adapt itself to these changed and changing conditions would out-distance its rivals; and its capacity to adapt itself to them would largely depend on the strength and flexibility of its national organization. It was the achievement of the New Monarchy [of the Tudors] to fashion this organization, and to rescue the country from an anarchy which had already given other powers the start in the race and promised little success for England.

"Henry VII had to begin in a quiet, unostentatious way with very scanty materials. . . . His

[1] The following excerpts are taken from A. F. Pollard's *History of England,* pp. 88-116.—Ed.

reign is dull, because he gave peace and prosperity at home without fighting a battle abroad. His foreign policy was dictated by insular interests regardless of personal glory; and the security of his kingdom and the trade of his people were the aims of all his treaties with other powers. At home he carefully depressed the over-mighty subjects who had made the Wars of the Roses; he kept down their number with such success that he left behind him only one English duke and one English marquis; he limited their retainers, and restrained by means of the Star Chamber their habits of maintaining lawbreakers, packing juries, and intimidating judges. By a careful distribution of fines and benevolences he filled his exchequer without taxing the mass of his people; and by giving office to ecclesiastics and men of humble origin he both secured cheaper and more efficient administration, and established a check upon feudal influence. . . . He left his son, Henry VIII, a stable throne and a united kingdom.

"The first half of Henry VIII's reign left little mark on English history. . . . In 1529 Henry began the process, completed in the acts of Annates, Appeals, and Supremacy, by which England severed its connexion with Rome, and the king became head of an English church. It is irrational to pretend that so durable an achievement was due to so transient a cause as Henry's passion for Anne Boleyn or desire for a son; vaster, older, and more deeply seated forces were at work. In one sense the breach was simply the ecclesiastical consummation of the forces which had long been making for national independence, and the religious complement of the changes which had emancipated the English state, language, and literature from foreign control. The Catholic church naturally resisted its disintegration, and the severance was effected by the secular arms of parliament and the crown. The nationalism of the English church was the result rather than the cause of the breach with Rome, and its national characteristics . . . were all imposed by parliament after, and not adopted by the church before, the separation.

"Catholicity had broken down in the state with the decline of the empire, and was fast breaking down in the church; nationalism had triumphed in the state, and was now to triumph in the church. In this respect the Reformation was the greatest achievement of the national state, which emerged from the struggle with no rival for its omnicompetent authority. Its despotism was the predominant characteristic of the century, for the national state successfully rid itself of the checks imposed, on the one hand by the Catholic church, and on the other by the feudal franchises. But the supremacy was not exclusively royal; parliament was the partner and accomplice of the crown. It was the weapon which the Tudors employed to pass Acts of Attainder against feudal magnates and Acts of Supremacy against the church. . . .

"Henry VIII confined his sympathies to the revolt of the nation against Rome and the revolt of the laity against the priests. . . . His real services were political, not religious. He taught England a good deal of her insular confidence; he proclaimed the indivisible and indisputable sovereignty of the crown in parliament. . . . He carried on the work of Henry II and Edward I, and by subduing rival jurisdictions stamped a final unity on the framework of the government.

"The advisers of Edward VI embarked on the more difficult task of making this organization Protestant; and the haste with which they, and especially Northumberland, pressed on the change provoked first rebellion in 1549 and then reaction under Mary. . . . Capital amassed in trade was applied to land, which began to be treated as a source of money, not a source of men. . . .

Small tenants were evicted, small holdings consolidated, commons enclosed, and arable land converted to pasture. . . . But even this high-handed expropriation of peasants by their landlords stimulated national development. It created a vagrant mobile mass of labor, which helped to meet the demands of new industrial markets and to feed English oversea enterprise. . . . Elizabeth was a sovereign more purely British in blood than any other since the Norman Conquest; and to her appropriately fell the task of completing her country's national independence. . . .

"The astonishing success of England amid the novel conditions of national rivalry requires some attempt at explanation. It seems to have been due to the singular flexibility of the English character and national system, and to the consequent ease with which they adapted themselves to changing environment. . . . Certainly England has never suffered from that rigidity of social system which has hampered in the past the adaptability of its rivals. . . . On the Continent, however, class feeling prevented the governing classes from participating in the expansion of commerce. . . . Hence foreign governments were, as a rule, less alive and less responsive to the commercial interests of their subjects. . . .

"There was no feeling of caste to obstruct the efficiency of English administration. The nobility were separated from the nation by no fixed line; there never was in England a nobility of blood, for all the sons of a noble except the eldest were commoners. And while they were constantly sinking into the mass of the nation, commoners frequently rose to the rank of nobility. . . . This social elasticity enabled the government to avail itself of able men of all classes, and the efficiency of Tudor administration was mainly due to these recruits, whose genius would have been elsewhere neglected. Further, it provided the government with agents peculiarly fitted by training and knowledge to deal with the commercial problems which were beginning to fill so large a sphere in politics; and, finally, it rendered the government singularly responsive to the public opinion of the classes upon whose welfare depended the expansion of England. . . .

"So far Tudor monarchy had proved an adequate exponent of English nationalism because nationalism had been concerned mainly with the external problems of defense against foreign powers and jurisdictions. But with the defeat of the Spanish Armada, the urgency of those problems passed away; and during the last fifteen years of Elizabeth's reign national feelings found increasing expression in parliament and in popular literature. . . . In domestic politics a rift appeared between the monarchy and the nation. For one thing the alliance, forged by Henry VIII between the crown and parliament, against the church, was being changed into an alliance between the crown and the church against the parliament, because parliament was beginning to give expression to democratic ideas of government in state and church which threatened the principle of personal rule common to monarchy and to episcopacy. . . . Popular acquiescence in strong personal monarchy was beginning to waver now that the need for it was disappearing with the growing security of national independence. People could afford the luxuries of liberty and party strife when their national existence was placed beyond the reach of danger; and a national demand for a greater share of self-government, which was to wreck the house of Stuart, was making itself heard before, on March 24, 1603, the last sovereign of the line which had made England a really national state passed away."

The period of quasi-absolute monarchy in England ended practically when Queen Elizabeth died, for the attempts of her immediate successors to prolong it only hastened and perfected the restoration of constitutional law. If the crown had passed to an English-born heir, acceptable to the loyalty which Elizabeth had inspired, the arbitrary tenor of government probably would not have had an early check; but here, again, we have a singular concatenation of events, helpful to the renewed investment of the people with controlling political power. The king who came to the throne was not only unwelcome, as a Scot, but personally incapable of commanding reverence, affection, or even respect. The twenty-two years of his reign were a trial to English loyalty which left it very weak. His son, the first Charles, had winning personal qualities which might have restored the prestige of the crown if he had not been so intolerably arrogant, and if his tyrannical temper had not been excited especially against the rising Puritanism of the time. His was the one challenge to rebellion that could not fail to call it out; and the doubling of the animus of revolt, by religious and political provocations, insured its success. The transiency of the ensuing overthrow of the monarchy, and the restoration of the Stuart kings with nothing of their old pretensions withdrawn, are facts of the least possible significance in English constitutional history. They come by accident, we may say, as an interruption between the trial and execution of Charles I, in 1649, and the throning of William and Mary by act of parliament, in 1689. The revolution of 1689, with its Bill of Rights and its Act of Settlement, were the outcome, the completion, of the revolution of 1649; and in both there was only a slow execution of the doom that lay on absolutism in England from the day that Queen Elizabeth died.

The English people had now, at the end of the seventeenth century, established, for all time and beyond question, that their parliament could make and unmake kings; that the real sovereignty resided there; that the seat of its power was more in the Commons than in the Lords; that nothing could be law without parliamentary enactment. that no law could be suspended in operation, no money exacted from the nation, no army raised or maintained, without due authority from parliament; that meetings of parliament must be frequent, the election of its members free, and freedom of speech in its proceedings unquestioned outside of itself. The fundamental conditions of a government controlled representatively by the public will were thus completely fixed in principle[1]; but the means of control were in legislation only. The administration of government remained still the prerogative of royalty, reached only by defining enactments of law. Its practical transfer to parliament, and to the Commons in parliament, was yet to come.

How immeasurably, nevertheless, had the English, when they reached this point, advanced beyond all other peoples! France, under Louis XIV and under a corrupt nobility that bore no share of the crushing taxation which it helped the "Grand Monarch" to devour, was at the lowest depths of her political degradation and social misery. The States-General of the kingdom,—the old national council,—in which a very limited third estate had been represented on a few occasions in the distant past by delegates from towns, had had no meeting since 1614. Some provincial Estates had been permitted to meet in the interval, but the king was now perfecting his autocracy by suppressing them, one by one. "The provinces," says Tocqueville, describing the conditions

[1] Cf. Stubbs, *Constitutional History of England,* Vol. II, p. 653: "[Most of these] were claimed under Edward III; they were won during the Rebellion, at the Restoration, or at the Revolution."—Ed.

that preceded the Revolution, "had lost their franchises; the rights of the towns were reduced to a shadow. No ten noblemen could meet to deliberate together on any matter without the express permission of the king." "In the rural districts none remained but such of the gentry as their limited means compelled to stay there. . . . Perhaps in no other part of the world had the peasantry ever lived so entirely alone."[1]

Among German peoples there seem to have been less visible signs of political life, outside the petty courts of its innumerable princelings, than there had been in the days of Luther and Charles V. There was still an active commercial life in the free imperial cities, but nothing of political life. The oligarchical character of their municipal freedom had become complete. In the provinces of the Austrian dominion, including most of Italy, and in Spain and the Spanish Netherlands, despotism was still unrelieved. The government of the Dutch Netherlands, conducted with singular liberality in many matters, was a government, nevertheless, in which the people at large had no voice. Popular elections there were as yet unknown. The States-General of the so-called re-

[1] Quoted from Tocqueville, *On the State of Society in France before 1789*, pp. 205, 223.—Ed.

public, and the provincial assemblies, too, were composed of members chosen by self-elected magistrates of the cities; the stadtholderships had been made hereditary in the house of Orange, and the prerogatives of the office were superior to those of the English king. In Sweden, the national Estates were so broken in spirit that, in 1693, they proclaimed King Charles XI as "an absolute sovereign," "who had the power and right to rule his kingdom as he pleased." In Switzerland, outside of the three old Forest cantons where the confederacy had its birth, the peasantry—the bulk of the people—were struggling, in frequent insurrections, to escape from conditions which made them little better than serfs.

Nowhere, at the best, had other peoples won a footing in the body politic as substantial and as safely affirmed to them as that which had come into the possession of the English about three centuries before. In the passage of western Europe from mediæval to modern conditions of life, the English had found openings for political improvement which no other people could use. Says Tocqueville, with his fine political discernment: "In England the feudal system was substantially abolished in the seventeenth century; all classes of society began to intermingle, the pretensions of birth were effaced, the aristocracy was thrown open, wealth was becoming power, equality was established before the law, public employments were open to all, the press became free, the debates of parliament public; every one of them new principles, unknown to the society of the middle ages. It is precisely these new elements, gradually and skillfully incorporated with the ancient constitution of England, which have revived without endangering it, and filled it with new life and vigor without endangering its ancient forms."[1]

Down to the close of the seventeenth century and even into the early years of the eighteenth, the political advance of the English had been wholly toward the upbuilding of legislative independence and authority in their parliament and of judicial independence and authority in their courts. But now there began a movement in the evolution of popular self-government along new lines,—a movement which led to the actual transfer of all executive responsibility and power from crown to parliament, reducing the monarchy to a fiction and proving convenient in many practical ways. This new departure in constitutional construction was made without any deliberate planning or intent.

[1] Quoted from Tocqueville, *On the State of Society in France before 1789*, pp. 29-30.—Ed.

["It is [1] so much easier, in discussing the causes and stages of a political contest, to generalize from the results than to trace the growth of the principles maintained by the actors, that the historian is in some danger of substituting his own formulated conclusions for the programme of the leaders, and of giving them credit for a far more definite scheme and more conscious political sagacity than they would ever have claimed for themselves."] If we have warrant for saying that circumstances, thus far in English history, had favored the political aggrandizement of the middle classes of the people, we may now say, with equal warrant, that circumstances became dictatorial and compulsory to that end. They brought, first, a woman to the throne, in the person of Queen Anne, who lacked the force of character necessary for independence in the exercise of her regal functions, and then after Queen Anne, a foreign prince who was hopelessly disabled by total ignorance of the English language, by equally total ignorance of England and its affairs, and by his dependence on one supporting party against another which denied his right to the crown. Queen Anne could sit in council with her ministers, listen to their dis-

[1] Cf. Stubbs, *Constitutional History of England,* Vol. II, pp. 537-538.—Ed.

cussions, take some part in them, perhaps, and possibly form opinions of her own. George I could not. She deferred to her ministers, and gave them a generally free hand; consequently, during her reign of twelve years, royalty slipped considerably into the background of English politics. In the thirteen years of her tongue-tied successor, who was never anything but an alien and a stranger to his nominal subjects, the royal figure went quite into eclipse, behind the Prime Ministry and the cabinet which Walpole then organized. That cabinet ministry became the responsible and real executive of the government,—responsible to parliament but not to the king. [Macy and Gannaway summarizes the stages in the evolution of cabinet government as follows:[1] "(1) There was the inner circle of the Privy Council and of the earlier Continual Council on whom the king relied for advice in government. The name Cabinet was applied to this group as early as the reign of Charles I. (2) Charles II began to substitute the inner circle in place of the Privy Council. (3) William III and Anne identified the Cabinet with party leaders. (4) George I ab-

[1] Cf. Macy and Gannaway, *Comparative Free Government*, p. 433; cf. also A. L. Lowell, *Government of England*, Vol. I, pp. 27-32.—Ed.

sented himself from Cabinet meetings. (5) Robert Walpole created the office of Prime Minister which served as an entering wedge in the transfer of the exercise of royal prerogative from the King to the Cabinet. (6) The Cabinet, supported by the House of Commons, forced George II to give Cabinet places to Pitt and Chesterfield. (7) After George III had for twenty-five years tried to discredit and destroy the Cabinet, its authority was restored under the leadership of the younger Pitt as head of the Tory party, thus committing both parties to the system. (8) Finally, beginning with the act of 1832, the nation is becoming enfranchised, the people are recognized as the source of final authority, there are frequent changes in party rule, and the people express their will by alternate choice between two competing Cabinets. The mechanism is such that the people retain the continuous services of both groups, one as actually governing, the other as pointing out methods of improvement."]

The evolution of parliamentary government was now nearly complete, in form if not in spirit, though the evolution of parliament itself was not. For the crown there was no recovery of the executive authority that had slipped away from George I. The influence of the first two Hanoverian kings in the government of Great Britain was almost naught, except in so far as they strove with some success to turn its foreign policy to the advantage of their German duchy. The strenuous effort of George III to master the new ministerial system produced some temporary disturbance and some national misfortunes, but had no reactionary effect. And even in that royal revolt there was no revival of the pretensions of the Stuart kings. It was little more than an attempt on the part of the sovereign to secure pliant ministers, and to control parliament by his own use of the methods of corrupting influence which recent ministries had employed. Later, in 1834, William IV exercised what had been, in former times, an undoubted prerogative of the crown, by dismissing a ministry which commanded the support of a majority in the House of Commons. But his action was condemned as unconstitutional,—condemned so decisively that no sovereign has essayed it since. This was the last attempt on the part of the crown to resist the supremacy of parliament, whether practically or theoretically understood, in the administration of government no less than in the laying of taxes and the making of laws. Thus the passing of executive functions from the king to a ministry, responsible to parliament and practically independent of the crown, has been made final and complete.

["The origins[1] of political parties in England fall clearly within the seventeenth century. It was the judgment of Macaulay that the earliest of groups to which the designation of political parties can be applied were the Cavalier and Roundhead elements as aligned after the adoption of the Grand Remonstrance by the Long Parliament in 1641. The first groups, however, which may be thought of as essentially analogous to the political parties of the present day, possessing continuity, fixity of principles, and some degree of compactness of organization, were the Whigs and Tories of the era of Charles II. Dividing in the first instance upon the issue of the exclusion of James, these two elements, with the passage of time, assumed well-defined and fundamentally irreconcilable positions upon the essential public questions of the day. Broadly, the Whigs stood for toleration in religion and for parliamentary supremacy in government; the Tories for Anglicanism and the prerogative. And long after the Stuart monarchy was a thing of the past these two great parties kept up their struggles upon these and other

[1] Quoted from F. A. Ogg, *Governments of Europe*, pp. 38-39. —Ed.

issues. After an unsuccessful attempt to govern with the coöperation of both parties, William III . . . fell back definitely upon the support of the Whigs. At the accession of Queen Anne, in 1702, however, the Whigs were turned out of office and the Tories (who already had had a taste of power in 1698-1701) were put in control. They retained office during the larger portion of Queen Anne's reign, but at the accession of George I they were compelled to give place to their rivals, and the period 1714-1761 was one of unbroken Whig ascendency. This was, of course, the period of the development of the cabinet system, and between the rise of that system and the growth of government by party there was an intimate and inevitable connection. By the close of the eighteenth century the rule had become inflexible that the cabinet should be composed of men who were in sympathy with the party at the time dominant in the House of Commons, and that the returning by the nation to the representative chamber of a majority adverse to the ruling ministry should be followed by the retirement of the ministry."

"The English Cabinet and party system [1] is es-

[1] Quoted from A. L. Cross, *History of England and Greater Britain,* pp. 614-615; cf. also A. L. Lowell, *Government of England,* pp. 449-461.—Ed.

pecially notable from the fact that its machinery is the most perfect which has yet been devised for speedily and peacefully voicing the will of the people and because it is the system which has been adopted, with more or less variation, by the chief European governments in recent times. It is essentially a government by an executive committee of Parliament whose members represent and are responsible to the majority of the House of Commons, which, in its turn, represents the qualified voters of Great Britain. Just as soon as the majority withdraws its support the Ministry either resigns, or dissolves Parliament, and submits to the verdict of a general election."]

Meanwhile in the middle of the eighteenth century, a few thoughtful minds in continental Europe had begun to study the lessons in government which England had been setting before them for so long a time. In this movement Montesquieu led the way in his "Spirit of the Laws," pointing to England as the "one nation in the world that has, for the direct end of its constitution, political liberty," and proceeding from that statement to an examination of the English constitution and its embodiment of "the principles on which this liberty is founded." It was a timely exposition and made a deep impression, especially in France, where it succeeded in arousing a feverish activity in political thinking. But French political thought, while taking a strong impulse from Montesquieu, departed from his wise historical method of investigation. The most influential of the political writers, Rousseau, Diderot and his colleagues of the "Encyclopedia,"—were, as Tocqueville described them, predisposed by their position to relish general and abstract theories upon the subject of government, and to place in them the blindest confidence. The almost immeasurable distance in which they lived from practical duties afforded them no experience to moderate the ardor of their character; nothing warned them of the obstacles which the actual state of things might oppose to reforms, however desirable. They had no idea of the perils which always accompany the most needful revolutions; they had not even a presentiment of them, for the complete absence of all political liberty had the effect of rendering the transaction of public affairs not only unknown to them, but even invisible. They were neither employed in those affairs themselves, nor could they see what those employed in them were doing. They were consequently destitute of that superficial instruction which the sight of a free community, and the tumult of its discussions, bestow even upon those who are least mixed up with government. Thus they became far more bold in innovation, more fond of generalizing and of a system, more disdainful of the wisdom of antiquity, and still more confident in their individual reason than is commonly to be seen in authors who write speculative books on politics; and "the same state of ignorance opened to them the ears and hearts of the people."

And so it was that the desperate French people, looking to England and to the English communities in America, with longing for their free institutions, but heedless of the time and the patience that went to the making of those institutions,—blind to the slow training that prepared Englishmen and English-Americans for the use of them,—were led into the riot and wreck of their terrible Revolution.[1] In the end, however, when the madness was spent, and when the reaction from it was likewise spent, there came a school-time for Europe, in which it took up the constitutions of England and English-America and studied them with good effect.

[1] For an eminently sane discussion of "The Principles of 1789," see J. H. Robinson's essay on this subject in *The New History,* pp. 195-235.—Ed.

For a whole generation the excesses of the French Revolution were deplorably prejudicial to democratic doctrines of government; so much so, even in England, as to check for that period the further development of the national constitution on popular lines. Otherwise the broadening of the representation of the people in parliament would have had an earlier beginning. From the late thirteenth century to the early nineteenth, it is proper enough to call the English government a representative one, because the will of a very effective and important section of the people was voiced in parliament; but the constituents of that section were still far from being the commons of England, in any right sense of that term. [For those millions of the understratum of English society, whose rights had been so vainly championed, five hundred years before, by the "visionary" Wycliffe, had not even yet been able to impress their will upon the councils of the nation. But again that strangely favoring combination of geographic influence and historic circumstance enabled the English people to make yet further gains in their struggle toward a more truly democratic government. For it was this strangely favoring combination that made possible the Industrial Revolution[1]; and it was the Industrial Revolution, which, in turn, made possible those social and political reforms of the nineteenth century in which the English people have so markedly led the world.

This spirit of reform was first manifested, at the beginning of the nineteenth century, in the reconstitution of the House of Commons.] This branch of parliament embraced, in 1831, the whole titled aristocracy of the kingdom below the peerage, and the untitled but aristocratic "gentry," along with a part of the well-to-do class; but none of the landless population of the rural districts, whether farmers or laborers, and few of the working class of the towns, had votes. Out of a total population of 22,000,000 in the United Kingdom, the voters numbered less than 450,000.[2] Most of the boroughs and towns represented were not the later growths of modern industry and trade, but the decayed country market-places and hamlets of a long-past age. Fifty-six of these, with less than 2,000 of total population, were electing 111 of the 658 members of the House of Commons,

[1] For discussion of this point, see, in this volume, the essay on "The Geographic Factor in English History," by Donald E. Smith.—Ed.

[2] Based upon W. Heaton, *The Three Reforms of Parliament,* chap. I.—Ed.

and 30 others, having less, altogether, than 4,000 of population, were electing 60 more.[1] But that was not the worst of the facts. Most of these "rotten boroughs," as they were styled, were enveloped in the estates of the great land-owning lords; the voters were their tenants, and a free election in them was never known. Such cities of modern origin and great importance as Manchester, Birmingham, and Leeds, had no representation, and that of London itself was small. What bore the name of the House of Commons had its representative commission, we can see, from a small fraction of even the well-to-do middle class, and not at all from the toilers of the commonalty.[2]

This dearth of democratic element in the English representative system was persistent until 1832, when an almost revolutionary excitement of popular feeling compelled the adoption of the first measure of parliamentary reform. This went far enough to disfranchise the most rotten

[1] Based upon T. E. May, *Constitutional History of England,* Vol. I, chap. 6.—Ed.

[2] For an account of the Industrial Revolution and its effects upon problems of government, see E. P. Cheyney, *Industrial and Social History of England,* pp. 199-276; F. W. Tickner, *Social and Industrial History of England,* pp. 530-540; and F. S. Chapin, *Historical Introduction to Social Economy,* pp. 147-260.—Ed.

of the boroughs and to give representation to forty-two towns and metropolitan districts which had had no voice in parliament before.[1] It lowered the property-owning or rate and rent-paying qualifications for voting enough to popularize the elections considerably, and to lessen materially the aristocratic character and spirit of the House of Commons; but the greater mass of the people were left still without votes. For another third of a century they remained unrepresented, but not unconscious of their rights. Agitations to secure a broader popular enfranchisement were soon started, taking form in what is known as the Chartist movement, which disquieted the country, more or less, from 1838 to 1848. The demand made was for the passage of an act, styled the People's Charter, embodying constitutional changes on six points,—universal manhood suffrage, equal electoral districts, vote by ballot, annual parliaments, no property qualification for parliament, and payment to members for parliamentary service. Of these six demands two have since been fully satisfied by the introduction of the ballot in 1872 and by the removal of the property qualification for a seat in parliament. Manhood suffrage was

[1] Supported by T. E. May, *Constitutional History of England,* Vol. I, chap. 6.—Ed.

made nearly universal and electoral districts nearly equal by the second and third Reform Bills, passed, respectively, in 1867 and 1884-5. Service in Parliament has not yet been salaried, and the demand for an annual election of parliaments is not likely to be renewed. Otherwise, the Chartist agitators were only a few years in advance of their time. [The Chartist movement, far from losing strength in the twentieth century, seems to be gaining in vitality all the time. Obscured by the war, the Electoral Reform Bill of 1918 must, nevertheless, take its place alongside the great Reform Bills of the nineteenth century, for the sweeping away of many of the disqualifications for the male franchise, and the endowment of between five and six million women with the right to vote is no insignificant achievement. Another Chartist demand recently satisfied is the payment of salaries to the members of the House of Commons. Thus far four points of Chartism have been adopted altogether, and a fifth, advocating annual elections of Parliament, has been approached somewhat in the Parliament Act of 1911, which reduces the maximum duration of Parliament to five years. Such legislation is a splendid justification of Carlyle's statement, made in 1839: "The matter of Chartism is weighty, deep-rooted, far-extending, did not begin yesterday; will by no means end this day or to-morrow."]

[Ever since the Reform Bill of 1832, England has been engaged in the refinement of those democratic institutions which she had evolved through the centuries, proving to an admiring world that such institutions are the best instruments for further political progress. In 1835 was accomplished the reform of town government, the abuses of which had been as notorious as those of Parliament before 1832. The Municipal Corporations Act of 1835 not only did away with the corruption in the towns, but also established for the first time the principle of local self-government within the kingdom. Supplementing, but not completing the work of this act, comes the County Councils Act of 1888, which democratized the administration of county governments. The last step in this direction is the Parish Councils Act of 1894, which extended the principle of local self-government to smaller units of the nation than had been treated in the two preceding acts. The system of local government in England is now one of the best examples of the democracy of English institutions. In the first place, local government is close to the daily life of Englishmen. The county divisions in England are much smaller than those of our

American states, and the spirit of community is consequently stronger. Besides, in England there is no tendency, as there is in other countries, either purposely or from slipshod habits of political thinking to confuse local with national issues. The result is a cleaner, more responsible and more intelligent system of local self-government than any other state has evolved. It was quite natural, in a century of reform of the machinery of government, that a coincident step should be the appointment to positions in the Civil Service on the basis of standing in open competitive examinations. The reform of the Civil Service in England gave an impetus to a similar movement in America, with the result that the Civil Service of the two great English-speaking peoples is based on as democratic a system of appointment as has yet been devised. A third line of reform, leading to simplification in the organization of the courts, is indicated in the great Judicature Act of 1873, which together with an Amending Act, consolidated the higher courts of the realm into the Supreme Court of Judicature, whose two great branches are the High Court of Justice and the Court of Appeals. But the most far-reaching of all, one that goes back to the constitution of parliament, something not so much a reform as a recapitulation of previous tendencies from the days of Magna Carta, is the Parliament Act of 1911. The open intention of the Act is to render powerless the present upper house, so that the substitution of a "Second Chamber constituted on a popular instead of hereditary basis," to quote the Act itself, may be more easily obtained. According to the terms of this Act, money bills become law within one month after passing the Commons, with or without the concurrence of the Lords; all other bills passed by the Commons in three successive sessions, sent up to the Lords at least one month before the end of each session and rejected each time by the Lords, are to be presented for the royal signature, provided that two years have elapsed since their introduction into the Commons. The spirit of this Act is the spirit of the English people throughout their constitutional history, a summing up of past progress, an intimation of future progress, a milestone in the free expression of English political thought.]

We have now traced the evolution of popular self-government by the agency of elected representatives, and find it to have been a process that worked almost exclusively in the political experience of the English peoples, producing institutions of constitutional monarchy in Great Britain which in the course of her expansion were to become models for the democratizing and constitutionalizing of government in every other part of the world. Without doubt, this pioneering and leading of all civilized society into or toward the democratic state has been the most important and distinguished function of the English peoples in history. By getting the first training that self-government gives to the self-governing multitude, they were the first of Europeans who could make much, in a substantial, lasting way, of the great opportunities for expansive action, influence and power that, three hundred years ago awaited the use of man.

The Old World was then entering on the third of the three stages of civilization which Carl Ritter, the geographer, defined as (1) the *potamic,*—developed in extensive river valleys, such as those of the Nile, the Tigris and Euphrates, and the Ganges; (2) the *thalassic,*—nourished by the influences and commercial stimulations of a great inland sea, like the Mediterranean; and, (3) the *oceanic,*—which opened to Europe when exploration of the broad Atlantic was launched from its western coast. Egypt and Babylonia led the march of civilization in its first stage; Phœnicia, Greece, Rome and mediæval Italy in the second; what peoples would be in the van of the third? Nobody, at the beginning of the sixteenth century, could have looked for that leadership to the inhabitants of the British Isles.

When Europe discovered America, the South Sea, and the ocean-way to the Indies, and found the earth to be really a globe, the English had less apparent preparation than most of their neighbors for exploiting these discoveries and becoming workers in a new construction of the general circumstances of human life. Islanders though they were, and of Saxon and Norman blood, their sea-going activities were slight. They took a minor part in the commerce of the time. Their trade with the Continent was conducted mostly by the Hanseatic and other leagues organized by enterprising merchants of the German towns. English character showed singularly little of the spirit of adventure. After a long series of French and civil wars, they seemed to be settling down to a rather unambitious career,—busied in the main with their sheep pastures and their farms.

A sense of free individuality, however, a consciousness of responsibility, and capable habits of associated action, acquired, through many generations, in their parish vestries, their courts and their parliament, had fitted these industrious farmers and burghers, as nothing else could, for that prosperous transplantation of themselves which has rooted young nations of English stock in all quarters of the earth. In their schools of self-government they acquired many superior qualities which were to overcome France in America and supplant the Dutch in South Africa, found this great federal republic of the United States, dominate India and Egypt, and give a lead to English influence in history such as no other race is likely ever to over-ride or even to overtake.

At the opening of the modern era, the Portuguese and Spaniards were in the forefront of the colonial movement, both in achievement and in opportunity. That they did not make the most of their primacy, and maintained it but a little time, was consequent, no doubt, on more than one cause. The tropical regions to which they were led for their colonial undertakings could hardly, under any circumstances, have nourished communities of European vigor and pith. Moreover, the success of the Spaniards in finding precious metals might have spoiled the constitution and the character of any young colony of that age. Furthermore, in losing all experience of political freedom, the Spaniards had also lost the power to generate the least degree of organic self-activity and self-nourished vitality in their colonial society. It had to be a piece of political mechanism, officially constructed and officially worked, from the central source of all power, at Madrid. By this fact alone it was made impossible for the Spanish settlements in America to become self-dependent political organisms such as the English settlements there and elsewhere became at a later day.

The wars of the Elizabethan age with Spain started the English on a maritime career; but the ultimate expansion of their little kingdom into the world-wide empire of a world-spread race grew from nothing in the half-piratical exploits of Hawkins and Drake. Nor can it be said to have grown from the undertakings of Raleigh, the one Englishman of the sixteenth century who, with the sagacity of a statesman, the imagination of a poet, and the spirit of an adventurer, looked abroad and divined the future of the New World. Even the first attempt of the Virginia Company to plant a settlement at Jamestown was too near failure to be taken for the true beginning of English achievement in colonization. ["English piracy in the Channel was notorious in the fifteenth century, and in the sixteenth it attained patriotic proportions. Henry VII had encouraged Cabot's voyage to Newfoundland, but the papal partition of new-found lands between Spain and Portugal barred to England the door of legitimate, peaceful expansion; and there can be little doubt that this prohibition made many converts to Protestantism among English seafaring folk. Even Mary could not prevent her subjects from preying on Spanish and Portuguese commerce and colonies; and with Elizabeth's accession preying grew into a national pastime. Hawkins broke into Spanish monopoly in the West Indies, Drake burst into their Pacific preserves, and circumvented their defenses; and a host of followers plundered nearly every Spanish and Portuguese colony. . . . National unity and the fertile mingling of classes had generated this expansive energy, for the explorers included earls as well as humble mariners and traders; and all ranks, from the queen downwards, took shares in their 'adventures.' They had thus acquired a body of knowledge and experience which makes it misleading to speak of their blundering into empire. They soon learnt to concentrate their energies upon those quarters of the globe in which expansion was easiest and most profitable." [1]]

Here, again, as in the shaping of the English polity within England itself, helpful and guiding

[1] Quoted from A. F. Pollard, *History of England,* pp. 108-109, 150.—Ed.

circumstances arose, strangely effective and opportune,—circumstances which carried Englishmen of the freest spirit, of the strongest character, of the best political training, out from their old beloved homes, to inhospitable wildernesses, across a forbidding sea, not for gold-seeking or for conquest, but for the resolute making of new homes, a new country and a new citizenship for themselves and their posterity. The circumstances which contributed to this great end were those that brought the English government into contention with religious beliefs among the people, as well as into assaults upon their political rights. In successive movements, first of the Pilgrim Independents to Plymouth, then of Puritans to Massachusetts Bay, of Catholics to Maryland, and of Quakers to Pennsylvania, this contention exiled four bodies, well picked from the best of English folk, such as could not have been won in any other way for the pioneering task which they took upon themselves. It is inconceivable that a settlement of the uninviting region of New England, by people of so sterling a class, could ever have been brought about by any other influence than this; or that an equal development of that region by people of any class could have been accomplished otherwise within the next hundred years. Then, again, by a different turn of the same circumstances, when large numbers of the beaten royalists of the Civil War left their English homes, another rare selection from the best bred manhood of England was sent over to the struggling colonies of Virginia and Maryland, to leaven them with new spirit and new strength. [The thought that Mr. Larned evidently had in mind was that these beaten royalists were from the governing class in England,—men trained, by experience that was in turn backed by centuries of family tradition, to be leaders of the commoners. This characteristic of the Virginia settlers, coupled with the development of a representative, county type of government necessitated by their widely scattered plantations, doubtless explains to a large extent the marked leadership shown by Virginia in the events leading to the framing of the American Constitution. [1]]

These favors of circumstances were the most extraordinary that ever attended the pioneering of colonization; but let us not forget how entirely their operation depended on the moderation of temper which even an oppressive government in

[1] Facts in support of such a view can be gathered from Turner's *The Rise of the New West,* Farrand's *The Framing of the Constitution,* and Beard's *Economic Interpretation of the Constitution.* Cf. A. F. Pollard, *History of England,* pp. 151-152.—Ed.

England was compelled to preserve. From religious persecution in Spain and France there was no such escape. Spanish America offered no refuge from the Inquisition to heretic Christians or to Moriscos or Jews; and the Huguenots were shut out from New France. Thus England alone, by virtue of the liberalizing influences in her political system, could limit her own oppression by opening her colonies to the oppressed, and could obtain therefrom so powerful and so determining an impetus to the fulfillment of her destiny.

"If France," says Parkman, "instead of excluding Huguenots, had given them an asylum in the west, and left them there to work out their own destinies, Canada would never have been a British province, and the United States would have shared their vast domain with a vigorous population of self-governing Frenchmen." But in the government of France, there was more than despotic intolerance to make it ruinous to colonial undertakings. As in the case of Spain, the centralized absolutism of France, robbing the people of all freedom and capacity for self-action, made successful colonization from that country impossible. French settlements in America were trading stations, religious missions, military posts,—everything except the social and political "plantations" of the English. There was nothing spontaneous about them, nothing organic and vital, nothing growing in a natural way. "Root, stem and branch," to quote Parkman again, New France "was the nursling of authority." The colony in all its parts and in all its workings, was an official, artificial structure. In the main, its white inhabitants were officially collected in France and shipped out on official requisitions from Quebec; and when these recruited colonists wanted wives, they, too, were officially recruited and shipped. Of course, colonists of that make-up could not be the founders of such communities as the English were planting farther south.

Even the Dutch, with all their apparent liberty of spirit and action, were disabled by their political constitution from prosperous rivalry with the English in colonization. There was an absolutism, in their case not royal, but commercial, which blighted their colonial plantings. Dominated in their government at home by the manufactures of the towns in their outer settlements, they were still more under subjection to the great corporations which monopolized trade. All their claims and holdings in America were controlled by the Dutch West India Company, which had almost unlimited powers of government, as well as exclusive commercial rights; and the colony, in turn, was ruled autocratically by governors whom the company appointed and who acted under orders from its directorate at Amsterdam. This autocracy explains the readiness with which the Dutch colonists soon surrendered to the more liberal domination of the English.

When France and England, in the eighteenth century, began their struggle for the possession of the great interior valleys of North America, active enterprise and formal procedure had given the French a much superior position on the continent. They had explored the country, overrun it with their traders and missionaries, opened friendly relations with the natives, and established many well-planned military posts. Logically they had much the better claim to the great prize of dominion for which the two nations fought,—within the disputed ground, the whole strength of position and preparation for the contest was on their side. But they were very far from France, and they had to fight, not only a far-away England, but a transplanted section of England, entrenched in the long line of colonies on the ocean coast, and as vigorous and self-inspired as England herself. Their own New France was but a name; not much of France had been brought to it, except the commissions and mandates of the French king and court. This, principally, was the cause of their defeat.

In the meantime, while the English of England, from the reign of the first Stuart to that of George V, had been slowly perfecting their monarchical constitution of representative government, the emigrant English in American settlements had been molding the same elements,—of tradition, common law, historical habit, and the free spirit of their race,—from the same primitive Teutonic sources into other constitutions of government of a purely republican form. Making new homes for themselves and a new structure of society in a strange land, as their Anglo-Saxon ancestors had done twelve centuries before, and organizing their communities under conditions much the same, the early English settlers in America reverted most naturally to the same type of structure, wherever they could act with independence and spontaneity. To the colonists of New England as to no other, fortune had given such independence, and the new fabric of English society grew there as it had originally in Britain, from the town or township as its political base; the beginnings of governmental action were thus put at the very doors of the people, and the old Anglo-Saxon system of political education by local training in self-government, revived and modernized, was once more set to work in a new land. Forms of government in other colonies than New England were dictated by royal or proprietary authority; they, consequently, had a less perfect early schooling in popular government; but the teaching reached them all in the end, and when they broke their colonial relation to the mother country, assuming political independence, in States which grouped them as they had been colonially grouped, but in a nationalized federation of their States, they offered, to the observation of the world, another very different and very striking example of constitutional and representative government. The English model was now republicanized and popularized to a degree far beyond its original; far beyond any trial of representative democracy then known outside of the three Forest Cantons of the Swiss.

The development of the idea of systematic constitution-making had been strangely tardy and slow. As we see in English history, the most definite constitution of government that existed anywhere, before the seventeenth century, was but a crude accumulation of royal concessions and parliamentary and judicial precedents, out of which certain fundamental principles of representative government were extracted and became established in the English practice of such government; but what we speak of as the English or British constitution was and is simply a legal and historical abstraction of the mind. Only in outline have its principles ever been systematically defined.

Down to the seventeenth century there had been no conception of a constitution of government derived otherwise than by grants and concessions from some royal or ducal sovereignty above the governed people. The first communities in modern times to constitute a system of government for themselves by written agreement were those of the English colonists in America. If the simple Mayflower compact of the Plymouth Pilgrims could be called a political constitution, it would be the first; but the "Fundamental Orders" and "Fundamental Agreement" of the Connecticut settlers are nearer to the idea. In England, a few years later, two attempts at the framing of a written constitution were made, under the Cromwellian Protectorate; but the operation of each was short-lived. Then, for more than a century, there seems to have been no more writing of systematic constitutions, excepting John Locke's for the Carolinas and William Penn's for Pennsylvania, and excepting, also, the important additions made to the old English constitutional documents, in the *Habeas Corpus* Act and the Bill of Rights.

The era of constitution-making consequently cannot be said to have opened until the Declaration of Independence was drawn up in 1776. Between that year and 1783 each one of the thirteen newly independent United States discarded its former character of government and framed a constitution for itself. In 1787-88, by the framing and adoption of the Federal Constitution of the United States, the greatest of such models of political art was exhibited to the world.[1]

Here in this republic of English America, for the first time in world history, the adaptation of popular government in representative form to a large structure of federal nationality was tried and proved. The Greek federations had been unions of represented states, not of represented peoples; the Swiss confederation was yet to be made a really nationalizing union; and in all preceding instances the federal structure of a political system had been attempted in but small ways. Now, the scale was large, the result impressive and the success in many aspects complete. This constitution crowned the work of the English peoples as the

[1] For a detailed account of the framing of the Constitution, see Max Farrand, *The Framing of the Constitution*.—Ed.

political teachers and leaders of the world. Let us see, then, how far and how successfully its lead has been followed.

Up to this time Europe had not half learned nor half understood the lessons of English political teaching. On the contrary the French Revolution, partly the outgrowth of earlier English influence, had discredited all democratic doctrine, though the idea of systematic constitution-making had fairly lodged itself in the European mind, and could not be long inactive. With the exception of the Spanish American countries and Sweden, the political constitutions originating throughout western Europe in the half-century after the rise of Napoleon, were all of the old charter type, not derived from the people, but granted to them from a sovereignty above. Still, they *were constitutions,* which in many cases served as the bases for their liberalized constitutions of to-day. When at last, following the revolutions of 1848, a resolute and general demand for liberalized and constitutional government was made throughout Western Europe, success was so great that the seeming failure of the revolutions promised to be temporary. For, in 1861, the constitution of Sardinia was extended to the Kingdom of Italy; in 1867, the dual monarchy of Austria-Hungary was created, with a separate constitution for each of its national parts; in 1871, the German Empire was organized under a written constitution; and in 1875, the Third French Republic was established, with a definite constitution adopted by an assembly representative of the national will. From Europe the movement spread eastward. Even the Sultan of Turkey was forced to capitulate, and conceded to his subjects in 1876 a short-lived constitution, which was revived by the Young Turk Revolution in 1908. Among Oriental peoples the Japanese were the first to receive a written constitution, proclaimed by their ruler in 1889. The Persians were likewise favored by their Shah in 1907, and have confirmed his action by the revolution of 1909.[1]

And now let us see how much of the precise architecture of the English and the Anglo-American constitution of popular government has been adopted by these nations, whose conceptions of constitutional and representative government were all derived from the political experience of the English race.

There are three essential features of the system of popular government developed among the Eng-

[1] Since this essay was written, China, too, has joined the ranks of constitutional government through the revolution of 1911-12.—Ed.

lish peoples: (1) a real representation of the people in the legislative department of their government, secured by a broadly general suffrage and by directness in the election of representatives; (2) control of public revenue and expenditure by the representative branch of the legislatures; (3) a real responsibility of the executive department of government to the people, secured either indirectly by the ministerial agency of the British system, or directly by election to the executive office, as in the United States.

Originally, as we have seen, the English elective franchise was limited strictly to the owners of property in land, and that rule prevailed till the last century, when the suffrage was extended by successive acts to tenants, householders, rate-payers and finally to lodgers, coming to be exercised at present in Great Britain by nearly the whole body of male citizens, as well as by women for many purposes of election, though not for parliamentary representation. Still, however, the conditioning or qualifying of the elective franchise, by some required ownership of property, some tax-paying, or some hire of a residence, to indicate a substantial footing in the community, even if slight, is a principle maintained in the United Kingdom, and in many of the colonies of the British Empire.

[By the franchise law of 1918 the British parliament has abolished the remaining limitations based on property and on sex, and thus again placed England in the vanguard of democratic liberalism.]

The same principle was adhered to for some time in the thirteen British colonies which assumed independence and formed the republic of the United States. It was not until new States began to arise in the West that property qualifications of the suffrage were first dropped. The original States then followed the example of the new commonwealths, some quickly, some slowly, until adult male citizens of the United States (criminals, paupers, the insane and the idiotic excepted) had received generally the right to vote. A few States require ability to read as a qualification, a few exact the payment of a small poll-tax, and a few have extended the right to women, in whole or in part. [Since 1912 those few have been joined by several others, raising the total number of full and partial suffrage states to 21.]

Outside of the political communities which the English peoples have formed, representative institutions have been constructed most frequently upon the basis maintained in Great Britain, namely that of a more or less limited franchise. Either a property-owning or a tax-paying qualification is prescribed in Prussia, and the great majority of the secondary states of the German Empire; in Spain, Italy, Holland, Hungary, Servia, Roumania and Japan. But in Prussia the franchise is narrowed still more in effect by a classification of the tax-payers in such a way as to secure political ascendency to the wealthy class. The indirect mode of election is practiced likewise, to some extent, in Italy, Baden, Bavaria, and some other states. Spain has made provision for a representation of minorities. And so one might continue indefinitely to cite examples of constitutional gains in the franchise. It is obvious enough, however, that the general tendency in Europe, on the whole, is plainly toward universal suffrage.

But in every instance of such constitutional gains, the nations have been largely following in the footsteps of England and America. [France, it is true, at the time of the Revolution, was the first to conceive the idea of universal manhood suffrage. But it was the English-speaking peoples who first put the principle into practice and perfected the instruments for its application.] In nothing else have the lessons of English example and experience impressed the world so forcibly and so effectually as in teaching that the people can safeguard their liberties only by securing control of the public purse. Generally, in the modern constitutions, this has been provided for with especial care.

Responsibility of the Executive is secured according to the British mode in all the British colonies and in most of the constitutional governments of Europe. That is to say, the immediate administration of those governments is entrusted to a cabinet of ministers whose tenure of office depends upon the approval of their measures by the representatives of the people. If they lose the confidence of a majority in the popular branch of the legislature, as shown by an adverse vote, they must either resign or obtain a dissolution of the legislature, thus appealing to the judgment of the people in a fresh election of representatives.

Executive responsibility is secured in the United States by centering it in an elected President, to whom all executive authority is given. The American republics in general have adopted this, which seems to be the natural republican mode; but the French, in their republic, have preferred to endow their President with little of personal responsibility, and to have him chosen in the National Assembly, instead of by popular election, making his functions and his place in the government much like those of the English king. In the Swiss Confederation "supreme direction and executive authority" are exercised by a Federal Council of seven members, elected once in three years by the Federal Assembly, which also elects one from the membership of the Council to be the President of the Confederation. But this produces more division and more indirectness of responsibility than either the British or the American scheme.

Many, also, of the monarchical constitutions of Europe contain formal declarations that the King's "ministers are responsible," which means, simply, that they are not sheltered by the irresponsible authority of the sovereigns but are subject to impeachment and trial for wrongful acts. This, however, does not touch the real executive power with which the King, who appoints and dismisses ministers, is clothed, and is therefore something very different from the responsibility of an English minister or an elected President of the United States.

From this review we learn that one or the other of the two types of representative popular government developed by the English peoples, in Great Britain and the United States respectively, have been copied approximately, if not exactly, in large parts of the civilized world. In the old monarchies there is still much resistance to the concession of a really responsible executive; but all kings and princes will have to yield it in the end, as the English kings have done, and content themselves with ceremonial functions, or else make way for elected chiefs of state, as America has done. Nothing in prospective history is more plainly certain than the final constitution of all civilized governments, in essential features, on English lines.

[In our survey of English leadings, thus far, we have considered only one field of political experience,—the internal constitution of government; and in this unquestionably the experience of the English peoples has been the forcing-house in which practically all the great principles of democracy and republicanism have been generated and nourished, and from which they have later been transplanted to nearly every nation of the civilized world. There remains one other field of political experience,—the imperial; and in this, too, English experience has generated still other great principles of government,—principles which will go far toward solving the perplexing problems of international association and interdependence which the world is now facing.]

In colonial expansion, as in discovery, exploration and settlement, it was not promptitude of enterprise that seated English folk so imperially. Neither in America nor in any other of their far-flung dominions were they the first to grasp opportunities of trade or empire, or dominating advantage of any sort in the world. Always deliberate, always slow, always behind some race of more alertness, they have been late-comers in every field of foreign enterprise, commercial or political; but once arrived, and their places secured, they, more than any other people, have been able to make effective use of it. And they have always had a strange help of fortune in finding some vantage-ground awaiting them in the field. It is by the force of that remarkable combination,—of favoring circumstances with rare capability and rare training for the best use of it,—that English folk, instead of Spanish or Portuguese or Dutch or French, are in possession of the North American continent, are dominant in Australasia, are masters of the best parts of Africa, rulers of India, administrators of Egypt,—the only people who exercise what can truly be called a world-power.

Apart from America, it was in India that English colonial claims first came into conflict with those of other nations. For there the French too had entered as traders, organized in similar companies, but acting in that incorporated, private capacity, under authorizations from their government which involved some ultimate support. The English East India Company and its agents in India could act with greater freedom, however, than was permitted to the French, and could organize action more efficiently by their own initiative and within themselves. This resulted necessarily from the less prescriptive and dictatorial spirit of English government, and from the more independent action in which the Englishmen had been trained.

In India, as in America, the French, at the outset of their rivalry with the English, were much the more alert in securing advantages of position and of circumstance. They were the first to take sides in the native wars, making themselves important as allies, and winning prestige and influence in southern India, while the English, by comparison, were considerably despised. "England," says one of her own historians of British India, "owes the idea of an Indian empire to the French," who likewise showed her how it could be won. But when the English of the East India Company took the idea, and saw that they must do as the French were doing, or lose all that they had come to India for, they soon outdid their teachers in the application of the arts and energy by which native rulers were superseded, or made subservient to European control.

The Anglo-French conflict of colonial ambitions came practically to an end in both India and America, in 1760, the year of the accession of George III to the English throne. England was then at the height of her supremacy among the European nations, and fully entered on her imperial career. Between 1764 and 1779, with what seemed to be a new conception of her destiny, she commissioned a series of official expeditions to explore the Pacific Ocean, resulting in a vast enlargement of her territorial claims in that part of the world. The greatest harvest of territory was gathered by Captain Cook, whose official instructions were to take possession, "with the consent of the natives, in the name of the king of Great Britain, of convenient situations in such countries as you may discover that have not been discovered or visited by any other European power." It was Cook's exploration that enabled the English to establish permanent claim to Australia, and later to New Zealand. It was his explorations, more than any other, which led the way for that wider establishment of English dominion which has taken place during the past two centuries.

In the exercise of their sovereignty over these wide dominions, it may be said with fairness that, on the whole and in the long run, the English, more often than otherwise, have been leaders in the modern culture of those altruistic feelings which check oppressive uses of power. The European enterprises of territorial acquisition and of colonization that were set on foot in the sixteenth century by the discovery of the western hemisphere, were all purely commercial in motive, and were ruled for about three centuries by narrow, unenlightened commercial ideas. These were ideas which tended, as Professor Seeley has shown in his lectures on "The Expansion of England," to put both colonies and conquered dependencies on the footing of so much national property, to be worked as estates for the pecuniary profit of the proprietary nation. Tracing the extension of that theory from captured possessions to colonies, he writes: "In the sixteenth century there was no scruple in applying it to conquered dependencies, and, since the colonies of Spain were in a certain sense conquered dependencies, we can understand that unconsciously, unintentionally, the barbaric principle crept into *her* colonial system, and that it lurked there and poisoned it in later times. We can understand, too, how the example of Spain and the precedents set by her influenced the other European states, Holland, France and England, which entered upon the career of colonization a century later. In the case of some of these states, for example, France, the result of this theory was that the mother country exercised an iron authority over her colonies." [1]

Politically the barbaric Spanish theory could not be put into practice in English colonies, because of the more liberal political institutions under which English colonists had been bred, and because of its repugnance to all English experience and thought; but it could be applied commercially, and it was. Hence the old colonial system of England,—the system that was broken down by the revolt of her American colonies,—"gave unbounded liberty except in one department, namely trade, and in that department it interfered to fine the colonists for the benefit of the home traders." "Thus," says Seeley, "this old system was an irrational jumble of two opposite conceptions. It claimed to rule the colonists because they were Englishmen and brothers, and yet it ruled them as if they were conquered Indians. And, again, while it treated them as conquered people, it gave

[1] Quoted from J. R. Seeley, *The Expansion of England,* pp. 78-79.—Ed.

them so much liberty that they could easily rebel." [1]

When the old system had been wrecked by the discordancy of its commercial with its political principles, and England constructed her colonial policy anew, she honestly yielded her mind to the conviction that freedom is a universal good,—the condition of all prosperity,—and that the more perfectly the terms of freedom could be brought into her relations with her colonies, the more beneficial in all ways those relations would become, equally to herself and to them. So the theory of colonial expansion was civilized in her hands, during the last century, and she introduced new precedents and examples to supersede those of Spain. [There is, however, according to Pollard, still a "distinction between colonies used for exploitation and colonies used for settlement" which "has led to important constitutional variations in the empire. Only those colonies in which large white communities are settled have received self-government; those in which a few whites exploit a large colored population remain subject to the control of the home government." [2]]

Even a hundred years ago the temper of men

[1] Quoted from J. R. Seeley, *The Expansion of England,* pp. 80-81.—Ed.

[2] See A. F. Pollard, *History of England,* p. 152.—Ed.

was harder than it is now, and the breach of sympathy between higher and lower races in the scales of culture and capacity was far more difficult to overcome. In the whole movement which has covered the later-found parts of the world with European masters, selfish motives have remained, no doubt, just the same in force and in quality from the early years of the sixteenth century, when the Spaniards took possession of Mexico and Peru, down to the last years of the nineteenth, when Africa was divided up and the Americans laid their hands on the Philippine Islands; but the temper in them has been greatly softened. It has been softened, too, in some of the dominating races more than in others, and most of all, seemingly, in the peoples of English stock.

Down to the last century, however, the English had quite as much heartlessness to answer for in their treatment of some, at least, among their alien subjects, as can be charged to the account of any other western European race. True, there have been instances, in earlier English rule, of a sordid, callous selfishness and a cold religious bigotry that are almost without a parallel; but so, too, without a parallel, have been the later penitent efforts toward reparation. That India had small experience of anything but rapacity in its government, during a long period of its subjection to an English mercantile corporation, is beyond dispute; though recent historical studies have taken something from the blackness of the pictures that were drawn by Burke. [It is of interest here to note the modern tendency to emphasize the fact that the maladministration of India took place only during the unrestricted rule of the East India Company, and that, with the growth of the influence of the home government, the management of affairs became more ethical, and material conditions began to improve. On the other hand, as Larned says, it must not be supposed that the administration of India under the company was altogether reprehensible. There is no doubt that the actions of men like Warren Hastings were prompted almost entirely by a desire to preserve India for England; and that the misdeeds of their terms of office caused men to forget many of their beneficial public measures. [1]] But the later British rule has been, certainly, as irreproachable as any government by right of conquest, without consent of the governed, can be. [Seeley's comment on

[1] For further discussion on this side of the question, see the article on Warren Hastings, in the Encyclopædia Britannica, 11th edition; Stephen, *Story of Nuncomar;* Strachey, *Hastings and the Rohilla War;* and Cross, *A History of England and Greater Britain.*—Ed.

this subject is pertinent. He claims that England did not *conquer* India in the generally accepted sense, and then goes on to say: "And thus the mystic halo of marvel and miracle which has gathered around this Empire disappears before a fixed scrutiny.[1] It disappears when we perceive that, though we are foreign rulers in India, we are not conquerors resting on superior force, when we recognize that it is a mere European prejudice to assume that since we do not rule *by* the will of the people of India, we must needs rule *against* their will."] Much that the British have done has been from pure intentions of good to the country and the people. Even though there has always been an unconfessed check on such intentions, proceeding from the demand of British industries and trade to have their interests considered before all else, even though this has discouraged the economic development of India in industries that would lessen the market for British goods, nevertheless, in nearly all conditions of peace, order, and even-handed justice between individuals,—in organized systems of education and benevolence, and in public agencies of every description, for trade, travel, and communication,—the country and its people have been immeasurably

[1] See J. R. Seeley, *Expansion of England*, p. 264.—Ed.

benefited in recent times by their British masters. Possibly the taint of self-profiting and self-aggrandizement may be removed in time, by the moral processes that have diminished it so much as they have. [A step toward the democratic government of India is indicated by an article in the *American Review of Reviews* of August, 1918. The article says, in part: "It would be far from true to assert that England looks forward to a future of selfish exploitations in the great Asiatic empire over which the British crown holds sway. . . . Mr. Montagu, Secretary for India in the Lloyd George ministry, has recently spent six months in India, studying all the problems of that vast country. He has returned to London with a report which proposes the beginnings of a very considerable system of native home rule. It is not expected to go as fast in India as we Americans have gone in the Philippines, but the plans proposed constitute a good beginning, and India can go forward towards full self-government on the Canadian plan by the simple process of making wide use of the initial powers conferred upon her."]

[Hopes for the realization of this ideal are justified by England's treatment of her dependencies in another quarter of the world. When the South African problem arose through the outbreak of the Boer War, the fundamental issue was not one of financial gain, but rather of racial equality against racial ascendency. In such an issue Britain's traditions made inevitable her alignment on the side of racial equality. But that Britain's great self-governing colonies should take a voluntary part in helping her to establish this ideal, is indication of the fact that there was developing in the British Empire a unity of sentiment and of aim which had never before been realized.

In this concerted action of England and her colonies in the Boer war, the growth of the idea of imperial federation is discernible. The Imperial Federation Society had been founded in 1878; but it was not until the Boer war that the colonies, which had once been regarded as "millstones around England's neck" came to be recognized as having a vital part in the British imperial organism. In the two Jubilee celebrations of 1887 and 1897, there may have been "a suggestion of blatancy and of mere pride in dominion." But the events which followed the Boer war have proved that this was only a temporary manifestation quite out of accord with the deeper and more permanent conception of imperial responsibility. No surer proof can be found of this new attitude than the note of profound sincerity which is sounded again and again through all of Kipling's poetry, and the acclaim with which that poetry was received among all English-speaking peoples was indication of their growing realization of that responsibility.

This eminently English conception of empire is embodied in the common councils between English statesmen and colonial prime ministers, in which the great problems of imperial policy and administration are discussed with new frankness and a new spirit of coöperation. Coincident with this tendency toward a greater unity on the part of the members of the British Empire has been the development of a more marked national spirit among the peoples of the self-governing colonies, a development which does not, however, as many may have feared, endanger the growth of imperial unity. On the contrary, the sense of nationality is an essential element in the fullest achievement of empire. It is only when each individual organ performs its own particular function that there can be attained the highest efficiency in concerted action toward common ends. As Ramsay Muir has so well said, "The essence of the British system is the free development of natural tendencies, and the encouragement of variety of types; and the future towards which the Empire seems to be tending is not that of a highly centralised and unified state, but that of a brotherhood of free nations, united by community of ideas and institutions, coöperating for many common ends, and above all for the common defense in case of need, but each freely following the natural trend of its own development."[1]]

If there is anywhere a promise of realization of such an empire it is in the governments that are conducted by the English and their kin; for whatever may have been the former fact, they hold the lead now on all lines of progress that tend away from oppression, toward freedom and toward that just law which is its surest guarantee. No claim of the English people is less disputable than that they, more than others, yield an unreserved allegiance to law. Law, in itself, as the interdiction of license and disorder, apart from all its sanctions and all the forces of authority behind it, commands them more generally than it commands other peoples. Some influence in their past has planted and cultivated in their minds the loftiest conception, yet attained among men, of the social purpose for which human ordinances of government are framed. When Hooker said of

[1] Quoted from Ramsay Muir, *The Expansion of Europe*, p. 189.—Ed,

Law that "her seat is the bosom of God, her voice the harmony of the world," he did not exaggerate the impassioned reverence of enlightened feeling which he expressed for his fellow-countrymen. English literature, unlike any other, contains many similar exaltations of the thought and spirit of Law.

As we traced the main incidents of the long, slow evolution of democratic institutions of government in England, we could see how often and how much it depended on reaffirmation and vindications of law, with some broadening and extension, always, of its previous scope,—some deepening of its effect on personal securities and rights. The Norman conqueror found it prudent to base the government of his new subjects, with no greatly disturbing change, on their old cherished law. His son, Henry I, won their loyalty to himself by a charter which confirmed the laws of Edward the Confessor; this, in turn, became the basis of the Great Charter, in which a definitely constitutional structure of law began to take form. Confirmation after confirmation of Magna Carta established the foundation for the grand edifice which successive generations of Englishmen, working sometimes by shrewd uses of opportunity, and sometimes by bold strokes of revolution, have been able to erect. It seems plain, then, that the evolution of the English system of free government involved a training of the people to be vigilant wardens of the law, with an enlightened appreciation of its import, such as no other people have received.

["This amazing political structure,[1] which refuses to fall within any of the categories of political science, which is an empire and yet not an empire, a state and yet not a state, a supernation incorporating in itself an incredible variety of peoples and races, is not a structure which has been designed by the ingenuity of man, or created by the purposive action of a government; it is a natural growth, the product of the spontaneous activity of innumerable individuals and groups springing from among peoples whose history has made liberty and the tolerance of differences their most fundamental instincts; it is the product of a series of accidents, unforeseen, but turned to advantage by the unfailing and ever-new resourcefulness of men habituated to self-government. . . . Almost every form of social organization and of government known to man is represented in its complex and many-hued fabric. It embodies five of the

[1] Quoted from Ramsay Muir, *The Expansion of Europe*, p. 232-234.—Ed.

most completely self-governing communities which the world has known, and four of these control the future of the great empty spaces that remain for the settlement of white men. It finds place for the highly organized caste system by which the teeming millions of India are held together. It preserves the simple tribal organization of the African clans. To different elements among its subjects this empire appears in different aspects. To the self-governing Dominions it is a brotherhood of free nations, coöperating for the defense and diffusion of common ideas and of common institutions. To the ancient civilization of India or of Egypt it is a power which, in spite of all its mistakes and limitations, has brought peace instead of turmoil, law instead of arbitrary might, unity instead of chaos, justice instead of oppression, freedom for the development of the capacities and characteristic ideas of their peoples, and the prospect of a steady growth of national unity and political responsibility. To the backward races it has meant the suppression of unending slaughter, the disappearance of slavery, the protection of the rights and usages of primitive and simple folk against reckless exploitation, and the chance of gradual improvement and emancipation from barbarism. But to all alike, to one quarter of the inhabitants of the world, it has meant the establishment of the Reign of Law, and of the Liberty which can only exist under its shelter. In some degree, though imperfectly as yet, it has realized within its own body all the three great political ideas of the modern world. It has fostered the rise of a sense of nationhood in the young communities of the new lands, and in the old and decaying civilizations of the most ancient historic countries. It has given a freedom of development to self-government such as history has never before known. And by linking together so many diverse and contrasted peoples in a common peace, it has already realized, for a quarter of the globe, the ideal of internationalism on a scale undreamt of by the most sanguine prophets of Europe."]

THE GEOGRAPHIC FACTOR IN ENGLISH HISTORY

DONALD E. SMITH

THE GEOGRAPHIC FACTOR IN ENGLISH HISTORY

THE Serbians have a motto: "One travels the world over, to return to Serbia," which applies, obviously, as most nationalistic mottoes do, in the case of every country on the face of the globe. The English version of it, though not crystallized into epigram, is none the less deeply felt by Englishmen of all time, with what justification the traveler in Great Britain can easily recognize. Viewed externally, England has a simple, well-bred beauty, never flagrant nor extravagant, yet rich and colorful, revealing on all sides the touch of an art that does not distort nature. The rural districts suggest a vast park, with their hedgerows, their fresh woods and gardens, their abundant sunshine and innumerable narrow streams whose placid surfaces little betray the depth of the waters beneath. The rough but low-lying mountains of Wales, northern England and Scotland supply the bold note in the landscape of Great Britain, wild yet nowhere savage, strong yet nowhere gigantic or Alpine.

To get back to less striking details of geography, —the island of Britain is separated from the northwestern coast of Europe by narrow seas which have served sometimes as a barrier, at other times as a link, between the Continent and England. The subsidence of her coast ages ago has made its outline very irregular, and converted the mouths of the rivers into estuaries of great value as harbors. The eastern shore, the edge of a plain, lies low and flat; the other shores are high, steep banks, difficult of access, except at the deep indentations of the rivers. Rising ghost-like out of the sea, the chalk cliffs of the southern coast of England give no suggestion of the character of the land that lies beyond their pale edge. In the olden time, that beyond was a mass of virgin forest, dark, forbidding, and as uninhabitable as the vast fens that stretched for miles around at the mouths of the rivers, interspersed with a few openings that permitted cultivation. The progress of settlement in time has cleared the forest land and reclaimed the swamps, till England stands to-day revealed as a country of rolling hills, smooth plains, and low mountains, a country level and green, immensely varied in activity and resources.

The well-watered downs and valleys of southeastern England, favored by an equable climate, are utilized both for sheep-pastures and for agriculture. Beyond these lies the midland region, or the great Central plain, as it is more often called. This, next to London, is the center of English wealth, population and industry, the scene of a wide variety of human activity,—mining, manufacturing, dairying, grazing,—all knit together in a network of railroads, rivers and canals, and opened to the outside world through its two great seaports, London to the southeast on the estuary of the Thames, Liverpool to the northwest at the mouth of the Mersey.

Back of this great Central plain rises the irregular mass of hill and mountain which forms the western rim of Britain, an almost continuous wall from Land's End to the Hebrides,—nowhere vast and massive, everywhere rough and difficult of access except through its three natural gateways, Bristol Channel, the Mersey, and Solway Firth. The extreme southwestern section, cut off by Bristol, springs precipitously from the stormy Atlantic, the far-jutting, rockbound promontory of Cornwall, whose rich mines of tin and copper first attracted to Britain the trading ships of ancient Phœnicia. Between Bristol Channel and the Mersey lie the low, rugged peaks and ridges of Wales, often veiled in mists from the moisture-laden winds of the west, a land of many flocks and numerous small villages, but richly endowed with a variety of mineral resources. To the north of the Mersey, the western wall rises again in the long, straggling ridges of the Pennines, behind which lies hidden one of the most beautiful spots in all Britain,—the wooded and picturesque mountains of Cumberland, silent, secluded, mirrored in numerous lakes,—the only region in England which has escaped the transforming hand of man. This, the celebrated Lake District, so securely cut off from the rest of Britain, seemed destined by nature to be the home of English romantic poetry. Still farther to the north the mountain rim, broken by Solway Firth and the Firth of Clyde, rises abruptly to the Scottish Highlands, covering the whole northern end of the island,—a massive wall of peaks and crags deeply trenched by glen and fiord,—Britain's bulwark against the winds and waves of Northern seas.

Back of the larger island of Britain, and cut off from easy communication with Europe, lies Ireland,—brilliantly green and attractive, but lonely and poor in natural resources,—encircled by its rim of low-lying mountains, beaten by cold, angry seas, and drenched by continuous rains which render the greater part of its flat central plain an untillable bog, barrier alike to internal communication and to the agriculture and industry from which alone the necessities of life might be secured. Small wonder that the Irish are an emigrating people!

These two large islands, with a number of small and dependent ones, constituting the British Isles, may be regarded as the predestined home of a great people. Surely, few regions of the earth's surface, of equal area, are so favored by natural conditions for the home of so vigorous and progressive a nation. Lacking though they may be in the bland climate and the sheer physical beauty of the most favored Mediterranean lands, the general aspect of nature is here altogether conducive to the highest human development. While it is true that the great scientific observer, Humboldt, regarded France as the most highly endowed of all European lands, from a point of view of natural advantages, we must dissent from his too sweeping generalization. Probably no portion of the earth's surface of equal area possesses such a profusion and variety of sources of wealth. Greater fertility of soil and greater facilities of purely agricultural wealth can be found in many historic river valleys such as the Nile, the Tigris-Euphrates and the Mississippi; and yet the English have been the teachers of the modern world in scientific agriculture. Certain arid mountain regions in Chile, Mexico and Peru, and in Colorado possess untold mineral wealth, but square mile for square mile the coal measures, and the iron, copper and lead mines found in one-half of the area of Great Britain surpass any one of these regions in economic value. Moreover, there can be found nowhere else, another condition markedly peculiar to Britain,—the juxtaposition, within a very limited area, of vast and varied mineral deposits, rich agricultural land, excellent forests, and well-nigh perfect interior water communications, combined with a climate which permits the white man to work under most favorable conditions.

Even if all these natural advantages were not apparent in the earliest historical times, yet the British Isles were attractive to the simple barbarians of the neighboring lands on the Continent, particularly those of what is now the Netherlands and northern Germany. These, before dikes had been built, were bleak regions of alternate forest and marsh, flanked by waste stretches of sandy shore, subject to constant inundations. There were no minerals, like the tin of Cornwall, to encourage commerce, while the level, exposed plains were swept by warring tribes in one desolating invasion after another.

Strange as it may seem to the traveler from America or from Mediterranean lands, the climate of England has been a natural endowment which encouraged immigration in times long past as it does industry in the present. As the geographer Kirchhoff has observed, the winds which sweep over this region from the North Atlantic are heavily charged with ozone so that the sea-air is felt over the whole archipelago, while the abundant moisture which they carry sustains the water supply of the rivers and the brilliant verdure of the landscape at nearly every season of the year. Besides giving essential aid to British agriculture, the high humidity of this region of mists and fogs, combined with its hilly character and abundant water power, has provided in the western part of the island all the conditions essential to the remarkable development of the Lancashire textile industry. Likewise the cyclonic storms of these latitudes have helped to rear a race of skillful, hardy mariners who have been disciplined in the severest school of navigation. There is, however, none of the terrific extremes of rainfall and tempest which have oppressed and discouraged men in the tropics, nor has the climate of these islands permitted the stunting of man's growth as has occurred in wide areas of the same latitudes in Asia and North America. Moreover, British climate has had a peculiar effect upon the relative importance of the neighboring islands of Ireland and Great Britain. The rainfall of Ireland is excessive when considered in connection with the drainage system. Consequently agriculture in Ireland is severely limited through the inability to grow cereals, while central England is in part protected from excessive precipitation by the wall of Welsh mountains in the west.

It is, of course, impossible to state precisely just what motives actuated the Germanic tribes of Angles, Saxons, and Jutes to begin their invasions of Romanized Britain in the fifth century of our era. Probably it was a combination of desire for adventure and conquest for its own sake with the pressure of hunger and dangerous neighbors in their home on the Continent. Suffice it to say that once embarked upon their low, dark ships they found the new land of southern and eastern England more attractive than their old homes, and the work of conquest not too difficult. As every school boy knows, these Teutonic barbarians easily established themselves at various points on the coast and afterwards pushed up the rivers into the interior and gradually mastered the country as far west as Wales and as far north as the Tyne. To what degree these Anglo-Saxons exterminated or assimilated the original inhabitants is not known. We do know, however, that in some cases they used both methods, depending in large measure upon the obstinacy of the resistance. The result was undoubtedly a mixed people, made up of uncertain proportions of Celtic Britons, Romans, and Teutons, whom we, for lack of a better name, call Anglo-Saxons.

Just what the historical bearings of this ethnic fusion have been, it is impossible to say. Professor Haskins in his "The Normans in European History," is not disposed to attach too much importance to it. "Only a formal and mechanical view of history," he says, "seeks to ticket off particular races against particular regions as the sole sources of population and power; only false national pride conceives of any people as continually in the vanguard of civilization. Races are mixed things, institutions and civilization are still more complex, and no people can claim to be a unique and permanent source of light and strength." Professor Goldwin Smith concurs in this view: "The further we go in these inquiries the more reason there seems to be for believing that the peculiarities of races are not congenital, but impressed by primeval circumstance. Not only the same moral and intellectual nature, but the same primitive institutions, are found in all the races that come under our view; they appear alike in Teuton, Celt and Semite. That which is not congenital is probably not indelible, so that the less favoured races, placed under happier circumstances, may in time be brought to the level of the more favored, and nothing warrants inhuman pride of race. But it is surely absurd to deny that peculiarities of race, when formed, are important factors in history."

In Green's "Short History of the English People," the "fair-haired Saxon" was held in great admiration and it has become almost traditional, at least until very recent years, to attribute to the early Teutonic conquerors of England most of the admirable, distinctive qualities of the modern Englishman. Mr. Larned was inclined to refer back to the primitive Teuton the germs of many English institutions. Without attempting to decide between the respective claims of the Anglo-Saxon and Norman schools of historians, it is easy to see that the position of Great Britain was the principal determinant of what the eventual racial amalgam was to be. If England had been as remote as Iceland, it certainly would now have a far greater ethnic unity and in all probability would never have undergone the Norman conquest. As a result of what actually happened the English were conquered without being destroyed; the Norman invasion meant the infusion of a new element without the total supplanting of the original population. "Outside of Normandy," according to Professor Haskins, "the Normans were but a small folk, and sooner or later they inevitably lost their identity. They did their work preëminently not as a people apart, but as a group of leaders and energizers, the little leaven that leaveneth the whole lump. Wherever they went they showed a marvelous power of initiative and of assimilation; . . . The penalty for such activity is rapid loss of identity; the reward is a large share in the general development of civilization. If the Normans paid the penalty, they also reaped the reward, and they were never more Norman than in adopting the statesmanlike policy of toleration and assimilation which led to their ultimate extinction."

After the completion of the Norman conquest the racial identity of the population of the British Isles was finally determined. Henceforth, in their island home they were to work out their historic destiny undisturbed by any further violent intrusion of the foreigner. The process of the modification of nature by man was to continue. In the succeeding centuries, steady encroachments upon the forests and the drainage of the fens were to bring larger and larger areas under cultivation, but there were to be no such striking transformations in the aspect of the land as resulted from the deforestation of many historic regions in North Africa and the Near East or such extensive reclamation as has taken place recently in Egypt and in the western part of the United States. The principal conditions of habitat were now fixed, and in this island home the English people were destined to work out the problems of their arduous but glorious future.

The path of one who would trace the influence of the geographical factors in English history is by no means smooth. The influence of physical environment on human affairs, or the reciprocal action of man and nature, has been discussed ever since the days of the Greek philosophers. Perhaps the first adequate statement of the problem was made by the French thinker Bodin in the last quarter of the sixteenth century. In recent years, the controversy has waxed warm over the question as to whether man or his homeland, nature or nurture, race or habitat, heredity or environment has been the prevailing influence in the life of the individual and society.

Before considering the specific geographical factors which have played so large a part in the history of England and the British Empire, it is only fair to admit that there is great disagreement among historians as to the general nature and direction of geographic influence. Some would even deny any important influence of habitat on historical development and assert that race is the great fundamental fact of history. In other words, an Englishman remains an Englishman wherever he makes his home, in whatever climate and under whatever physical conditions he chances to live. Carlyle went even further in proclaiming the Great Man theory of history and denied to either race or physical environment any power to modify essentially the course of human history. To him, the individual genius of a few contributes all that is noteworthy in the progress of mankind; and Emerson in his "Representative Men" supports Carlyle in this view.

Quite opposed to all this are the theories of the naturalistic or materialistic school of geographers and historians. This philosophy of history with more or less important modifications has been defended and popularized more recently by such writers as Lecky and Bryce in England, and by Professor Shaler and Miss Ellen Churchill Semple in America. Through their writings the modern view of the philosophy of history has been modified imperceptibly but completely, so that it is well-nigh impossible for us to conceive the course of English history, which is now under our consideration, apart from its relation to the broad geographic facts which have indelibly impressed their influence upon it.

Assuming then, as a working hypothesis, that "history is the modification of man by nature and of nature by man," acting through the influence of climate, food, soil, and the general aspect of nature, we will be able to observe some of these effects in the history of England.

If we can agree with Lord Bryce in attributing to physiography and the conditions affecting human industry a marked influence in the shaping of a people's history we will find no more striking exemplification of the workings of these factors than in the British Isles. It is true that these influences are here not always the most obvious, nor as simple in their discernible effects as may sometimes be seen in the life of a nomad community living in the desert, or in the case of a mountaineer folk like the Swiss and Scotch highlanders, but the geographical factor will, nevertheless, become apparent on the slightest analysis. A study of the physiography of the British Isles will explain not only the backwardness of Ireland, and the marked characteristics of the people of Wales and the Scottish Highlands but will also enable us to understand the course of the migrations and conquests and consequent racial distribution of the inhabitants of these islands, past and present. Whether man is now more dependent upon the natural conditions which surround him than he was in the past need not enter into the discussion. But the distribution of the forests, fens, rivers, and mountains has always affected the density of population and the conditions of life. It is physiography, not the accidents of history, which has dictated that the English must be not a nation of nomadic shepherds, nor of mountaineers, nor indeed an exclusively agricultural people, but rather a society with a complex industrial and commercial life.

The question of the influence of the geographical environment upon the ethnic composition and character of the English people has not escaped much learned discussion. Speaking of the influence of the configuration of the land upon its inhabitants, Professor Hinsdale has said, "Nothing can be more evident than that these facts almost wholly controlled the early movement of races, such as migration, and that they powerfully affect military operations, the character and extent of conquests, the size and the boundaries of states, the location and character of cities, and the direction, kind, and abundance of facilities for travel and transportation." The situation of England as it fronts the shores of north central Europe was an invitation to the nearest Teutonic people to come over and occupy the land. Even in the days of primitive seamanship the distance from the mouths of the Rhine and the Scheldt to the estuary of the Thames was very short, while less than thirty miles separates the Dover cliffs from the mainland opposite. It was a more serious matter for a large body of people to cross the North Sea from Scandinavia, but the difficulty was partially obviated by the much shorter distance from the Norwegian fiords to the coast of Scotland. Natural harbors were to be found in the estuaries of the English rivers and the Northmen found easy access to the interior of the country simply by following the river courses. There is no difficulty, then, in realizing how readily the island of Great Britain became a meeting place of all races of northwestern Europe. Whether it is true or not, as some biologists assert, that such an amalgamation of different racial stocks produces a more vigorous people, need not concern us here. The patent fact is before us that British geography brought upon the original Celtic inhabitants wave after wave of the more daring, adventurous, and energetic peoples of Europe,—Romans, Teutons, Danes, and Normans, —which have in unknown proportions been fused into what is called the Anglo-Saxon race. Britain, by her island position, selected her own inhabitants; the resulting interaction between these inhabitants and their environment has determined the course of English history.

What can be asserted, in general, of the result of insular life upon a people? Having in mind such islands as that ancient seat of Ægean civilization, Crete, or the island of Sicily, that meeting place of three great historical peoples, the Phœnicians, the Greeks and the Romans, what general inferences may be drawn regarding the characteristics of islanders? Miss Semple, in her "Influences of Geographic Environment," points out that island life tends to develop marked national individuality which is developed by isolation and accompanied often by a precocious civilization. This marked individuality of island folk is regularly seen "in combination with the opposite fact of the imminent possibility of an expansive unfolding, a brilliant efflorescence followed by a wide dispersal of its seeds of culture and empire." After remarking that these island peoples rarely originate the elements of civilization, Miss Semple adds, "For that their area is too small. But whatever seed ripens in the wide fields of the continents the islands transplant to their own forcing-houses; there they transform and perfect the flower. Japan borrowed freely from China and Korea, as England did from continental Europe; but these two island realms have brought Asiatic and European civilization to their highest stage of development. Now the borrowers are making return with generous hand. The islands are reacting on the continents. Japanese ideals are leavening the whole Orient from Manchuria to Ceylon. English civilization is the standard of Europe. 'The Russian in his snows is aiming to be English,' says Emerson. 'England has inoculated all nations with her civilization, intelligence and tastes.'"

The British Isles, as Kirchhoff has said, are especially suited to be the home of a hardy, resourceful people. This is in agreement with the view held by the English writer, Goldwin Smith, who maintains that islands are more likely than continental areas to be settled by a bold and enterprising race. Migration by land has more often been the result of some outer compulsion such as the pressure of hostile neighbors, or simply the consequence of the wandering habit, and need not necessarily betoken any particular activity or enterprise. On the other hand, the migration of peoples by sea in ancient times was not only a hazardous enterprise but one likely to weed out the timorous and the inefficient. History has no record of a people endowed with more magnificent daring than the Norsemen. The Greeks and the Phœnicians were timid navigators, by comparison, and regularly hugged the shore in their fear of what Homer called the "unfruitful" sea. As Goldwin Smith says, "The Northman evidently felt perfectly at home on the ocean, and rode joyously, like a seabird, on the vast Atlantic waves." The population of the island of Great Britain is made up almost entirely of a highly selected race,—daring, resourceful, adventurous seekers after freedom, yet willing and loyal followers of a proved and acknowledged leader.

Readers of Wordsworth are familiar with the

ode in which he associates human freedom with the mountains and the sea. The mountaineers of Wales and Scotland have sustained the Celtic tradition of liberty; the Anglo-Saxons brought with them a similar spirit. But this spirit of liberty, in itself a product of historical evolution, must be securely protected during the early stages of its growth. Such a protection the sea affords to an island population. The most easily recognized advantage of an insular position is freedom from invasion. No country can be absolutely secure without being utterly remote from the regions of civilization, but remoteness is a relative matter. England is remote enough behind her sea barriers to render invasion exceedingly difficult,—her lands have not been harried by a foreign invader for seven hundred years. This advantage, moreover, is not merely one of immunity from foreign conquest. It has also contributed to the political liberty and prosperity of the country by reducing the need of a standing army and militaristic institutions. In addition, the orderly development of national life had not been arrested by having forced upon it an alien civilization.

The insularity of England has of course resulted also in a certain cultural isolation. This has tended to foster the self-sufficiency and the peculiarities of the Englishman and has prevented the ready influx of foreign ideas. But England is nevertheless essentially a part of Europe, while standing somewhat aloof and exercising a moderating influence upon the affairs of the Continent. She has been "the asylum of vanquished ideas and parties." Spanish and Portuguese Jews fleeing from the Inquisition, French Huguenots, after the revocation of the Edict of Nantes, and Netherland fugitives from Spanish tyranny have in turn taken refuge in England and given their talents to the common store of English national life. Thus English insularity has been tempered by the very nearness of the island to the Continent. England has been spared, by its situation, the extreme isolation of Iceland or that of Norway and Ireland. Foreign ideas can penetrate by the slow process of infiltration; they cannot overwhelm with a sudden rush.

Nor can it be denied that the actual area or extent of the British Isles has in itself had a peculiar influence. It has always been recognized that the mere fact of the greater size and natural wealth of Great Britain as compared with Ireland have determined very largely the relations of the two. The larger island, more fortunately situated in regard to the rest of Europe, was bound to be the dominant partner. Ireland was too near to escape the orbit of British influence and too small and poor to resist successfully. Likewise, the superior size and resources of England pointed unmistakably to her ultimate triumph over both Wales and Scotland. The division of Scotland into highlands and lowlands, unfortunate from the point of view of Scotch independence; and the poverty of the Welsh in their remote mountain home all contributed to the unavoidable predominance of the English. Furthermore, the area of these islands must have had curious negative effects. It is unthinkable that the course of English history could have run as it has, if the total area of the islands had been no more than that of Crete, or, on the other hand, if it had been as great as that of Australia. In the former case, England must have remained a mere dependency of one of its powerful continental neighbors, another Corsica, or at best Sicily; while if the island had been very much larger we must imagine it seeking to dominate its continental neighbors much more successfully and, in a sense, more ruinously than has actually occurred. It is quite possible, also, that if England had been as small as the island of Crete it might have had a brilliant history as a purely maritime state, a kind of Tyre or Athens, but without the solid backing of a large agricultural population, the only source of a man-power adequate to play a great rôle as an empire-builder. A greater area, on the other hand, must have destroyed the balance between the agricultural and the maritime population as it has actually existed; and the close articulation of the sea and land which is more marked in Great Britain than in any other similar area in Europe could not be so dominant a characteristic of the country. Under these circumstances, the national life might have approximated more nearly that of France or Germany, while the greater mass of such an enlarged England would probably have rendered a Norman conquest utterly impossible.

Perhaps the most obvious geographic fact about a country is its situation with reference to other lands. The position of the British Isles has long been recognized as peculiarly advantageous to her power and prosperity. Although these islands are on the extreme verge of the Continent they are not a mere outpost or frontier station. Lying, as they do, close to the principal countries of central and western Europe and athwart the mouths of the great rivers which constitute the natural highways of commerce, England is rather the gateway of Europe than a detached and isolated portion of it. The present war has emphasized the tremendous importance of those islands in their commanding position to close the northern shores of central Europe to the trade of the world; ships from the Baltic ports, Scandinavia, Hamburg, Rotterdam, and Antwerp can find egress from the North Sea only by passing under the guns of the British fleet and shore batteries. English seaports have been natural entrepôts of commerce for the greater part of Europe ever since the opening in the sixteenth century of the new trade-routes to America and the Far East. It has not been merely the innate mercantile superiority of Englishmen that has made the greatness of Liverpool and London. The avenues of sea-born trade for the northern hemisphere have their natural focus in the British Isles—a fact which has not been altered by the opening of the Suez Canal and the consequent restoration of the Mediterranean to something like its former commercial importance.

It has often been remarked that the British Isles have a highly favorable location on the earth's surface, not only because of their immediate situation near the European continent but also because of their relation to the great land

and water masses of the globe. If New Zealand lies near the center of the water hemisphere, so Great Britain lies in the center of that hemisphere which contains the largest extent of land. If a spectator could be raised above London to a sufficient height to see half the globe beneath him, his view would embrace all Europe, Asia, Africa, North America and the greater part of South America; only Australia, New Zealand and a small part of South America, would lie beyond the horizon. This central strategic position, while it has, of course, a geographic basis, is also largely a historical product. In classical times Britannia and Hibernia lay upon the uttermost fringe of the known world. Their isolation from the great currents of early historical times was greater than that of New Zealand in the present. Even as late as "the spacious days of good Queen Bess" England was, in a sense, an out-of-the-way land not unlike the Far West of fifty years ago. "It would be difficult to find in all history a more convincing proof of the influence of the geographical position of a country on the fate of its inhabitants than is that of Britain. Englishmen of the prediscovery days formed, in spite of the genius and valor displayed by their race on the fields of war, of poetry and science, but a small population of comparatively little influence on the march of universal history. The discoveries of the great navigators of Latin blood enlarged our knowledge of the globe, revealed the central position of Britain on the land hemisphere, and led unexpectedly to the expansion of this little kingdom into the world-wide British Empire." [1]

Nor is the effect of geography less marked in the internal development of England. The island of Great Britain, unlike the schoolboy's Gaul, is divided into five parts, determined by the conformation of its mountains and hills, reënforced by the trend of its principal rivers. Wales and the highlands of Scotland stand apart as two independent regions strongly marked by their rugged mountain character and relative inaccessibility. Of the remaining three sections, by far the larger and most important part of the island, the northernmost is the Scottish Lowlands, separated from England by the Cheviot Hills and Solway Firth. England, proper, is in turn divided into two equal areas by the valleys of the Trent and the Severn—the land lying to the north and west of these rivers being higher, more wild and picturesque, and more turbulent in its history, while to the south and east of this line are the fertile agricul-

[1] Kirchhoff, "*Man and Earth,*" p. 147.

tural lands, the old commercial cities and earliest centers of wealth and culture. Nearer to the mainland, southeastern England was always first exposed to those civilizing influences that spread from the Mediterranean world to the outer edge of the Continent. European culture therefore took root in southern England and afterward spread northward, so that it is here that we find London and Westminster, Canterbury and Winchester, Oxford and Cambridge.

Taking then as a line of cleavage between southeastern and northwestern England the diagonal drawn from the mouth of the Severn on thc Bristol Channel to the mouth of the Trent on the Humber, it will be found that the differing geographical features of the two regions have had a potent influence on English history. Even though this line is not hard and fast nor marked by any distinct or impassable barrier, it separates two regions as opposed in their historical development as the North and the South in the United States of America. In the beginning, invaders from across the Channel and the North Sea, landing in the southeast, pushed the earlier inhabitants toward the northwest. Hence the Romans, then the Angles and Saxons, and finally the Normans made the lands south of the Humber more completely their own and left Wales and Scotland almost untouched. The Celtic tribes in the remote west and north were consequently not exterminated but have survived to contribute to the population of Great Britain an element not alien but different.

Furthermore, the richer agricultural region of the southeast with its commercial towns and more direct communication with the outside world was quicker to emancipate itself from the economic and social conditions of the Middle Ages. The Peasants' Revolt of the fourteenth century scarcely touched the rude, undeveloped peoples of the north. The southland, populous, wealthy and progressive, was until the eighteenth century the home of English radicalism, while the feudal northwest, dominated by the nobles and clergy, stood faithfully by the king and the established order. London was the sheet-anchor of the Parliamentary party in the struggle against the crown in the days of Cromwell. The south, too, had been the first to feel the new ideas of the Renaissance and Reformation. Here republicanism and puritanism throve, while the landed aristocracy of the pastoral north remained staunchly conservative in politics and religion.

But a curious inversion of these respective rôles

has been effected by geographical factors unrealized before the Industrial Revolution. Before the eighteenth century, when England was a commercial and agricultural country, geography favored the economic superiority of the southern portion of the island; but when the new processes and inventions of Hargreaves, Arkwright and Watt made possible the extraordinary development of English manufactures, the industrial center of gravity shifted to the northwest. The vital part played by iron and coal in modern industry gave new value to the mines in the neighborhood of Newcastle, Sheffield and Birmingham. Factories and population began to cluster around the northern coal measures. The infertility of the soil in the northern part of England, in South Wales and in Scotland was not an impediment to the growth of factory towns and a great urban population; in the rising seaports of Liverpool and Glasgow new industrial regions found gateways for their incoming raw materials and for outgoing finished products.

These economic changes were likewise reflected in the political life of the country. English liberalism gravitated with the mass of the population toward factory cities like Manchester and Birmingham; the great Reform Bill of 1832 was in part a response to changes in social conditions which had in turn resulted from the rise of the new industrialism based on the natural resources of the northwest. London and the southeast, which as late as the Glorious Revolution of 1688 had been the progressive commercial district, was soon outdistanced by these rapidly growing industrial cities of the north, and finally has come to be the center of English conservatism. A closely packed population of artisans in factory towns forms an ideal substructure for the building-up of a liberal party with a radical wing. It need not surprise us, therefore, that Manchester, three generations ago, should have given its name to a new school of political and economic thought, or that the northwest, later, should produce Gladstone, Bright, Chamberlain and Lloyd-George.

Geography, as we have seen, has been a potent factor in determining English political affairs; it has been even more potent in the upbuilding of England's maritime supremacy. In the first known theater of maritime activity, the inhabitants of the Ægean Islands, notably the Cretans, were the great seafaring people. Some time later this primacy passed to the Phœnicians and their great colony at Carthage; but the Greeks had already emerged as a rival power in trade and colonization. Under Roman rule the Mediterranean was a highway of peaceful commerce. It was not until after the barbarian invasions that warfare on the sea was resumed and we read of the predatory Vandals establishing a temporary supremacy over the western Mediterranean basin. During the mediæval period the northernmost wing of the Teutonic race, by their oversea expeditions, laid the foundations of England, while later still the maritime communities in and about northern Italy dominated the trade-routes of the Mediterranean. But of all the peoples who have used the sea in peace and war nonc havc so identified themselves with it or utilized it so successfully as the English.

The two factors, race and geography, are fundamental in explaining the expansion of England. However, it is well in this connection to speak a word of caution. As Professor Seeley has so clearly pointed out, the primacy of England among the maritime nations was not established until comparatively recent times. The fact that the world has become so accustomed to acknowledging the superiority of the British islanders in all activities relating to the sea, has led to the general belief that this was always so and that from the nature of the English people it could never have been otherwise. There is great danger in thus taking for granted the innate racial superiority of the Anglo-Saxons in this as in other fields of human endeavor, and in ascribing to inherent necessity that to which we have become accustomed. It may seem clear to us that the Anglo-Saxons, descended from sea-rovers and Vikings, are by nature's degree foreordained to follow the highways of the sea to subdue and replenish the earth. As a matter of fact it is impossible to speak of England as a maritime power until long after the discovery of America. "Our insular position," says Professor Seeley, "and the fact that our island toward the West and North looks right out on the Atlantic ocean, may lead us to fancy that the nation must always have been maritime by the necessity of the case. . . . But after all England is not a Norway; it is not a country which has only narrow strips of cultivable land, and therefore forces its population to look to the sea for their subsistence. England in the time of the Plantagenets, was no mistress of the seas; in fact she was scarcely a maritime state at all. Occasionally in wartime we find mediæval England in possession of a considerable navy. But as soon as peace arrived the navy dwindled away again. The constant complaints of piracy in the Channel show how little control England was able to exercise even over her own seas." Under the Plantagenets the English were more warlike than at any later time, but they exercised their fighting spirit in campaigns in France. "The glories of the English army of those days greatly eclipsed those of the English navy; we remember the victories of Crécy and Poitiers, but we have forgotten that of Sluys."

In spite of the latent capabilities of maritime adventure which lay deep in Anglo-Saxon nature, geography dictated that these powers must lie dormant until the more modern world should open up a new field of opportunity. As late as the fifteenth century the English were narrowly circumscribed on the frontier of Europe while the cities of the Hanseatic League and the northern shores of the Mediterranean were more advantageously placed nearer the centers of the world's commerce. The trading activities growing out of the Crusades had deeply stirred many localities on the Continent but it only barely touched the remote British Isles. It was not till the middle of the seventeenth century that the amphibious Blake, once a general, later an admiral, led an English fleet into the Mediterranean. When in the sixteenth century the changed commercial interests of Europe shifted the business center of gravity from the Mediterranean to the Atlantic coast, it was Cadiz and Lisbon, not the English seaports, that took the places of Venice, Genoa and Barcelona. It is not to be assumed, of course, that all maritime life must wait upon and be regarded as identical with colonization and empire. Even in the sixteenth century, life in the British Isles was more maritime, more closely connected with the sea than was that of Spain. The waters which wash the British shores abounded in fish, and the English as well as the Dutch were rearing a hardy population of fishermen and sailors engaged in the local coasting trade, while English ships plied actively on the narrow waters between England and France and the Low Countries. All this was natural enough, but what seems strange to us was the postponement of England's participation in the epic of discovery and exploration. But the early preëminence of the Italians, Portuguese, and Spaniards must not drive us to the other extreme of being too apologetic of the English. In spite of Professor Seeley's modest claims for his countrymen, the English were not long behind-hand in the race for dominion over-seas. And if they were belated, they were in good company. The French and the Dutch were likewise late in feeling the new impulse, while the great merchant seamen in the Hansa sphere of influence were hopelessly sluggish in realizing the new opportunities. Moreover, we can now see how the English were becoming fairly launched upon their Atlantic period of history even in the Tudor period, although they could make no pretension of taking the lead in the unrivaled explorations of the fifteenth and sixteenth centuries. It was a ship from Bristol which anticipated Columbus in actually reaching the American continent, and before the sixteenth century was over the Elizabethan sailors were playing a conspicuous part in opening up the New World. Nor was the defeat of the Armada a mere flash in the pan, an accidental victory, due to the genius of an individual commander. It was primarily a victory of seamanship, of men bred to the life of the sea, of professionals over amateurs. That England did not immediately thereafter become a great naval power in a technical, military sense was due to a new tendency in national policy rather than to any incapacity. Conditions of insular life had been at work long enough to endow the English with all the potentialities of maritime supremacy and time only was needed to exhibit them on a magnificent scale.

There is no need to dwell upon the individual

achievements of English navigators and admirals in subsequent times. We are not concerned with personal talent but rather with the genius of a race as conditioned by its geographical environment. Even an indelible predilection for trade and travel might have been stifled during the ages by unfavorable conditions of habitat. The Swiss are scarcely more inhibited from maritime development than an island population denied access to the sea by an unfavorable articulation of land and water. But in this regard the geographical factor was altogether favorable to the English. A profusion of natural harbors, almost perfectly distributed around the whole circumference of the island, with rivers leading back from them, was only one element. The land was abundantly supplied with ship timber and skilled artisans to utilize it, while the population was large enough and rich enough to feel those commercial needs which impelled them to trade with their neighbors. Perhaps all this might not have been sufficient to give the United Kingdom over two-thirds of the ocean-going tonnage of the world. Less than a century ago, when a general progress in the mechanic arts led to a revolution in ship-building, the English took every advantage of the changed conditions. The Industrial Revolution had given them what was nearly a monopoly in the building of steam machinery so that the transition from the age of sailing ships to steam navigation only confirmed their superiority. The change from wooden to iron and steel ships, which came still later, could only help that nation which led the world in iron and steel production. Nature again conferred an inestimable boon upon England's shipping interests when she gave her the Welsh coal fields. Coal suitable for fuel on steamships is distributed very sparingly around the world, so that the presence of excellent bunker coal in South Wales, near tidewater, has been a benefit beyond all calculation to English shipping interests.

It would be unprofitable in this connection to enumerate further the advantages which this island people have derived from the situation, physiography and natural products of their island home. But there is another consideration which now forces itself upon our attention. Mr. Larned in his essay refers to the peculiarities of English emigration and colonization. Industries connected with the sea and even extensive trade relation with distant countries need not necessarily lead a nation to found a colonial empire, as witness Norway. But we can now with our historical perspective perceive how certain geographical considerations led to the foundation of a Greater Britain. The fascinating subject of the political organization of the British Empire is already preëmpted by Mr. Larned, but the geographical substructure upon which that imposing edifice is reared deserves some discussion in this essay.

It is a well-known fact that one-fifth of the land surface of the globe and something like one-fourth of the earth's population are in the British Empire. Its various shores are washed by the Seven Seas and it enjoys or endures every variety of climate and every degree of fertility and aridity from the polar regions to the tropics. The component parts of the empire are nearly equally divided between the northern and the southern hemispheres and among the various continents so that there is a complete diversification of industry. The settlements of the English-speaking people not only completely encircle the globe but they have taken possession of the choicest land from the point of view of productivity as well as suitability for the homes of white men. It is a mere truism to say that the British Empire is based upon the sea-power of England and that its highways of communication are the sea. That this empire has an economic foundation and is knit together by a multiplicity of commercial interests rather than held down by brute force goes without saying. Our question is, then, what geographical factors have entered into the production of this imperial fabric?

This question can not be answered by reference solely to the maritime instincts of the English people, together with their insular position and accessibility to the sea. In a general sense all Europe with its peninsular lands and its large and intelligent population is peculiarly fitted to expand its commerce, civilization, and political rule over the rest of the earth. This is just what has been happening during the last four centuries and the English have only been in the lead and forefront of this movement. Some one has said that ancient Hellas was "the most European of European lands." If this is literally true the British Isles stand next to ancient Greece in the possession of especially European attributes with the further important advantage of possessing extraordinary natural resources. It may be said then that England is Europe only more so, and differs from its continental neighbors only in possessing the European character in a higher degree. If the geographical advantages possessed by the English people in combination with their own good fortune and the ill-luck of some of their principal rivals have somehow given them a unique position in the world to-day, this can only be understood in the light of the actual facts of the evolution of the empire.

The first step in the territorial evolution of the British Empire was the unification of all the British Isles under one political sovereignty. This in itself was a long, slow process and could not be undertaken until the period of foreign invasions was over. We cannot think of the present imperial domain as based upon England alone. English invasion into extra-European lands could only be safely begun after the solution of the Welsh, Scotch, and Irish question. At the same time it is more than likely that the preservation of distinctive qualities among these junior members of the British family has contributed to the richness as well as variety of the resultant civilization. We now all agree with Matthew Arnold in appraising highly the Celtic element in the British population. Vexatious as these domestic problems have been to English policy they have probably helped to save the life of these islands from a monotonous uniformity. The evils of disunity were substantially overcome before the young empire was forced to meet the great external dangers personified in Louis XIV and Napoleon. Nature had placed the several British Isles too near together to become eventually anything but one family, but they were divided by the sea and the mountains sufficiently to perpetuate interesting and extremely valuable individual characteristics.

Confronting successive foreign enemies at the threshold of her entry into the imperial estate, geography selected for England not only her friends but her enemies and profoundly influenced her foreign policy. Leaving to one side the futile struggle of the Hundred Years' War at the close of the mediæval period, we can see how the location of England projected her into a conflict with any great military power controlling the Low Countries. Even before the Tudors the French overlordship of Flanders brought them into conflict with the English kings. In the sixteenth century the inclusion of the Netherlands in the Spanish dominion, rather than the differences between the Protestants and Catholics, precipitated the struggle between Philip II and Elizabeth. The buccaneering exuberance of England's young sea-power furnished added complications and later experience made the control of the narrow seas between England and the Continent a settled feature of English policy. So consistently have the English followed this national policy that it now seems inevitable that they should become involved in international difficulties if not actual war with any great military power that seeks to dominate Holland or Belgium. After the war with Spain in the time of Philip II, the ambition of Louis XIV to secure the Low Countries brought England into the conflict, and a similar situation arose a century later with Revolutionary France and Napoleon. There is, therefore, ample precedent for the British defense of Belgium against Germany in the present war.

Mr. Mackinder has remarked that England was "of Europe but not in Europe" and this is true enough to explain a certain aloofness of the English from ordinary European rivalries and her devotion to the principle of the balance of power. The progress of military science and the formation of powerful centralized states in western Europe discouraged active participation by the English in continental wars and steadily diverted them to a more thorough pursuit of commercial interests. England's steadily growing strength was henceforth to be thrown more exclusively against any nation that appeared in the lists as a commercial rival. The growing importance of the mercantile class likewise deflected England from militaristic adventures, and with enlightened selfishness made their country's foreign policy conform to its economic interests. To be sure individual initiative and enterprise has usually preceded government aid, or even protection, in the carving out of new territory for the British Empire. But seldom have the pioneers in trade and colonial enterprise failed to win a sympathetic backing from the government. This has been illustrated repeatedly in India, Africa and Australasia, where foothold has been secured by private persons engaged in business to be followed up later by active governmental protection and participation, until finally a new colony was founded or a new territory conquered.

This apparently planless and happy-go-lucky up-building of the English dominion beyond the seas has excited the wrathful scorn of the Germans. They have pointed out repeatedly that the English have succeeded only by the most undeserved good luck, combined with occasional flashes of intelligent brutality. It must be conceded that good fortune has often attended on English ventures in imperialism. It was no merit of the English but the most fortunate circumstance of their isolation which spared them the desolation which the Thirty Years' War brought upon Germany, and this is only one example of the sort of affliction which was visited upon the peoples of the European continent. English military prowess, even though it helped, was not the principal cause of the decline of Spain in the seventeenth century nor the squandering of the resources of France in the later dynastic wars. Geography not only helped England directly in countless ways, but it indirectly promoted British interests by helping to destroy her enemies. Wars not only crippled rival industry on the Continent but drove to England thousands of skilled artisans who became an integral part of English industry. At a time when France was England's principal rival, the illiberal treatment by France of her Huguenot population injured French manufactures and sent these talented exiles to seek an asylum in England; while a similar illiberality of the English government toward its religious nonconformists sent admirable colonists to become empire-builders in the New World.

Good luck and geography combined often facilitated British progress toward world dominion in most curious ways. By intrinsic merit and heroic endeavor the Portuguese deserved to be a formidable rival. However, they lacked the population and natural resources to give them, in Europe, the broad basis of a colonial empire. Their ultimate failure, moreover, was assured by their being exposed without natural frontiers to the military power of Spain. The sixty years' "Babylonian Captivity" as a conquered Spanish province was not only a check to the country's development but made Portugal thereafter dependent upon foreign support to maintain her independence. Thus Portugal became a client state of England's instead of a serious opponent. Indeed, by a curious turn of fortune, Bombay passed from the hands of the Portuguese to the British as a dowry of the Portuguese wife of an English king. This was soon to strengthen the position of the English in India and proportionately injure their rivals. Again it was good luck rather than intelligent policy that secured Gibraltar and so led the way to England's becoming a great Mediterranean power. A fortunate combination of circumstances rather than foresight took the English to Malta and to Egypt; but enough has surely been said to illustrate this point. Geography, which often made the mistakes and misfortune of England's rivals fatal, often rendered her own innocuous. A temporary weakness of the government of England, due to the incapacity of the king or a civil war, did not immediately lay the island open to easy conquest. Her rapidly growing population nourished by the productivity of the soil and the varied facilities of industry furnished a reservoir from which to stock her colonial possessions. Thus she could make full use of whatever opportunity chance or manifest destiny brought to her.

In no part of the world has the work of England as a colonizer and empire builder been more strikingly exemplified than in North America. The late start which the English made in the actual establishment of colonies, might under different circumstances have proved fatal to their ultimate success. For over one hundred years after the discovery of America the Spanish and the Portuguese were permitted to select the sites of their colonies and occupy as much of the land of the new continent as they desired, undisturbed by any interference of the English or French. Fortunately for the future Anglo-Saxon supremacy in North America, the Portuguese directed their efforts to South America, Africa, and southeastern Asia. The Spaniards followed in a general way the tracks of Columbus and concentrated their efforts upon the West Indies, and Central and South America. The initial impulse which was given to exploration and settlement in this region was reënforced by the finding of precious metals in Mexico and Peru. For generations afterwards, the energies of Spain were concentrated here, leaving the northern part of the American continent to others. This was largely accident, although the winds and ocean currents had been the chief factors in taking Columbus over the course which he sailed and bringing him to the particular portion of the newly discovered lands which he actually reached.

Similarly, the claims in the New World which were staked out by the English, French, and Dutch were determined in the first instance mainly by geographical considerations. The North Atlantic is relatively narrow between Newfoundland on the one side and Ireland and Brittany on the other. Knowledge that the Spaniards had already preëmpted the lands for the south also directed the later arrivals to the more northern portion of North America. All these influences combined to apportion in a rough way the newly discovered lands among the maritime powers.

The new conditions of life which the English and French found awaiting them were arduous enough to discourage the timid and weed out the unfit, without absolutely discouraging immigration from Europe. The climate of our Atlantic seaboard is more rigorous than that of France and the British Isles but it is a white man's country and makes no impossible demands upon a European's powers of adaptation. South of Chesapeake Bay many districts suffered from malaria which, combined with the hot summers, put a premium upon negro slavery. On the northern end of the habitable area, in the St. Lawrence region, agriculture was made difficult by severe winters and a thin soil. Physiography and climate, therefore, discouraged the growth of a dense population in what is now lower Canada and hampered the growth of the French settlements there, despite the profits in the fur trade.

The main outlines of the growth of the English colonies were also fixed fairly early by these same natural features. The climate, the configuration of the land, the presence or absence of natural harbors, the fertility of the soil, and the fauna and flora directed industry into this or that channel. The mountain wall of the Appalachians flanked by dense forest growths opposed a mighty barrier to westward migration, while the warlike aborigines assisted the mountains and forests in hemming in the English colonists close to the Atlantic shore-land.

The struggle was not decided by these natural features alone, but they contributed mightily to the victory of the English. Mr. Larned has pointed out how the policies of the home government of France and England affected the conflict in America and we will not labor the point further.

The English colonial institutions were worked out principally in connection with the growth of the American colonies and this experience has been utilized wisely in the governance of similar settlements in other parts of the world.

The geographical advantages enjoyed by the British Empire in the Great War are hard to exaggerate. The fervent loyalty of the Dominions is a tribute to English political achievement, but the direct bearing on the struggle of British sea-power is closely correlated with her strategic position astride all the chief lines of water communication. Reference has been made before to the many advantages of the location of the British Isles relative to the neighboring coast of Europe. But the possession of such key-positions as Gibraltar, Malta, the Suez Canal, Aden, Ceylon, Singapore, and Hong-Kong—not to mention a multitude of coaling-stations and naval bases in every part of the world—enormously facilitates the operations of the Allied fleets. The instinct for maritime exploration and discovery which led Drake, Cook, and Vancouver into distant seas not only gave England title to the richest portions of the earth for colonization but also secured to her the best natural harbors and military and commercial positions. Two places of supreme importance for ocean transportation which the English barely missed acquiring have fallen to their American kinsmen, so that Hawaii and the Panama Canal now perfectly supplement the previously won British possessions in the working out of Allied naval strategy.

Perhaps it is not too much to claim that the hope of the world now rests in the continued control of the sea by the Anglo-Saxon, at least until a new world-order shall have brought about its internationalization. The uninterrupted flow of men and supplies to Europe from America and the British Dominions is surely a condition precedent for the success of the Allied arms. If the natural advantages of the British Isles in the selection of their inhabitants in the beginning, plus the later triumphs in trade and colonization, have aroused the fear and envy of modern Germany, it is but the irony of history that this island people by their spirit of high maritime adventure should break the power of the land despotism. A hundred years ago, men talked of England as the modern Carthage and they spoke of "perfidious Albion" as the equivalent of "Punic faith." Even now Prussian militarism can see only weakness in an empire held together chiefly by commercial interests and a spirit of voluntary association. But when the day came, England kept her faith with Belgium and with France; and the Dominions—the "Lion's Whelps" of Kipling—needed neither compulsion nor exhortation.

Geography and an historical evolution continuously influenced by the geographical factors of the sea and insular life have made Great Britain the heart of a mighty empire, bound together by a community of interests and ideas. Political liberty of the individual citizen and of the several self-governing dependencies is fundamental to its prosperity and permanence. Imperial federation, with its unity based upon the common heritage of democratic institutions and the unrestricted use of the ocean highways, gives us the pattern of a newer and better ordering of the relations of all the peoples of the earth. The Englishman, Tennyson, has expressed it perfectly in the "Parliament of Man, the Federation of the World."

ENGLISH CONTRIBUTIONS TO SCIENTIFIC THOUGHT

GRACE F. CALDWELL

ENGLISH CONTRIBUTIONS TO SCIENTIFIC THOUGHT

THE English mind, we are often told, has two pet aversions,—a joke and a work of art. Whatever may be their shortcomings, however, in wit and humor, or in the arts, the English certainly hold no inconsiderable place in the evolution of scientific thought, particularly of that practical and altruistic thought which looks toward social betterment. Nothing could be more characteristic of the English attitude toward science than the words spoken by Sir Humphry Davy, that never wearying champion of the "cause of humanity,"—words spoken nearly a hundred years ago, when, at a meeting of the Royal Society for the Advancement of Science, he presented the Copley medal to the French physicist, François Arago, in honor of his discovery of the property possessed by bodies in general to be affected by magnetism: "As one of our Fellows, his discoveries have the same interest for us that they have for his brethren of the Royal Academy of Sciences. We, I trust, shall never be behind them in dignity and nobleness of sentiment; far be from us that narrow policy which would contract the minds of individuals and injure the interest of nations, by cold and exclusive selfishness; which would raise the greatness of one people by lowering the standard of that of another. As in commerce, so in science, no country can become worthily preëminent except in profiting by the wants, resources and wealth of its neighbors. Every new discovery may be considered as a new species of manufacture, awakening novel industry and sagacity, and employing, as it were, new capital of mind. When Newton developed the system of the universe, and established his own glory and that of his country on imperishable foundations he might be regarded as giving a boon to the civilized world for which no adequate compensation could ever be made; yet even in this the most difficult and sublime field of discovery Britain has been paid, if not fully, yet fairly, by the labors of Euler, La Grange, and above all, Laplace; perfecting the theory of the lunar motions and planetary perturbations, and affording data of infinite importance in the theory and practice of navigation. Fortunately science, like that nature to which it belongs, is limited neither by time nor by space. It belongs to the world and is of no country and no age. The more we know, the more we feel our ignorance and the more we feel how much remains unknown; in philosophy, the sentiment of the Macedonian hero can never apply,—there are always new worlds to conquer."

Such a conception of science has been characteristic of the English-speaking peoples throughout their history. They have given out to the world discoveries and inventions which have changed the whole face of the earth. They have covered its seas with ships, and its land with a network of railways and trolleys, telegraphs and telephones. They have brought together products from remotest parts of the earth, and built factories filled with machinery for transforming these raw materials into manufactured articles which increase man's comfort, add to his leisure, multiply his powers, and so provide almost unlimited opportunity for world-wide social betterment. But all these things the English-speaking peoples could never have done, had they not always been eager searchers after truth and willing benefactors of mankind,—had they not been, as have no other people, the great "melting-pot" of culture, in which has been blended, fused and clarified all that is of permanent value in human experience, from that of primitive man to the present.

In the assimilation of these cultural elements, the geography of England and later of America has been in large measure a determining influence. In ancient times, when the center of civilization was in the Mediterranean world, England was off on the outermost rim of the civilized area,—a remote island cut off from the Continent and completely out of the current of civilized thought, an island in which the rest of the world was interested only because of its mines of tin and copper. These it was which first attracted civilization to British shores. Visited by the Phœnicians, then by the Greeks, and finally conquered and occupied by the Romans, England was first introduced to Mediterranean culture and so promised to become the inheritor of all that man had learned in ages past. But for nearly twelve centuries the promise was not fulfilled. During that time England remained almost stagnant so far as material and intellectual progress was concerned. She, like the rest of the world, was awaiting some great impulse which would rouse her to intellectual activity.

Here again Britain's geography stood her in good stead. Had she been far removed from Europe she would not have been swept into the current of European interests and consequently of European culture. As it was, however, England was, in the first place, near enough to France to invite the Norman conquest with all that it signified,—the introduction not only of more advanced forms of government, literature and art, but also mediæval Christian learning. In the second place England was near enough to Spain to be brought in touch, through trade and travel, with the highly developed Arabic culture which was being fostered by the Moors in the powerful kingdom of Granada. It was England's nearness to France and to Spain which made possible the first commingling of these two currents of thought, the Christian and the Mohammedan, at the University of Oxford, then in its infancy. It was this contact with European culture which, from the thirteenth century to the sixteenth, poured into the English melting-pot all that humanity had learned in the ages that had gone before. It was this knowledge, confused and fragmentary, which in the thirteenth century stimulated Roger Bacon to see "the Vision of the world and all the Wonder that would be"; it was this knowledge, fused and clarified, which from the sixteenth century on enabled Francis Bacon and his successors to realize that vision and to work out the wonders of modern science.

It was thus England's geography which brought to her the impulse necessary to waken her dormant intellectual powers. As one looks back over human history such great impulses to intellectual progress seem to come only at rare intervals. Imagine what a sense of power must have thrilled the hairy, almost brute ancestor of ours who first learned to use a club! Thousands of centuries later, when some man first thought of replacing his wooden club by a weapon made of stone, what must have been the awe and admiration inspired in his fellows! For such another impulse to progress we look in vain through several hundreds of centuries until one day, not more than six thousand years ago, some ancient Egyptian, wandering in the neighborhood of Sinai (to use Mr. Breasted's illustration), happened to bank his fire with stones containing copper-ore, and next morning discovered in the ashes a brilliant globule of pure metal: "Without knowing it, this man stood at the dawning of a new era, the Age of Metal, and the little bead of shining copper which he drew from the ashes, if this Egyptian wanderer could have seen it, might have reflected to him a vision of steel buildings, Brooklyn bridges, huge factories and vast stretches of steel roads. For these things of our modern world and all they signify would never have come to pass but for the little bead of metal which the wandering Egyptian held in his hand for the first time on that eventful day," six thousand years ago. Such an impulse to constructive thinking made possible the development of that material civilization without which any great intellectual growth is impossible. From the glittering surface of the copper globule there might have been reflected not only the image of a material civilization, but also a vision of all the brilliant discoveries in science and invention, made possible by the use of metal, which have so immeasurably bettered man's estate, added to his intellectual enjoyment and opened to him new vistas of conscious progress toward an unlimited perfectibility.

During the five thousand years, however, which elapsed between the Egyptian wanderer and the English Roger Bacon,—between the beginning of the Age of Metal and that next great impulse to intellectual activity, the Renaissance,—the human race had only begun to accumulate its present vast store of knowledge; only a few seeds of pure science were gleaned by the ancient world, and even these, painfully and almost secretly raised by a few isolated Greek thinkers, remained practically unknown to the people as a whole. They were even lost to the world altogether for nearly a thousand years following the Germanic invasions which in the fourth century disrupted the whole Roman Empire. But it was these very seeds of pure science—some unearthed from the ruins of ancient libraries or from mediæval monasteries, others carefully treasured and handed down from generation to generation of learned Arabs,—it was these very seeds which, disseminated over Europe during the Renaissance or Revival of Learning from the thirteenth to the sixteenth century, were finally to bear fruit in the almost incredible achievements of modern science.

In the meantime, however, up to the Renaissance, there existed in England only the four pseudo-sciences popularly known to the ancient world,—the mystical astrology, magic, and alchemy and a practical but crude geometry, which was nothing more than the simple rule o' thumb methods of measurement and computation worked out by the ancient Egyptians. If we would appreciate fully the greatness of the English contribution to scientific thought, we must not forget that there is a radical difference between what, on the one hand, we moderns call science,—that is, definitely systematized knowledge of natural or social phenomena and of the relations between them,—and what, on the other hand, the ancients understood by the term. To them it was the cloak which covered a multitude of ideas rooted for the most part in myth and legend, superstition, magic and religious observances. "No study of Nature for her own sake," as Professor Botsford has phrased it, "but only for practical ends or from religious motives—this was the vital weakness of ancient science." All primitive thinking, as Professor Robinson would have us remember, is either practical, or mystical and romantic. Mankind, surrounded by forces and phenomena which he could neither control nor even understand, sought to explain them by attributing them to the action of beings higher than himself, beings whom he must therefore propitiate if he would live in peace and harmony.

In modern times man in large measure controls the external world by turning to his own uses the laws of nature revealed by science; but the mediæval Englishman, like ancient man, in the absence of scientific knowledge, resorted to magic, the attempt to influence by wonder-working the forces which controlled his fate. By charms and incantations, accompanied by the use of amulets, potions, symbolic herbs and all sorts of fetishes from a lock of hair to a toe-nail, he sought to propitiate the good and to ward off the evil spirits or to avert an unpleasant fate, particularly disease or death. Some, on the other hand, like Faust, sought to court the favor of the Evil One by direct invocation, a practice which rarely failed to accomplish its purpose. One can understand why the mediæval Englishman who wore a piece of chrysolite in his right ear in order to acquire wisdom, would be very slow to realize that the charm was ineffectual; but oftentimes either by suggestion or by hitting upon the right herb or drug the charm worked. By discarding the futile and retaining the useful, there had been gradually built up a number of recipes and "prescriptions" which, developed by the ancient Greeks and brought to England by Arab and Jewish physicians, later formed the nucleus of the modern science of medicine. But along with the practice of magic there had also grown up, through experiment and observation, and through concrete investigation into properties, a considerable body of knowledge of natural phenomena which had given birth to other pseudo-sciences, particularly astrology and alchemy, the twin daughters of magic.

In his struggle with external forces ancient man

had soon learned that to be forewarned is fore-armed. Consequently by omens, auguries, and divinations, he sought to learn the will of the gods, so that he might regulate his actions accordingly. Out of this belief had grown the practice of astrology, or the forecasting of the future of human beings from indications given by the relative positions and movements of the stars, the planets, and the moon,—a pseudo-science destined in its turn to become the mother of astronomy. The fixed stars, grouped in constellations, formed a belt about the earth called the zodiac, which was divided into twelve parts or "signs." To each sign was attached a certain significance, favorable or unfavorable, that just rising at the time of birth being the dominant one. The beneficent or maleficent influence of the planets, including the sun and moon, was modified by the particular sign in which they happened to be at the date of birth. A mediæval book called the "Secreta Secretorum" describes the brilliant career of a weaver's son, who, chancing to be born when Venus and Mars were in their most propitious signs promising wisdom, beauty and love, rose accordingly, in spite of most adverse circumstances, to be vizier to his king. The astrologer was also consulted for advice as to the proper time for doing any important business, be it a bargain or marriage or both. In consequence he not only carried on a very profitable business but incidentally acquired no inconsiderable amount of real astronomical knowledge. This practice, originated by the Babylonians, adopted and elaborated by Greek and Roman, Christian and Mohammedan, had been passed on to England, where in the thirteenth century it was flourishing in full force, implicitly believed in by all classes,—by the learned as well as the ignorant, by a Roger Bacon no less than by the humblest peasant. But its importance in the history of English science lies in the fact that it aroused an interest in astronomical phenomena which prepared the way for the truly scientific achievements of a Newton or a Herschel.

In addition to his eagerness to know and to control his future, man has another very marked desire, that of transmuting into gold or silver whatever comes into his possession, be it a "Tin Lizzie" or a leaden Russian bond. On the basis of this universal trait, there grew up among the ancients the practice of alchemy,—in its narrower sense, the art of making gold or silver from the baser metals. More broadly, it signified among the Greeks, at least, the theory of the composition of all matter. By the study of all sorts of substances, and by the combination of various chemical elements, the mediæval alchemist sought to produce genuine gold and silver coins. When he finally became convinced that this was impossible, he, like the modern druggist, tried the argument that his was "just as good or even better." Finally when people refused to be any longer imposed upon, the practice was forbidden, but in the meantime much well-founded knowledge of chemical substances had been evolved from the alchemist's experiments,—a knowledge which was later to develop into the modern science of chemistry.

Such then was the so-called science which existed in England before the Renaissance,—magic, astrology, alchemy, and simple rules of measurement and computation. Only by keeping clearly in mind the utter formlessness and chaos of early English knowledge, its enslavement to all sorts of superstition, prejudice and ignorance, and the obstacles thus placed in the way of true science, only by keeping all this clearly in mind can we appreciate the full significance of English achievement in scientific thought. For those masses of confused and unsystematized knowledge, either devoted to the merely practical on the one hand, or involved in mystical and fantastic notions on the other, lacked the vital principle of abstract thinking, the broad observation, and orderly arrangement which alone could transform them into true science. No such result could be hoped for so long as knowledge was passed down from old to young on bases of superstition and miracle, tradition and authority.

Some new impulse was needed to stir the English mind to a truly intellectual activity. That impulse came just before the dawn of the thirteenth century, when England was swept into the religious wars or Crusades waged by the Christian West against the Mohammedan East. As a result of the Third Crusade, led by King Richard the Lion-Hearted, there was introduced into England through Jewish translators, all the wealth of Arabic learning, from Spain and from the East, bringing in its train those seeds of pure science which had been produced by the ancient Greeks and treasured by the Arabs for nearly a thousand years. Most important among these were the teachings of Aristotle on natural science, much distorted, however, by the many translations, Syriac, Persian, Arabic and Hebrew, through which they had passed. The first effect of the introduction of these new ideas was a feverish desire to reconcile them to the teachings of Christianity, for Aristotle was of course a pagan. In consequence the translations into Latin were still further distorted by the numerous omissions and interpolations of overzealous copyists. But the scholastics of the thirteenth century were so impressed by the breadth of his knowledge and so overpowered by his logic, "so fully convinced," as Professor Robinson phrases it, "that it had pleased God to permit Aristotle to say the last word upon each and every branch of knowledge, that they humbly accepted him, along with the Bible, the Church fathers, and the Canon and Roman law, as one of the unquestioned authorities which together formed a complete guide for humanity in conduct and in every branch of science."

Among the first to protest against the fondness for scholastic logic and the supreme respect for Aristotle, was that first of English scientists, Roger Bacon, a Franciscan monk of the early thirteenth century. "If I could have my way," he wrote, "I would have every book of Aristotle's burned (the Latin translations, that is), because the study of these is only a waste of time, a cause of error and an increase of ignorance." It was this same first English man of science who perceived the fundamental weakness of Greek scientific thought,—the fact that it was based upon mere reason rather than upon reasoned observation and experimentation. Instead of poring over bad translations of Aristotle, instead of relying upon authority and tradition, Roger Bacon with true English independence advised men to observe the common things of nature round about them, to make experiments, and to draw their conclusions from these. Even though Aristotle *was* very wise, Bacon contended, he had but planted the tree of knowledge and it had "not as yet put forth all its branches nor produced all its fruits." With prophetic vision this mediæval Englishman claimed that science could do more for man than all the magic of the ages, that some day it would enable men to fly, to construct horseless carriages, propel ships without oars, and build bridges without piers.

But this John the Baptist of modern English science, keen and systematic thinker though he was, was destined to remain only the voice of one crying in the wilderness of barren scholastic logic. For more than three hundred years longer the blind subservience of learning to classical authority and to mediæval theology, was to continue almost unbroken. Even Roger himself, though he was one of the first to break away from authority, nevertheless still believed that the chief service which learning could render was as handmaid to theology. It remained for his more famous namesake, Francis Bacon, living in a more favorable age, to further the emancipation of learning by elaborating, broadening and popularizing the ideas which Roger had formulated.

The time was now ripe for such popularization; for conditions in the early seventeenth century were radically different from those of the thirteenth. During those four hundred years there had occurred momentous events in world history, which had infinitely broadened the Englishman's intellectual horizon and in many ways completely changed his point of view. During these four hundred years Englishmen had established on English soil the principles of individual liberty, of representative government, and of the sovereignty of parliament over the crown; they had experienced the decay of feudalism and the abolition of serfdom, the growth of a free rural population and of wealthy commercial cities. At the same time they had watched the gradual failure of the Holy Wars of Christian against Mohammedan with all that such failure signified,—the downfall of the policy of theocratic government, the overthrow of other-worldliness and the passing of the temporal power of the Papacy; they had watched, too, with ever-increasing enthusiasm the spread of the great intellectual awakening resulting from the confronting and commingling of Eastern with Western civilization,—an awakening due not so much to the actual exchanges made as to the severance of bonds of fixity, intolerance and conservatism, the resulting liberation of thought and the stimulus to new ways, new ideas, new points of view. In consequence of the introduction of paper in place of parchment and of printing instead of laborious copying by hand, these Englishmen, chiefly through the efforts of scholars such as More and Colet, Grocyn and Linacre, had by the end of the sixteenth century very generally possessed themselves of the riches of Greek and Roman literature. Not only had they thus recovered what little of science the ancients had thought out before the Christian era, but they had acquired, also, many new instruments,—the mariner's compass and the lens, Arabic numerals, algebra and Euclidian geometry,—which were to guide them into realms of scientific thought which even their heretofore ignored Roger Bacon had never dreamt of.

Meanwhile these Englishmen had heard with breathless wonder of the great New World that lay beyond the western seas; thrilled by the discoveries of Columbus, Balboa, and Magellan, they had sent out their own Cabots, Drake, Hawkins, and Sir Walter Raleigh, and by the defeat of the Spanish Armada had established supremacy over the seas. In the midst of all this intellectual ferment had come the Reformation with its revolt from papal authority, the matching of faith against faith, of sect against sect, of one form of intolerance against another, and the consequent bewilderment, questioning and shaking of all faith, the breaking away from traditional moorings and the challenge to independent thinking. Such had been the events of the period from the thirteenth century to the seventeenth. Only such an age could have produced a Francis Bacon. Only such an age could have listened to his message, and profited by his teaching. Only such an age could have given to English thought that confidence, independence, and toleration, that impulse toward practicality and altruism, which constitutes the lasting glory of English achievement in science.

Thus at the beginning of the seventeenth century, the time was indeed ripe for the ushering in of a new age, the beginning of the age of modern science. Through discovery and exploration of the external world of nature, through travel and communication with the outside world of men, England had come to realize that there were many things altogether unknown to the ancients, many things in which they had even been in grossest error. Consequently, in science as in all other realms of thought, Englishmen were ready now, as they had not been in the days of Roger Bacon, to break away from classical and ecclesiastical authority and to rely upon their own observation and experience.

It was this new attitude which found eloquent expression in Francis Bacon's "Advancement of Learning" in 1605, and again in his "Novum Organum," published singularly in 1620, the year in which the Pilgrim Fathers landed at Plymouth. Like his predecessor, Roger, he warned his countrymen against the dangers of submission to authority, particularly that of Aristotle and the schoolmen. Like his predecessor, too, he foresaw the infinite possibilities of social betterment to be attained through the accumulation of knowledge about man and nature by means of direct observation, experimentation and research. Only through his indispensable preliminary work could man arrive at any sound conclusion as to the laws of the universe and his relation to them. Only so could man regain his power over nature. "Man, the servant and interpreter of nature," Bacon says, "can do and understand so much, and so much only, as he has observed in fact or in thought of the course of nature." "First of all, we must prepare a natural and experimental history, sufficient and good; and this is the foundation of all." But in his study of nature, Bacon reiterates, man must rely solely upon observation and experience as the only means of keeping his mind free from prejudice, error and preconceived notions, "for God forbid that we should give out a dream of our own imagination for a pattern to the world."

Man's guiding thread out of the labyrinth of natural phenomena was to be found in the method, originated by Bacon, of reasoning from a group of arranged facts, or observation through a series of eliminations, to an abstract or generalized truth. This, the famous "inductive method," was, however, more brilliant than useful; for neither Bacon himself nor any scientist since has ever arrived at any great discovery through its use. On the contrary the "natural method" of first forming an hypothesis or supposition and then testing it by application to observed facts is that universally followed. But Bacon's efforts to establish his method of reasoning were not entirely futile, for it is only by inductively taking into account facts already observed or experienced, that the scientific imagination can construct its hypothesis, from which to work back to experience. The significance of Lord Bacon's work lies not in the application of his method of reasoning, but rather in his insistence upon experimentation and observation of nature, instead of blind reliance upon a perverted logic and an unsubstantiated authority.

This insistence upon the experimental method is one of the two great characteristics of Bacon which entitle him to recognition as England's great leader in modern scientific thought. The other is his keen perception of the importance, the interdependence, and the social aim of all scientific endeavor. For he, too, has his dream of an ideal commonwealth, the New Atlantis, which, could he have his way, would be organized under the direction of an Academy of Sciences, his famous House of Solomon, or what we would call to-day a university of research endowed by the state for the promotion of social progress. With masterly skill Bacon shows up the obstacles that lie in the path of human progress,—the ignorance and prejudice, traditional views and blind worship of authority which hold man slave to nature. He would have man put aside all these, and cease making knowledge a servant of theology, which, to avoid trouble, he relegates to the realm of faith; nor would he have man make knowledge an idealistic end in itself, but rather a practical means to the end of social betterment. The great object of all science is to recover man's sovereignty over nature, "to endow the condition and life of man with new powers or works," "to extend more widely the limits of the power and greatness of man." "Is there any such happiness as for a man's mind to be raised above the confusion of things, where he may have the prospect of the order of nature and error of man? But is this a view of delight only and not of discovery? of contentment and not of benefit? Shall he not as well discern the riches of nature's warehouse as the beauty of her shop? Is truth ever barren? Shall he not be able thereby to produce worthy effects, and to endow the life of man with infinite commodities?" The whole spirit of Bacon's attitude toward science and philosophy is this bent toward the practical, the altruistic, the democratic, and in this it is typically English. For in spite of Bacon's nominal support of absolute monarchy and aristocracy, his ideas were essentially democratic; he believed that not only he himself, but each and every man, was "born to be of some advantage to mankind," and that, on the other hand, mankind must work unitedly toward the betterment of each and every man's estate.

It is this attitude which gives to Francis Bacon his unique position in the history of science,—he is the first to formulate the idea of modern progress through man's conscious adjustment to and scientific control over the natural forces of the universe. "To him," as Professor Robinson has said, "knowledge was above all dynamic and progressive; in his works our modern idea of human progress first appears in unmistakable form." It is true that Bacon did not himself make any real contribution to scientific knowledge and that his fear of accepting unproved hypotheses led him to reject the Copernican theory of the solar system,—led him also to underestimate and even disregard the work which was being done by some of his contemporaries, among them William Gilbert's description of the fundamental principles of magnetism, and Harvey's discovery of the circulation of the blood; "nevertheless," to quote Professor Robinson again, Bacon and his imitator, Descartes, "scotched authority, although they had not the heart to kill it, and the unprecedented intellectual clarification, accompanied by an unprecedented accumulation of facts in regard to man and his environment, which succeeding centuries have witnessed, is largely due to the attitude of mind which Bacon and Descartes encouraged."

That this influence of Francis Bacon on modern scientific and philosophic thought was both immediate and lasting is attested over and over again by acknowledgment on the part of later scientists, French, Italian and German, as well as English. His insistence upon observation and collection of facts directly from nature made a strong appeal to the Frenchman, Descartes, who in this deliberately adopted Bacon's suggestion; in a letter written in 1632 Descartes expressed the wish that "some one would undertake to give a history of celestial phenomena after the method of Bacon, and describe the sky exactly as it appears at present, without introducing a single hypothesis." Another French philosopher, Condillac, living one hundred and fifty years later than Bacon, is said to have remarked, "No one knows better than he the cause of our mistakes." Voltaire and the French Encyclopædists regarded Bacon as "the Father of experimental philosophy," and d'Alembert refers to him as "the greatest, the most universal and the most eloquent of philosophers."

But great as was Bacon's influence on Continental thought, his greatest service was rather to his own countrymen, and through them to the rest of the world, both in philosophy and in natural science. Bacon, as he himself remarked, "rang the bell which called the wits together." The fact that the fundamental principle of Locke's "Essay Concerning Human Understanding,"—that all our ideas are the result of sensation and reflection,—is found briefly stated in the "Novum Organum," entitles Bacon to distinction as a precursor of English psychological speculation. In ethics, too, Bacon may be regarded as the forerunner of all those systems, particularly utilitarianism, as we shall have occasion to note later on, which are based upon the application to conduct of the method of direct observation of human consciousness and of the results of actions. Baconian principles have thus undoubtedly exercised a powerful influence upon the whole trend of English thought in mental, moral and political philosophy.

But perhaps the most significant effect of Bacon's influence upon the progress of natural science, an effect due not to any contribution of his own, nor yet to his inductive method, but rather to the spirit of his work, was the impetus given by his "New Atlantis" to the organization of the Royal Society of London for the Advancement of Science, which took place in 1662,—less than forty years after his death; for this society, in its relation to the individual on the one hand and in its service to the state on the other, is, to some degree at least, a realization of Bacon's dream of an Academy of Sciences.

However great may have been the failure, politically, of the Puritan Revolution, which ran its course between the death of Bacon and the founding of the Royal Society, one permanent gain of supreme importance had been made,—the English people as a whole had come not only to realize but to demand their right to freedom of thought, and to the acquisition of that knowledge upon which alone rational thought can be based. True political freedom can only follow upon, not precede, intellectual and spiritual freedom. "Give me liberty to know, to utter, and to argue freely according to conscience, above all other liberties," Milton had cried in 1643. It was this spirit of Bacon and of Milton, this spirit of free inquiry, which characterized certain meetings held in London during the next twenty years, of "divers worthy persons, inquisitive into natural philosophy and other parts of human learning, and particularly of what hath been called the 'New Philosophy' or 'Experimental Philosophy' "; and it was these meetings which, largely through the efforts of Robert Boyle, a devoted though unconfessed follower of Bacon, finally resulted, in 1662, in the organization of the Royal Society of London for the Advancement of Science.

In striving to realize the aim of its founders, an aim which has since grown to be five-fold, this society has performed an inestimable service for English science. At its inception it sought to advance scientific thought by means of experiments performed before the members at the meetings of the society. Later there grew up a library and museum for the preservation of manuscripts and scientific correspondence, and for instruments and models of historical interest. The Royal Society furthermore seeks especially to promote scientific research by the encouragement of all worthy individual investigators, rich or poor, of noble rank or lowly, English or foreign, not only through channels of sympathy, recognition of merit and intelligent coöperation, but oftentimes through financial assistance as well. It has taken the lead in direction of attention to, and active support of the government in, many scientific undertakings of national importance, such as the equipment of the Royal Observatory at Greenwich, the ventilation of prisons, protection of buildings and ships from lightning, investigation of earthquakes and volcanic eruptions, upper atmosphere and deep-sea research, expeditions for scientific exploration in geography, geology and allied subjects,—these are only a few of its vast and varied activities all carried on in coöperation with the government. Lastly, what is perhaps more significant for the future than any other of its aims, the Royal Society has undertaken the promotion of international coöperation in scientific investigation, not only through its correspondence, its recognition of foreign merit, and its election of foreigners to membership, but also, of late years, by taking a leading part in activities connected with the International Catalogue of Scientific Literature and with the International Association of Academies for the Advancement of Science.

Such then is the framework of the Royal Society, the nearest approach which England has yet made toward the realization of Bacon's ideal House of Solomon. Though in its organization it does not, except in the most general way, accord with Bacon's scheme for an Academy of Sciences, nevertheless in its spirit and in its functions it has laid the foundation upon which that House may be erected in the coming day when man will put to practical use, for his own conscious progress, all the knowledge of natural and social phenomena which is awaiting acquisition, and on the organization and application of which that progress depends.

Up to very recent years, however, the Royal Society has in many respects failed to realize its opportunity. Though it has fostered some of England's greatest scientific achievement, it has not performed as great a service for England as the French Academy has for France, or the universities for Germany, in bringing about concerted action and scientific coöperation. Bacon's scheme has been more nearly realized in foreign academies; scientific discoveries and inventions of great importance, such as Adams' determination of the orbit of a hitherto unknown planet, or Babage's invention of the calculating engine, were for years left in neglect by Englishmen; Newton's astronomical discoveries were made known to the world through the Frenchman, Voltaire; Locke's school was founded in France; Dalton's theories of chemistry, Faraday's discoveries in electricity, and Darwin's theory of evolution have supplied the ideas for German university courses; English and American inventors, through the new machinery and processes which they have given out to the world, have unconsciously paved the way for German industrialism; and through the invention of modern artillery, aeroplane, and submarine, they have all unwittingly placed in German hands the tools of militarism. Facts, such as these, have at last brought to the English-speaking peoples a realization of their great mistake,—their failure to carry out Bacon's idea, to establish a real House of Solomon, some central organization for the collection and correlation of the work of individual investigators in widely scattered fields. Only now are we realizing the consequences of that lack of the historical and encyclopædic spirit, shown by continental nations, which must accompany and supplement individual genius, if the fullest benefit of thoroughness of research and completeness of coöperation are to be attained.

On the contrary, in spite of Lord Bacon's scheme for organization, English science has remained, from his day to this, a series of brilliant individual achievements rather than a corporate effort. But in this very fact, as we shall see, lies the peculiar distinction of the English contribution to scientific thought; and in this fact, too, lies the explanation of its greatness. English scientists have not yet realized Lord Bacon's dream of coöperation; but they did adopt and follow out, each in his own individual way, that experimental method which, as we have seen, was first suggested to a dormant world by an Englishman, Roger Bacon, in the thirteenth century, and four hundred years later was presented in its full significance by another Englishman, Francis Bacon, to a world aroused, ready to listen, and eager to seize upon this means of broadening their intellectual horizon.

Even the most casual glance over the three centuries of modern science which have elapsed since Bacon's time is sufficient to reveal to us three well-defined periods in the application of this experimental method. The first, approximately from 1600 to 1750, was distinctly a period of great generalizations during which natural laws of fundamental importance were worked out, particularly in the natural sciences of astronomy, physics and chemistry.

The earliest of the epoch-making discoveries of this first period was a treatise on magnetism, published in 1600, by William Gilbert, court-physician to Queen Elizabeth. Gilbert's work, the first to be characterized by a strict adherence to the experimental method, was likewise the first to describe accurately the phenomena of magnets, magnetized bodies, and electrical attractions; it constitutes not merely the first but also the most important single contribution ever made to the science of magnetism,—that science so vital to English navigation, commerce, and empire. It was

Gilbert, too, who invented the word "electricity"; and it was his observations and speculations on this subject, supplemented by those of Boyle, Newton, and Watson, which guided Benjamin Franklin in 1752 to his memorable identification of lightning with electricity, and all the revolutionizing discoveries and inventions which have followed in its wake.

In 1616, the year of Shakespeare's death, and only eleven years after the appearance of Bacon's "Advancement of Learning," another physician, William Harvey, brought forward his discovery of the circulation of the blood, and followed it up a few years later by the announcement of his theory that the formation of the embryo takes place by the successive addition of parts instead of by the unfolding of a miniature complete from the beginning. By these two discoveries, together with others of lesser importance, Dr. Harvey not only worked a revolution in the whole theory of medicine, but also won the distinction of being the founder of the sciences of anatomy and physiology, for the development of which the world had to wait, however, for nearly two hundred years longer. In that same memorable year, 1616, John Napier gave to the world his system of logarithms, a short method of multiplication and division for large numbers, which has ever since remained one of the foundation stones in higher mathematics. Within another fifteen years, Thomas Harriot, the tutor of Sir Walter Raleigh, gave more complete form to the outlines of modern algebra. These two great achievements, the logarithms of Napier and the algebra of Harriot, made possible thirty years later the working out of differential calculus and of complicated astronomical problems by Sir Isaac Newton.

The mention of Newton recalls to us one of the most illustrious names in the history of science. Visitors to Westminster Abbey never fail to seek out a certain monument which bears this inscription:—

Here lies
SIR ISAAC NEWTON, KNIGHT,
Who by vigor of mind, almost supernatural,
First demonstrated
The motions and figures of the Planets,
The Paths of the Comets, and the
Tides of the Ocean.
He diligently investigated
The different refrangibilities of the Rays of Light,
And the properties of the Colors to which they
give rise.

An Assiduous, Sagacious and Faithful Interpreter
of Nature,
Antiquity, and the Holy Scriptures,
He asserted in his Philosophy the Majesty of God,
and exhibited in his Conduct the simplicity
of the Gospel.
Let mortals rejoice that there has existed
Such and so great

AN ORNAMENT OF THE HUMAN RACE.

Born 25th Dec., 1642; Died 20th March, 1727.

Such was the estimate placed upon the importance of Newton's discoveries by Englishmen of his own day. But during the years, nearly three hundred now, which have marked the advance of science since his time, the world has come to realize that the significance of Newton's work lies not merely in the specific discoveries he made in physics, astronomy and mathematics, but more in the entirely new trend which he gave the whole course of modern thought.

The way had been well prepared for Newton not only by the labors of his earlier countrymen, Bacon, Napier and Harriot, but also by those of three continental philosophers, Galileo, Kepler, and Descartes. Even while Francis Bacon was formulating his deductive method, based upon experimental research, even while he was dreaming, too, of a living astronomy by which the physical laws of terrestrial relations should be extended to the realm of heavenly bodies, even then that first of great Italian thinkers, Galileo Galilei (1564-1642), was already opening up a new era in the history of descriptive astronomy by his invention of the telescope. This great event occurred in the year 1609,—the same year in which that intrepid English sailor, Henry Hudson, first entered New York Bay and discovered the river which bears his name. And just as Hudson's memorable voyage was followed by many another destined to establish an English civilization upon American shores, so Galileo's invention of the telescope was followed in bewildering rapidity by one discovery after another in the realm of science,—discoveries which filled men's minds with amazement and swept aside, as worse than groundless, fables and conjectures which for ages past had been accumulated regarding the appearance and the movements of stars and planets. The mediæval scholastics were now confronted, in the system of Jupiter and its satellites, by a visible example in miniature of the truth of the theory set forth in 1543 by the Polish astronomer, Copernicus,—the theory that the earth and all the other planets revolve about the sun as the center of our universe. Such an example, more convincing than all the tomes of mediæval logic, marks the downfall of scholasticism, the severance of bonds of perverted Aristotelianism, and the overturning of mediæval cosmogony. Galileo's telescope was destined not only to bring within the range of man's vision planets and stars never before dreamed of, but also to reveal to the eager gaze of later scientists a whole new world of scientific and philosophic thought.

In that same epochal year, 1609, Johann Kepler, imperial astronomer and astrologer of Rudolph II of Germany, completed his "great Martian labor," as he himself phrased it, "of leading the captive planet to the foot of the imperial throne," through the publication of a work on the orbit of the planet Mars. In this and later treatises Kepler established his three great laws of planetary motion: that each planet revolves in an elliptical orbit round the sun, whose center occupies one of the foci of the orbit; that the radius vector of each planet, drawn from the sun, describes equal areas in equal times; and that the squares of the periodic times of the planets are in the same proportion as the cubes of their mean distances from the sun.

By these three laws of planetary motion, Kepler had blazed out the trail which, toward the close of the century, was to guide Newton on into still greater regions of undiscovered truth. But before this could be accomplished, it was necessary that a bridge should be built from ancient to modern mathematics, more especially geometry and algebra. That bridge was begun by Napier who, as we have seen, contributed a system of logarithms; the bridge was extended still farther by Harriot's theories and methods in algebra. The main body, however, was built by the Frenchman Descartes who in 1637 published his "Geometry," a work which for the first time correlated geometry with algebra, established the principles of analytical geometry and made it possible for Newton himself to complete the mathematical bridge by his own invention of differential calculus. Thus had the way been prepared for Newton's transcendent discovery that the law of gravitation is applicable throughout the known universe.

Some vague conception of the existence of gravitation or the force by which bodies on or near the earth's surface are attracted toward the center, was present in the minds of the ancients. Some speculations had also been made in mediæval times as to why things fall toward the earth. But the first important step toward the investigation of this mysterious force was taken only when Galileo set himself to discover not *why* but *how* things fall. He had observed that a ball, starting from rest, falls toward the earth's surface with uniformly increasing speed. By experiment with such freely falling bodies, and also with balls rolling down an inclined plane, he proved mathematically that if the speed of falling is proportional to the time from the moment of starting, the space traversed must be proportional to the square of the time of falling. He discovered also that a ball, having acquired a certain speed by rolling down an inclined plane, will roll to the top of another plane of the same height, regardless of its inclination, provided that friction be slight. The logical conclusion to be drawn from this fact is that if the second plane be level, the ball will keep on rolling forever, provided there be no external interference. These observations of Galileo were first put into definite words by Newton and constitute what is known as the first law of motion,—that a body to which motion has once been imparted will continue to move in a straight line at the same speed, forever, unless stopped by some external force. Since this law now serves as the foundation of the whole science of dynamics, Newton may justly be regarded as the founder of this branch of modern physics.

Nor was this all. Philosophers had heretofore believed that the motion of the planets could be accounted for only by the application of some external force; in this idea originated the theory of vortices, which had been roughly drafted by Kepler and later (1644) set forth in detail by Descartes. According to this Cartesian theory, as summarized by William Wallace, the universe is infinite and infinitely full of matter of uniform character. This matter is divided into an infinite variety of forms, set in motion by God. The movement of any one particle in this closely packed universe is possible only when all the other particles move simultaneously. There will then inevitably result throughout the universe an innumerable host of more or less circular movements, and of vortices or whirlpools of material particles varying in size and velocity. In consequence of the circular movement, the particles will have their corners pared off by rubbing against each other. The finer matter thus formed, collecting in the center of the vortex, makes up the sun or star. The spherical particles continue their circulatory motion with a tendency to fly off from the center; these make up the atmosphere which envelops and revolves around the central accumulation. A star may be caught in a neighboring vortex. If its velocity is greater than that of the vortex, it escapes and, partially broken up, becomes a comet. If, on the other hand, the velocity of the star is less than that of the vortex which catches it up, the star is held by the vortex and becomes a planet, revolving about the central mass.

Such was the famous theory of vortices advanced by Descartes. As Wallace says, it is undoubtedly "one of the grandest hypotheses which ever have been formed to account by mechanical processes for the movements of the universe." It ended the old Aristotelian theory, and "banished the spirits and genii to which even Kepler had assigned the guardianship of the planetary movements." "The Cartesian theory, like the later speculations of Kant and Laplace, proposes to give a hypothetical explanation of the circumstances and motions which in the normal course of things led to the state of things required by the law of attraction." But in many ways the theory was inadequate to explain known facts. The true foundation of a mechanical theory of the universe was laid not by Descartes but by Kepler's three laws and by Galileo's dynamics. The Cartesian theory of vortices, however, unquestionably prepared the way for a more rational mechanical theory.

Its weaknesses were soon perceived by Newton who, by the formulation of the first law of motion, proved the supposition of vortices false. It now became apparent that it was not the continuous motion of the planet, but the deflection of its motion from a straight line, which required explanation. This was the problem which Newton now set himself. Its solution occupied him for twenty years. As early as 1666, the year of the Great Fire in London, it had occurred to him that the motion of the moon about the earth might be determined by the same law which governed the fall of an apple. Applying the law of falling bodies which he had previously worked out, to the motion of the moon, he computed the amount of deflection which would be caused by the force of gravitation or the attraction exerted on the moon by the earth. He found that his results did not entirely accord with observed facts, and with great disappointment laid his calculations aside. A few years later, a new determination of the size of the earth by Picard gave him new data for his problem. With feverish eagerness he applied himself again to the solution, and in almost uncontrollable excitement found that the force which determines the fall of an apple is the self-same force which holds the moon to its orbit. His discovery was announced to the world by the publication, in 1686, of his famous "Principia." This discovery meant that the moon, having a motion of its own which, if unaffected by any external force, would make it move in a straight line, must be deflected from a straight-line to a curvilinear orbit by the force of gravitation acting from the earth. And if this theory could explain the motion of the moon about the earth, the same theory could explain the movement of the earth about the sun and the movements of all the other planets. The force of this attraction of gravitation Newton stated mathematically to vary directly as the mass of the bodies and inversely as the square of the distance between them.

Newton was not alone in perceiving the possibility of such a solution. It had been foreshadowed in the third law of Kepler; it had also been conceived independently by three English friends of Newton's,—Sir Christopher Wren, the architect of St. Paul's Cathedral; Robert Hooke, who first suggested that the motion of heavenly bodies could be stated in terms of mathematics, and Edmund Halley, who first calculated the orbit of the 1682 comet which now bears his name. Far from detracting from Newton's fame, however, these facts, on the contrary, add luster to the brilliance of his achievement, for he alone had been able not only to recognize the law, but also to demonstrate its validity.

"Every particle of matter in the universe," we can hear Newton saying again and again, "attracts every other particle with a force varying inversely as the square of their mutual distances, and directly as the mass of the attracting particles." From this law he determined also the orbit of the moon and of comets; from it he deduced the fact that the earth is flattened at the poles; from it he explained the precession of the equinoxes, the tides, the ratio between the mass of the moon and that of the earth, between that of the sun and of the earth. He also demonstrated that a spherical body exerts the same attraction on an external planet as if its mass were concentrated at the center; and from his time since in all astronomical calculations, planets, stars, etc., have been regarded as points in space. Newton thus reduced the phenomena of the solar system to a mathematical basis of known dynamic principles.

By thus stating conclusively in terms of mathematics, not *why* but *how* the force of gravitation acts as the sole influence in governing the movements of planets and satellites, Newton established the science of gravitational astronomy, and demonstrated, to a world amazed, the possibility of a mechanical theory of the universe. The *why* of it all, however, the mechanism by means of which the force of gravitation is exerted, continued to remain a mystery which neither Newton nor any other scientist since his day has been able to elucidate. Nevertheless, the discovery that all the movements of the heavenly bodies can be described by one and the same simple formula, marks the greatest, the most significant, achievement in the history of science.

The extension of Newton's formula to explain the origin of the solar system was accomplished a hundred years later by the astronomer Laplace (1749-1827), "the Newton of France," who prophesied for Newton's "Principia" a lasting preeminence over all productions of the human intellect.

Laplace's "Nebular Hypothesis," though emphatically only a speculation, is to-day perhaps the most widely accepted theory as to the origin of the solar system. This theory, based on Newton's laws, presupposes a nebulous mass originally extending throughout the space now occupied by our solar system. This cloud of gaseous matter is further presupposed to be rotating upon its axis. In cooling it would contract toward its center, thus accelerating the rate of rotation and forming by increased pressure a solid mass at its center called the sun. As contraction continued and speed of rotation increased, a series of successive rings of matter were cast off by the shrinking nebula. Each of these rings, continuing its movement of revolution about the central mass, would develop a center of attraction of its own around which all the particles of matter that made up the ring would gradually accumulate in rotational movement. Thus from each ring would be formed a solid mass or planet having a movement of revolution about the sun and one of rotation about its own axis.

Such in barest outline is the Nebular hypothesis built up by Laplace upon the Newtonian law of gravitation. Unlike the Cartesian theory of vortices which it has displaced, the Nebular theory has not thus far been proved inconsistent with any observed fact. But as Simon Newcomb has said, "Should any one be skeptical as to the sufficiency of these laws to account for the present state of things, science can furnish no evidence strong enough to overthrow his doubts until the sun shall be found growing smaller by actual measurement, or the nebulæ be actually seen to condense into stars and systems."

Newton's name then stands as the greatest in the history of science. The importance of his work, though realized in a narrow way by his contemporaries, was not recognized in any broad sense till nearly one hundred years later, when a new period of activity in pure science was ushered in. The immediate effects of Newton's philosophy, as we shall see, were felt not so much in the field of natural science, as in the realm of more general philosophic thought.

Here, too, revolutionary changes were being wrought, chiefly through the labors of Newton's illustrious contemporary, John Locke (1632-1704), perhaps the greatest of philosophic exponents of civil and religious liberty, founder of the first continuous school of English philosophy, and herald of modern psychology, the science of individual experience.

This last quarter of the seventeenth century was an age peculiarly fortunate for the growth of a typically English school of philosophy. The air was rife with religious and political discussion. Catholic was striving against Protestant, monarchy against democracy, Divine Right against a stern Responsibility to Society. Bacon and Descartes had already "scotched authority," and others were eagerly waiting to strike the death blow. Following Bacon, but independently of him, Thomas Hobbes, in his "Leviathan" (1651), had already conceived the idea of applying the new "mechanical philosophy" to the whole constitution of society in such a way as to bring social phenomena within the same principles of scientific explanation as were found to apply in the case of natural phenomena. By his rational analysis of the moral nature of man as actuated by motives of self-interest tending continually to clash one with another, Hobbes had given the first great impulse to that utilitarian school of ethical speculation which was foreshadowed in Francis Bacon and which has ever since been so marked a characteristic of English social science; furthermore, Hobbes had commanded the respect of even his most violent opponents by insisting that the whole political system of a nation should be based upon a rational regard for the common weal. While he fearlessly attacked the Divine Right of Kings, he failed, on the other hand, to realize the need of religious toleration. His work on the whole represents a long step in the advance of English thought toward well-organized social science. Hobbes' preparation of the way for John Locke, however, was not that of path finding,—Locke was not a follower of Hobbes,—but rather that of map making; Hobbes charted out the lay of the land, over which Locke within the next fifty years was to hew his own path.

Other influences, too, were at work, preparing the way for a new philosophy. Gilbert had founded the science of terrestrial magnetism; Harvey had established the beginnings of anatomy, physiology and medicine. Napier, Harriot, Descartes and Newton had evolved a system of higher mathematics. Robert Boyle had formulated the law of gases and done much to transform alchemy into chemistry. Furthermore, Nehemiah Grew, the earliest vegetable anatomist and physiologist, through the study of seed germination in his "Anatomy of Plants" (1682), was working out the beginnings of botany. In the same year John Ray's "Methodus Plantarum Nova" earned for him the title of Father of modern zoölogy. Halley was soon to make the first calculation ever attempted of the orbit of a comet. And Galileo, Kepler, Descartes and Newton had created not only a new astronomy but also a whole new mechanical theory of the universe.

In the meantime the Royal Society had been founded and experiment in physics had become the fashion. Scientific knowledge was being rapidly diffused through a new custom of popular lectures. Aristotelianism had been dethroned and mediæval scholasticism at last put to rout. Freedom of the press was being gradually obtained and freedom of thought being demanded more and more insistently. And finally the Glorious Revolution had established the sovereignty of parliament over the crown, marked the triumph of the Commons over the Lords, and saw the ancient rights and liberties of Englishmen guaranteed by the passage of the Bill of Rights.

Under conditions such as these it was inevitable that a school of philosophy typically English should arise. It is inconceivable, too, that an English thinker living in such stirring times could abstract himself from the social, political and religious problems of his time. It was only to be expected then that John Locke would set himself in truly English fashion to work out practical solutions for the problems immediately before him. The two which appealed to him as most pressing were, on the one hand, the question of civil and religious liberty, and, on the other, the question of the origin of mental phenomena and their relation to the validity of knowledge. To the solution of these two problems he devoted his whole life. The results of his labors are embodied for the most part in his "Letters on Toleration" and in his "Essay Concerning Human Understanding."

Locke's early inclination toward politics had won for him the position of confidential secretary to the first Earl of Shaftesbury; between these two there developed an inspiring and lasting friendship based upon their common desire to advance the cause of liberty,—civil, religious and philosophical. Even in the earliest of Locke's essays, the bent of his mind is clearly apparent; for in these he set forth objections to the sacerdotal conception of Christianity, and made short work of ecclesiastical claims to infallibility in the interpretation of the Scriptures. In one of these earlier essays he also formulated a system of utilitarian ethics much more comprehensive than that of Hobbes. According to Locke's teaching, the distinction between right and wrong was dependent upon the results of actions in bringing about happiness or unhappiness. On these grounds later on he defended the principles of democracy and of constitutional law. His whole system of ethics, founded thus upon experience, is another milestone in the development of English rationalism.

The culmination of Locke's thought, however, on the value of experience is to be found in his

"Essay Concerning Human Understanding." The importance of the "Essay" in English philosophic thought is due not to any valuable contribution made by Locke himself, but rather to the fact that it formed the starting point from which all later thought developed. It is this fact which marks John Locke as the founder of the first continuous school of English philosophy. It was left for his successors, particularly Bishop Berkeley and David Hume, to work out the details of the system.

Whatever may be the world's estimate as to the value of the English school of philosophy, there can be no question that the "Essay" constitutes one of England's greatest contributions to purely scientific thought, for in it are laid the foundations of modern psychology. Descartes a few years before had announced a theory of "innate ideas," that is, that the mind is in possession of certain principles of knowledge prior to experience; but, as William Wallace has said, "Descartes's dubious phraseology anent innate ideas, found a witty executioner in Locke." According to Locke's theory the mind acquires knowledge only through experience, or, in other words, through sense-impressions received from the external world, and through the internal process of reflection. Each individual's knowledge consequently is limited and determined by his experiences. Since the experiences of no two people are exactly the same, it becomes evident that no two people will see the outside world from exactly the same point of view. Out of this belief grew Locke's theory of tolerance. In this conception of experience as the sole source of knowledge, Locke prepared the way for psychology, the science of individual experience.

Without going into a discussion involving highly technical phraseology, it is easily evident that this new theory of Locke's as to the origin of knowledge would lead inevitably to his theory of tolerance. While his "Letters on Toleration" are primarily pamphlets in support of free religious associations outside of the established church, there can nevertheless be deduced from them a thoroughgoing argument for intellectual freedom in general. Locke's theory of knowledge on the one hand and his theory of tolerance on the other are striking illustrations of the growing tendency to exalt reason at the expense of authority. The supremacy of reason and experience over faith and authority was so firmly established by Locke, that through all the theological warfare that followed between church and state, between science and religion, the theologians themselves relied upon reason rather than upon revelation. They, too, were becoming convinced of the truth of Locke's terse statement: "He that takes away reason to make room for revelation puts out the light of both; and does much the same as if he would persuade a man to put out his eyes, the better to receive the remote light of an invisible star by a telescope."

In the words of Alexander Fraser, Locke's "repugnance to believe blindly what rested on arbitrary authority, as distinguished from what was seen to be sustained by self-evident reason, or by demonstration, or by good probable evidence, runs through his life. He is typically English in his reverence for facts, whether facts of sense or of living consciousness, in his aversion from abstract speculation and verbal reasoning, in his suspicion of mysticism, in his calm reasonableness, and in his ready submission to truth. . . . Locke is apt to be forgotten now, because in his own generation he so well discharged the intellectual mission of initiating criticism of human knowledge, and of diffusing the spirit of free inquiry and universal toleration which has since profoundly affected the civilized world. He has not bequeathed an imposing system, hardly even a striking discovery in metaphysics, but he is a signal example, in the

Anglo-Saxon world, of the love of attainable truth for the sake of truth and goodness. 'If Locke made few discoveries, Socrates made none.' But both are memorable in the record of human progress."

Only a few years after Locke's death in 1704, George Berkeley, later Bishop of Cloyne, took up the work which his master had left, and developed his famous theory of vision which even now stands the test of rigid investigation, leaving him still the great discoverer in the psychology of vision. From psychological preliminaries, Berkeley went on to develop his metaphysical doctrine of Idealism and so established on a permanent basis the distinctly English school of philosophy founded by Locke. This school, as we shall see, was to come into much greater prominence in the nineteenth century warfare between science and religion.

It was in France, however, rather than in England, that the ideas of Newton and of Locke were first made the basis of definite schools of thought. Voltaire, during his famous sojourn in England from 1726 to 1729, had been very deeply impressed by the broad tolerance which characterized English thought and by the great achievements of the English in science and philosophy. Voltaire's return to France marks the introduction of both

Newton and Locke to continental schools of thought. Newtonian physics soon after displaced Cartesian philosophy and became, as we have seen, the basis upon which Laplace built his Nebular hypothesis; Locke's speculations on mental phenomena were elaborated and erected into the science of psychology by Condillac (1715-1780) and his followers, whence it later found its way back to England.

Thus the marvelous advance of pure science in England during the seventeenth century was already, in the early years of the eighteenth, making a most profound impression upon all European thought, social, religious, and philosophical. Perhaps the most striking effect of all was the impetus given by Newtonian physics to the development of the school of English Deists, which had been founded by Herbert of Cherbury as early as 1645. They sought to do away with all revealed religion with all its dogma and its ritual, to establish a rationalistic criticism of biblical documents, and to worship God as the manifestation of immutable law. The Deist movement soon died out, but not until it had produced Voltaire and Rousseau, and wrought far-reaching changes in the views of the French Encyclopædists and in German biblical criticism.

The achievements of Newton, Locke and their immediate followers mark the close of the first great period in the development of English scientific thought. It was, as we have seen, a period of beginnings during which through an amazing series of brilliant individual achievements, a few great English thinkers had laid the foundations of modern astronomy, physics, and higher mathematics, botany and zoölogy, anatomy, physiology and medicine, psychology, and ethics. All this had been accomplished in a period of less than one hundred fifty years since Bacon's "Advancement of Learning." This sudden and immense enlargement of man's intellectual horizon had been brought about through the application of Bacon's experimental method,—a minute observation of natural phenomena aided by suitable instruments and verified by experimentation. In all the ages of past civilization nothing had been accomplished in any way comparable to the advance of this first period of English science.

There has been a general notion, even among the best informed people, that the Greeks had engaged in practically all the forms of intellectual activity with which we are now familiar; that they had forecast nearly all of our fundamental discoveries in science; that their achievements of the intellect were equal, if not superior, to anything which man has since accomplished. But telescopes, microscopes, and all the other instruments of the modern scientist were unknown to the ancient Greeks. Their knowledge at the best was only a crude and haphazard observation unsupported by experimentation. By the middle of the eighteenth century our knowledge in all the branches of modern science, as Professor Robinson says, "greatly transcended, in its extent and precision, anything known to the Greeks and Romans. The diabolical superstitions associated with witchcraft . . . finally gave way, and the new spirit of unfettered criticism and the confidence in experimental science and its applications which it had begotten—which were ever reënforcing the conception of progress and were ever weakening the authority of the past—furnished the necessary preliminaries for a new series of achievements."

The second period, a comparatively short one, in the history of English thought was, by the very nature of its extent from the middle of the eighteenth century to the early years of the nineteenth, characterized by an entirely different type of scientific activity. The advance of pure science, dependent as it is upon unfettered criticism and freedom of thought, had now to await further steps in the general trend of English experience before it could enter upon another great period of generalization. For the next half century the English intellect was occupied, not by the formulation of new theories of natural science, but rather with the application to practical life of those already formulated. It constituted, therefore, the middle or transitional period in the growth of English scientific thought. But this does not mean that it is any less significant. The least active is often the most vital; the least sensational, often the most dramatic. So it was with this half century of transition.

At the beginning of the period, in the early years of the eighteenth century, England was on the verge of momentous changes in her social, industrial and economic life,—changes that were destined to transfigure completely the face of all later civilization. On the one hand they were to lead, through the practical application of scientific principles, to a series of epoch-making inventions which would revolutionize industry; on the other hand they were to bring forth the first great formulation of the principles of economic science.

In consequence of the greater liberty of individual action and broader tolerance of belief, which had been achieved through the Glorious

Revolution of 1688-89, England had become the asylum of oppressed peoples of the Continent, where freedom was as yet a thing unknown. Particularly was this true of France. In 1685, the Edict of Nantes, which had guaranteed protection to French Protestants, had been revoked, and thousands of Huguenots, mainly silk weavers, took refuge in Protestant England. This great tide of immigration had a profound effect on English industry. The stimulus to the silk trade was immediate and lasting. Slowly but surely trade secrets leaked out and English workmen learned to copy French methods. But the English artisan could not equal the French artist, and the fashion for French goods remained, so much so that materials not bearing the label, "French made," were sold with difficulty. This new stimulus to industry was felt, too, not only in silk weaving but in all the other industries brought over by the immigrants,—weaving of linen and of sail cloth, printing of calico and other cotton goods, making of hats, paper, glass and pottery, tapestry and furniture. The new trades took root very quickly and grew with astonishing rapidity, until England became a veritable beehive of domestic industry.

This tremendous increase in industrial activity

was, of course, in answer to a corresponding increase in demand, to be explained partly by the greater skill and taste of the newcomers, but much more by the fact that this period of immigration was coincident with a period of increased communication with the Continent, due mainly to political causes, which brought in its train a new fashion for things continental. If the Frenchman of the eighteenth century followed the English lead in science and philosophy, the Englishman on the other hand, followed the French in customs and manners, dress, art and literature. This, it must be remembered, was the age of Queen Anne, and of the Georges, the age of the coffee house, the essay and the beginnings of periodical literature, the age of Pope and of Johnson, the age when form and ceremony, dress and outward adornment, luxury and ease, were the highest ideals of a very considerable portion of a wealthy and prosperous population. Small wonder that English industry advanced by leaps and bounds, and that her products, protected by rigid navigation laws, soon found their way to all parts of the civilized world,—carried to England's rapidly growing colonial empire, carried moreover in English ships manned by English sailors, and controlled by English merchants, whose profits fast came to constitute the greatest source of the nation's wealth.

But before attempting to seek out the economic causes underlying this tremendous increase in manufacture and domestic industry, more especially in cloth making, we must be careful to remind ourselves that these words did not mean in those days what they mean to us to-day. "Manufacture" was still used by the eighteenth-century Englishman exactly as it had been by the ancient Roman, in its literal sense, "made by hand." The old spinning-wheel, which could produce but a single thread, the simple hand-loom, and all the tools used were of the same primitive type as those which had done service fifteen centuries before in Roman Britain. "Domestic industry" meant not that within the boundaries of a nation, but literally a trade carried on within the home. Each weaver's cottage was a separate and self-sufficing unit where the women and children of the family did the spinning, while the men were occupied in weaving and in tilling the little plot of ground, whose products supplied the family with food. These cottages, it must also be remembered, were for the most part rural, not urban. The ancient craft-guilds which all through mediæval times had practically controlled the various trades, were attempting to maintain their old-time monopoly by a rigid policy of exclusion, which prevented any considerable development of these new industries in the towns, within whose boundaries their jurisdiction was protected by royal charter. Fortunately under the primitive system then prevailing the new trades could be carried on as easily in rural districts as in urban, for the processes of manufacture were of the simplest, involving no use of costly machines, necessitating no interdependence of labor beyond that which the family itself could supply.

Methods of exchange were equally undeveloped. The northern districts, which during the eighteenth century were still largely pastoral, produced by far the greater part of raw wool; and here relations between the wool-raiser and the weaver were of the simplest,—the weaver bought the raw wool direct from the producer and sold the cloth he made directly to the consumer. In the southern districts, where materials were imported, the supply was controlled by "merchant manufacturers," who, instead of selling the raw material to the weaver, merely intrusted it to him for making into cloth which when finished was returned to the merchant. Such a system of manufacture and exchange undoubtedly had its advantages; but there was fast approaching a time when it could no longer supply the demand. It is only by keeping in mind, however, this primitive character of English industry during the eighteenth century that we can appreciate fully the revolution wrought by the introduction of machinery and of modern industrial processes.

This tremendous social and economic change, the earliest stages of which we now call the Industrial Revolution, took place in the last quarter of the eighteenth century. Its causes and the reasons why it came first in England rather than on the Continent are many, varied, and highly complex. There were, however, as Professor Ogg has pointed out, several obviously favoring conditions,—the greater abundance in England both of skilled labor and of capital, the gradual passing of the control of domestic industry into the hands of merchant-manufacturers, and the early and rapid progress of mechanical invention. In England many favouring circumstances, both geographic and historical, had opened the door to wider opportunities and greater rewards than in any other nation of Europe. England's early overthrow of the feudal system, the growth of enclosures, and her extraordinary accessibility to the sea had already brought the woolen industry largely under the control of merchant-manufacturers, particularly in southwestern England.

But English industry could not come into its own till the domestic system could be replaced by the factory, when all the materials could be kept under one roof, and all the laborers work together in one place. Only so could specialization of labor develop, only so could efficiency be realized. To bring about this result, one more factor was obviously necessary,—the improvement and increased utilization of machinery. It was just here that English science came to the rescue of English industry.

Of all the processes in cloth making, that of spinning had always been the slowest; anywhere from five to ten spinners were required to keep one weaver busy. This disproportion became still more perplexing when in 1738, John Kay of Lancashire invented the "flying shuttle," which enabled one man to do the work of two and at the same time double the productive capacity of the loom. The demand on the spinner, which now became greater than ever, finally in 1761 led the Royal Society for the Encouragement of Arts and Manufactures to offer two prizes for the invention of a spinning machine which could produce more than one thread at a time.

English practicality came at once to the fore in a wonder-working series of improvements. The earliest of these was the "spinning-jenny," invented in 1764 by a Lancashire weaver, James Hargreaves. This machine, which could be operated by a child, at first produced eight and later eighty threads, but these threads, lacking firmness, could be used only for woof. Seven years later Richard Arkwright, a peddler, put together his "water-frame," whose firm thread, substituted for the linen formerly used as warp, now enabled weavers for the first time to produce all-cotton cloth. This fact alone would mark it as an epoch-making invention; but its importance is still further increased by the fact that its cumbrous mechanism and dependence upon water power, making its use in the domestic system impossible, gave a powerful impetus to the growth of the factory system. A few years later Samuel Crompton, also of Lancashire, combined the merits of the "jenny" and the "water-frame" in a machine called the "mule," which has served as the basis for all modern weaving machinery. Crompton's "mule" made possible the spinning of a very fine soft thread, and thus led to the establishment in England of the manufacture of muslin. By his invention the productivity of the spinners was so increased that the burden of demand shifted now to the producers of raw cotton.

Up to this time cotton fiber had been separated from the seeds by hand; but in 1792 Eli Whitney's cotton gin, which enabled one man to do the work of ten, opened to the English spinners all the great resources of the American cotton fields. This in turn shifted the demand to the shoulders of the weavers. In 1784 Cartwright, a clergyman of Kent, had conceived the idea of a power-loom; but due to the unsatisfactory conditions of water power the machine did not come into general use until the early years of the nineteenth century, when the difficulty was removed by the application of steam power. Thus, by a series of three great inventions, the cotton gin, the spinning machine and the loom, the textile industry was carried from the cottage to the factory; cloth was no longer man-made, but machine-made. Thus in a brief period of fifty years had England introduced and established the first great principle of modern industrialism, the use of machinery.

The second great element in industrialism is that of power. Ever since the time of the ancients, the expansive power of steam had been known, but this knowledge had not been put to practical use until 1705 when the need of some means of pumping water from mines led the Englishman Newcomen, through the introduction of the principle of the piston and cylinder, to the invention of a crude steam engine. But Newcomen's engine which made use of steam only at one end of the piston was of very low efficiency; it remained for another Englishman, James Watt, sixty years later, to make the engine of practical use in industry by closing the cylinder and applying steam at both ends to increase efficiency; by introducing a separate condenser to avoid cooling the cylinder; a "governor" of revolving balls to secure regularity of motion; and a rod and crank arrangement which made possible the use of a belt to drive other machinery. It was these improvements made by Watt which first made possible the use of the steam-engine in the operation of machinery. From 1785 when it was first used to run a spinning machine, it was rapidly introduced wherever factories sprang up in all the newly born industrial centers of northern England. Watt's engine, therefore, marks the establishment of the second great principle of modern industrialism, the use of mechanical power to economize man power.

But in order that these two great principles of

the Industrial Revolution, the invention of machinery for the multiplication of human efficiency and the perfecting of engines for the application of steam power, might be worked out, two other fundamental elements were necessary,—an abundant supply of material for the manufacture of machinery and an equally abundant supply of fuel for the generation of power. Machinery cannot be made without metal nor can steam be produced without fuel. Fortunately large areas in northern, central and western England are underlaid with invaluable deposits of coal and iron ore; but it was not until the middle of the eighteenth century that proper methods of utilizing these resources were discovered.

In ancient and mediæval times ore had been melted by the use of charcoal, but this was a very expensive process, in the first place because by this means the full amount of pure iron could not be obtained from the ore; and in the second place because great quantities of charcoal were required for every ton of iron. Under such circumstances it was only natural that sooner or later measures would be taken to prevent the deforestation of England and in the end seriously cripple her iron trade. By 1750, in fact, export had practically ceased and Swedish pig iron was being imported in ever increasing quantities. It was necessary that some new method of smelting be evolved. Early in the seventeenth century attempts had been made to utilize coal for this purpose; but not till the middle of the century was any degree of success attained. Through experiments made by Dud Dudley and Abraham Darby a process of smelting by coke was developed, but the product obtained did not possess the desired malleability. Shortly afterward Smeaton invented his cylinder-blowing apparatus, which supplanted the crude bellows in supplying the necessary blast. But the most important discovery was made by Cort in 1784; this was the process called "puddling," by which for the first time it became possible to make malleable iron by the use of coal instead of charcoal. This discovery, the essential element of which is the purification of raw iron by means of oxygen, was supplemented by another also made by Cort, that of the substitution of grooved rollers in place of the hammer in making bars or plates. A few years later Cort's process came into general use through the annulment of his patent, and resulted in a marvelous increase in the production of iron through the kingdom, particularly in those regions of northwestern England where coal and iron are found in close proximity. By the end of the Napoleonic era England, instead of importing iron, was exporting it at the rate of 91,000 tons a year. The significance of this fact for us, however, lies not so much in the increase of England's export trade as in the fact that from this time on an adequate supply of machinery was assured. This development of the iron industry had also produced a corresponding stimulus to coal mining, which placed at the command of factory owners a seemingly inexhaustible supply of coal. Thus had England's natural resources made possible the permanent establishment of her industrial supremacy,—a supremacy which could not have been achieved, however, had not Englishmen in true Baconian fashion turned to practical use that knowledge of natural phenomena which her scientists had already placed at their disposal.

Thus was brought to pass that remarkable industrial transformation by which the agricultural England of the early eighteenth century became the leader in all those great social, industrial and economic movements, which have so distinctly characterized the last one hundred years. As Frederick Ogg, in his "Social Progress in Contemporary Europe," has pointed out: "There has been no small amount of speculation as to why England should have produced the unrivaled galaxy of inventors—Kay, Hargreaves, Arkwright, Crompton, Cartwright, Radcliff, Horrocks, Newcomen, Watt, Cort, and a host of others—by whom in the eighteenth and earlier nineteenth centuries the industrial leadership of the kingdom was so firmly established. It was not because the need of improved mechanical appliances was more keenly felt than in France, Germany, Switzerland, and other countries. It was not because England was a leader in pure science. It seems to have been primarily because of two things,—first the fact that the need was as keenly felt as elsewhere, and second, the pronounced tendency of English genius, at any rate in the period mentioned, in the direction of practical, applied science, rather than in that of pure science. While continental *savants* prosecuted their researches in light, electricity, and chemical reactions, Englishmen of scientific interests busied themselves with the application of knowledge already available. With but an exception or two, the English inventors were men of very ordinary education, and several of them were but tinkers and jacks-of-all-trades. Through an infinite amount of patient experimentation they contrived to bring to bear upon the problems of everyday industry the discoveries of their more brilliant continental contemporaries. Watt, for example, made practical use of the expansive power of heat, and the result was the steam-engine; but the idea that such a thing could be done seems to have originated with the physicist of Marburg. The steam-engine came in response to a very definite need—the need, that is, of pumps of greater power in mines which were reaching levels where the old hand-power or horse-power pumps could not be made to serve. Here and in scores of other cases the principle that necessity precedes invention was abundantly illustrated, even though continental experience demonstrated that necessity does not always produce invention."

This marvelous series of mechanical inventions and of industrial processes, which England, through the application of science, had brought forth during the last years of the eighteenth century was the culmination of one of the two main lines of development, which marked the second great period in English science. But its effects did not stop here. From England the Industrial Revolution spread to France, from there to Germany and other European nations, whence its influence has been felt throughout the whole civilized world. Meanwhile the marked inventive genius of the English-speaking peoples was finding expression in other ways. Their invention and development of the ocean steamer and of the locomotive, of the automobile and the aeroplane supplied the great means of communication and transportation which have brought together the uttermost parts of the earth. Their perfecting of the press has placed the newspaper in practically every home, while the telegraph and telephone have carried the mind of man to the remotest regions of the world. Their invention of the reaper and the sewing machine, together with a host of similar labor-saving devices, has not only lightened the burden of labor and multiplied man's power and efficiency in industry; these in themselves are achievements of no mean importance, but their full significance becomes apparent only when we realize that such relief from labor means also that leisure for self-improvement and for appreciation of the finer things of life which are destined more and more to determine the course of social progress.

These achievements, as Professor Robinson has said, "serve to explain the world in which we live, with its busy cities, its gigantic factories filled with complicated machinery, its commerce and vast fortunes, its trade unions and labor parties, its bewildering variety of plans for bettering the lot of the great mass of the people." It was the Industrial Revolution which brought about the great Reform Bill of 1832, and those which followed it with all their ramifications in English political history, a series by which the spirit of democracy was for all time established on English soil. It was that same Industrial Revolution, the problems of which served to waken and rouse men's minds to grapple with those great social, industrial and economic questions upon the solution of which our future civilization depends.

While the tendency to occupy the social point of view was greatly increased by the Industrial Revolution, and our general view of the world very materially affected by new ways of spinning and weaving, this tendency is nevertheless only a continuation of that decidedly ethical, utilitarian and economic bent, which has characterized all modern English thinking from Francis Bacon down through the centuries to Sir Francis Galton on the one hand, or to E. R. A. Seligman on the other. It was the attempt made by Adam Smith, late in the eighteenth century, to furnish a rational analysis of such problems, which led to that other great achievement which marked the second period of English scientific thought,—the foundation of the science of economics.

Up to the middle of the eighteenth century economic ideas had not been formulated into any definite body which could be called a science; they had instead been included within other bodies of doctrine, such as ethics or jurisprudence; to found a separate science of economics it was necessary to isolate these scattered ideas and bring them together in a definite and independent system of thought. Adam Smith was not the first of English thinkers who had attempted to formulate a definite body of economic laws. All through the seventeenth century there had been a steadily increasing number of pamphlets on this subject; but most of them had been written in consequence of some specific situation,—in defense of or in attack upon some monopoly or privilege or some particular legislation. Each one had his own ax to grind; but out of it all, nevertheless, had come a most profitable realization of the importance of the navy, of shipping, and of colonial development, for it was the theory of the Mercantilists, whose ideas had up to this time dominated the economic affairs of the nation, that the chief source of wealth lay in commerce, and in the actual supply of gold and silver coin. It was only natural that such a system as this with its narrow emphasis on foreign trade, should have found its greatest support in the maritime England of the sixteenth and seventeenth centuries. It can hardly be called a speculative doctrine; it was rather, as some one has said, a spontaneous growth resulting from the reaction of social conditions on minds not trained to scientific habits.

Of all writers of the period, however, the only one who can deservedly be called a forerunner of Adam Smith was Nicholas Barbon (1640-1689), for he, putting personal interests entirely aside, honestly tried to define those fundamental principles, the existence of which was either ignored or taken for granted by the pamphleteers. Barbon's work was the first real protest against the English Mercantilist policy, which had already outlived its usefulness. His ideas were the natural outcome of the agricultural improvement which took place in England during the late seventeenth century and which was to convince Englishmen of the profitableness of farming on a larger scale with greater capital and with the scientific application of the principle of crop-rotation. It was Barbon's protest against the Mercantilist theory which gave impetus to the emphasis placed by French economists upon the importance of agriculture. It is a matter worthy of note, too, that as early as 1685 this English thinker had already hit upon a fundamental assumption of modern political economy, which we find expressed in his own simple words: "To be well fed, well clothed, and well lodged, without labor of either body or mind, is the true definition of a rich man." Furthermore, his insistence upon the fact that "prohibition of any foreign commodity doth hinder the making of so much of the native" is a striking anticipation of the modern free-trade doctrine that any check on imports acts as a check on exports; but in no case did the seventeenth century pamphleteers touch in any illuminating fashion upon the question of the distribution of wealth now so universally regarded as the most important branch of economics. For them the great question was not distribution but production, or, in other words, the increase of the total national wealth. Barbon's ideas, on the other hand, were the natural expression not only of the agricultural changes being wrought in England during his day, but also of the general philosophical conceptions, the trend of which, as we have already seen, was being determined by his more famous contemporaries, Newton and Locke.

The significance of the whole school of English natural philosophy,—the philosophy of Newton and of Locke, of Barbon, and of Berkeley and Hume,—lies in their common belief that the conduct of men in society is subject to natural law in the same way that the equilibrium of nature is maintained by physical law. This mechanical conception of the universe, like everything else English, is very intimately bound up with the theory of utilitarianism, a system of ethical doctrine which asserts that conduct is morally good in proportion as it promotes the greatest happiness of the greatest number. Though the word "utilitarianism" was not coined until the nineteenth century, the first hint of the theory had been given by Lord Bacon, and his idea had reappeared in Hobbes' declaration that since man's natural state is one of warring self-interest, the function of government should be the furtherance of the common weal. A little later John Locke's strong assertion of individualism had done much to popularize the theory. It crept into eighteenth-century theology in the guise of the doctrine that all the movements of the universe were guided and controlled by divine wisdom and benevolence in such a way as to produce the greatest possible sum of human happiness. This dogma in turn was carried over into the realm of philosophy by Berkeley and Hume, the English successors of Locke, who developed it into the conception of a *jus naturae;* this "law of nature" they represented as a harmonious and beneficial code inherent in nature and antecedent to human institutions, whose laws are human and whose arrangements are the imperfect ones of existing governments. That nation was best governed, therefore, whose laws and institutions came nearest to expressing the constitution of the natural order. Such was the political philosophy of David Hume, whose ideas in particular acted as a subtle leaven to French thought, especially in his influence over Turgot and Rousseau.

Influenced by this English school of philosophy so markedly utilitarian in spirit, there arose in France about 1750 a group of thinkers, chiefly economists, known as the Physiocrats, one of whose leaders was Turgot, the friend of Hume. Following their English guides, Barbon, Locke, and Hume, they extended the mechanical theory into the economic world and conceived the production and distribution of goods as carried on according to fixed laws of nature. These, they asserted, must be sought out and strictly observed if men are to realize their highest social welfare. They preferred to call themselves the "Economists," because, taking the tillage of the soil as a starting point, they based their reasoning upon the conception of natural liberty, and "like our Locke," attached a new significance to the individual and his rights. Society, according to their view, is composed of individuals all of whom have the same natural rights; and even though all might not have the same capacities, nevertheless each individual, understanding his own interests best, would be more likely to act in accordance with the laws of nature than would the government. Whence their maxim, *laissez faire,* "let things alone." The state or community is only a contract between individuals, the object of which is to limit the natural liberty of each only as far as is necessary to secure the rights of others. The function of government, therefore, is not to extend control over the individual, but solely to protect his life, liberty and property. Since the ideas of liberty and of property inherent in the very nature of man are essential to his individualism, the chief function of human law should be to recognize, formulate and maintain these rights.

This economic theory of the French Physiocrats with its emphasis upon land and upon individualism followed the Englishman Barbon in protest against the Mercantilist theory that commerce was the measure of a nation's wealth. The Physiocrats held, on the contrary, that wealth came from nature; thus they placed the emphasis not upon commerce, but rather upon agriculture. The Mercantilist doctrine of trade regulation gave way before the *laissez faire* of the Physiocrat. One of their most important tenets was their emphasis upon the value of land and its surplus or *produit net;*—in other words the theory that only that labor is truly productive which adds to the quantity of raw materials, agricultural and mineral, thereby made available for use by man; the annual addition to the wealth of the community is measured by the excess of the mass of such products over the cost of production; and upon the amount of this excess, or *produit net,* depends the well-being of the state and its progress in civilization. In order to secure at the same time the maximum economic gain and the maximum individual liberty, they believed not only in the possession of private property but also in the greatest possible freedom for the individual in the disposition of his property; in other words there must be entire freedom of exchange, there must be unrestricted competition, there must be no control exercised through monopolies or special privilege.

The service of the Physiocrats on the whole was on the one hand largely negative in consequence of its insistence upon greater freedom from restraining regulations and burdensome taxation. On the other hand their idea of distribution was the source of many succeeding attempts to trace the round of production and exchange, distribution and consumption. But more than anything else their service to economic thought lies in the fact that their attempt, under English influence, to formulate a body of exact principles apart from morals, politics, and jurisprudence resulted in the founding of economics as a distinct and independent science.

But before this body of economic thought could receive permanent recognition as a science, it remained, still, for the great English thinker, Adam Smith, to modify, broaden and organize these fundamental principles into a unified and coherent system. This he did through the publication of his "Wealth of Nations," which appeared in 1776, the year of the Declaration of Independence. The same forces which had produced the American Revolution had also produced the

"Wealth of Nations," for Smith's insistence upon the economic freedom of the individual and upon the restriction of government control over production and distribution were but the inevitable outcome and expression of that general unrest and assertion of individualism which was, during this period, a marked characteristic of all thought, religious and philosophical as well as political and economic. Smith's "Theory of Moral Sentiments" shows how clearly he perceived the interdependence between the economic and all the other phases of social phenomena; in this work, as he says, he intends to give "an account of the general principles of law and government, and of the different revolutions they have undergone in the different ages and periods of society, not only in what concerns police, revenue and arms but whatever else is the subject of law." These words, as some one has pointed out, are "an anticipation, wonderful for his period, of general sociology."

The degree to which he was successful in the achievement of his purpose is a matter of considerable difference of opinion. But none can question his broad, keen, and discriminating observation of social phenomena and his markedly English tendency to draw from these their full significance, rather than to derive his conclusions by deductive processes of logic from previously postulated abstract principles. That he did, however, in some degree fall a victim to certain warping postulates must be admitted. His general acceptance of the tenets of the English school of philosophical utilitarianism represented by David Hume led him to a more or less optimistic conception of a system of economics based upon an enlightened self-interest. But on the other hand he sought at the same time to analyze and interpret existing institutions as results of social phenomena which had been actually observed in operation. His more or less mechanical interpretation of economic questions, together with a leaning toward materialism, have laid him open to severe criticism from an opposing school of thought which asserts that he failed to regard wealth as a means to the higher aims of life, failed likewise to keep in view the moral destination of the race.

It cannot be denied, however, that in the years following the publication of his "Wealth of Nations," Smith's ideas exercised a far-reaching influence in the assertion of personal freedom and "natural rights." It discredited completely the Mercantilist policy of the past, and gave a powerful impetus to the overthrow of institutions no longer suited to modern conditions of social life. It is a matter of interest to Darwinians, too, that both Turgot and Adam Smith mentioned the effects of the increase of population upon the wages of the laboring classes, and so pointed the way twenty-two years later for Malthus' memorable "Essay on the Principle of Population" (1798); for it was the attempt made in this essay toward the discovery and scientific treatment of laws governing such increase that guided Charles Darwin to his theory of natural selection. This is only one instance of the widely diverging currents of thought set going by Smith's "Wealth of Nations."

Whatever may be the present opinion of Smith's theories as a guide to future social reconstruction, he is nevertheless universally acknowledged as the Father of all modern political economy. Professor Haney, in his "History of Economic thought," has pointed out the merits which, according to his view, entitle Adam Smith to this distinction: "Building upon the thought of English predecessors and the Physiocrats, and influenced by a different environment, he turned from 'nature' or agriculture as the source of wealth, and gave to labor that position. While, on the whole, a believer in free trade and *laissez faire,* he was more of an opportunist, and was less rigid and absolute in applying his doctrines. Smith's work was fuller and more comprehensive than that of Quesnay or Turgot, and the firm establishment of political economy may justly be dated from the 'Wealth of Nations' (1776). Smith took the sole emphasis away from production, putting the consumer more to the front, and in doing so prepared the way for a broader treatment of economics. He also presented a more comprehensive discussion of value and the shares in distribution than any predecessor. Although some of his followers wrote more accurately and confidently than he, Adam Smith excels the great majority of them in breadth of view, and there came a time when many economists turned back to the Father of Political Economy rather than to his immediate successors."

One of the most notable instances, perhaps, of the effects of this utilitarian view of political economy upon the broader but closely related lines of political and philosophical theory, is to be seen in the teachings of Jeremy Bentham (1748-1832), whose far-reaching influence on English legislation has been pointed out by Mr. Larned in an unpublished part of his essay on

"English Leadings in Modern History." "In the home government of England," Mr. Larned writes, "this progress toward just law and large individual freedom received a remarkable quickening, within some early decades of the last century, from the influence of the teachings of Jeremy Bentham and the numerous disciples who took inspiration from him. The working of this influence on English legislation, between about 1825 and 1865, is traced with clearness by Mr. A. V. Dicey in his interesting Harvard lectures on 'The Relation between Law and Public Opinion in England.' Starting from the conception that all right objects in life are summed up in the promotion of 'the greatest happiness of the greatest number,' Bentham's doctrines, urged with tireless ardor and energy by him throughout a long life, acted slowly but powerfully and variously on English thought and feeling. They involved a philosophical belief in the utilitarian theory of morals, and a practical belief in the *laissez faire* or 'let alone' theory of legislation, grounded on the assumption that every person, as a general rule, is the best judge of his own happiness, and should be restricted in free action no farther than is necessary for securing equal freedom among his neighbors. All the springs of humanitarian feeling were fed by both these beliefs.

"Generally, within the range of European or western civilization, many influences had been working always and increasingly in these directions; influences which received a great stimulation in the latter half of the eighteenth century, and then were checked by the reaction which followed the French Revolution. All such genial and generous forces in modern civilization had come into activity again at the time referred to, and were universally felt; but the Bentham gospel of greatest happiness for the greatest number did undoubtedly bring a special stimulation of them to English feeling, and give a powerful impulse to rapid moral advances in politics and law. It had not a little to do with the transfer of the control of government from the land-owning oligarchy to the middle class in English society, by the parliamentary Reform Bill of 1832. It has even more, perhaps, to do with the compensated emancipation of slaves in British colonies, under the Act of 1833, and with the energetic activity of England against the African slave-trade, which she pursued with little help from other Powers until that infamy no longer shamed mankind. It must have been, moreover, among the reënforcements which came at this time to the doctrines of Adam Smith's 'Wealth of Nations,' contributing to the break-down of the English 'corn-laws,' and ultimately to the overthrow of the whole system of governmental 'protection' to prices and profits for a few at the expense of all.

"These are merely conspicuous among many results that come partly or wholly from the general movement of reform in legislation for which Bentham labored, to harmonize it with philosophical principles of humanity and right. Within the forty years which Mr. Dicey calls 'the period of Benthamism or individualism' the whole temper of the criminal law was changed; its penalties were mitigated; capital punishment was reserved for murder alone; imprisonment for debt was brought nearly to an end; important beginnings were made in legislation for regulating the hours and conditions of labor in factories, especially in the interest of women and children; cruelty to dumb animals began to be dealt with by law; and the right of workmen to combine in trade unions, denied formerly, was conceded to a limited extent."

The work of Bentham is a typical illustration of the growth and outspreading of that English political utilitarianism which we have seen foreshadowed in Hobbes two hundred years before. Though not confined to political and legislative fields, Bentham's activities were not particularly concerned, however, with the more strictly economic phase of English thought. A truer representative of the work of Adam Smith and of the ever widening circles of his influence, is to be found in that most ardent pupil of Bentham's,—John Stuart Mill (1806-1873), who set out to do for his own generation what Smith had done for the late eighteenth century. The monument to his attempt is his "Principles of Political Economy" (1848), for a time the most widely influential of all modern works upon that subject. Though his conception of the field of economics was less narrow and formal than that of Ricardo, who had been Smith's immediate successor, nevertheless Mill did not by any means achieve the ideal which he had set for himself. He never grew to the stature of a "modern Adam Smith,"—he succeeded only in becoming an elegantly lucid and overgrown Ricardo, with an acquired Malthusian complexion. Strenuous believer in rationalism though he was, he nevertheless was often inconsistent, uncertain and superficial, and his work in economics failed to stand the acid test of scientific criticism.

But while his actual contribution to the body of English economic science was neither great nor permanent, he nevertheless performed a most significant service for English philosophic thought in general and for ethics in particular. The system of thought which Mill set himself to expound was in the main the utilitarianism of his father and of Bentham. In philosophy John Stuart Mill is the final exponent of that empirical school whose foundations were laid in Newtonian physics, whose chief tenets were outlined by John Locke and later elaborated by Berkeley and Hume. The chief characteristic of this "typically English" school has continuously been the emphasis laid upon human reason,—an insistence, that is, upon the duty of every philosopher to investigate truth for himself, rather than accept the authority of another. In other words, knowledge must be rooted in experience. It is this individualism together with an increasing tendency to give first place to psychological problems which marks the school as so characteristically English.

But Mill's greatest service lies in the fact that he, more strongly than any of his predecessors, has emphasized the humanist element. His thought was for his fellow-men about him rather than for Man in the abstract. He early realized on the one hand the need of a broad and democratic education for the people as a whole, and on the other the need of greater harmony among philosophers in order that humanitarian reforms might be given that same basis of fundamental agreement which characterizes all other scientific advance. Though the general color of his thought may be in some respects quite justly called a "materialistic political utilitarianism," Mill is nevertheless an admirable example of the steadily increasing idealistic and humanitarian tendencies of the middle and later nineteenth century,—tendencies which were given their first great impulse in those conditions which had arisen out of the Industrial Revolution with its consequent development of the spirit of democracy. Mill's earnest plea for the abolition of slavery, the enfranchisement of women, and the alleviation of poverty, his belief, too, that the cultivation of altruistic feelings would offset the old "natural order" of innate self-interest, and his insistence upon the necessity of a well-safeguarded social order and security compatible with a complete intellectual liberty, and a broad toleration of individual action,—all these mark John Stuart Mill as one of England's most conspicuous leaders of thought in an age whose most remarkable feature was the development of humanitarian sentiment. Social sympathy was to him the mainspring of obligation and the sanction of morality; for "morality," he says, "consists in conscientious shrinking from the violation of moral rules; and the basis of this conscientious sentiment is the social feelings of mankind; the desire to be in unity with our fellow creatures, which is already a powerful principle in human nature, and happily one of those which tend to become stronger from the influence of alvancing civilization."

But Mill's altruistic ideals did not lead him to the present conception of sociology as a science, probably because the early establishment of political economy in England as an independent science had concentrated attention upon practical problems of legislation and administration connected with the subject, to the virtual neglect and exclusion of other social questions, the importance of which has not until recent years been recognized. As Merz has suggested, "the existing political Order in this country with its enviable constitution,—considered by many foreign philosophers as a model of political organization to be initiated by the aspiring peoples of the Continent,—relieved English thinkers from dealing with fundamentals or answering the abstract question of what society is or ought to be." But Mill was far from any smug satisfaction with the intellectual conservatism of the mid-Victorian period. "Where there is," he says in his essay "On Liberty," "a tacit convention that principles are not to be disputed, where the discussion of the greatest questions which can occupy humanity is considered to be closed, we cannot hope to find that generally high scale of mental activity which has made some periods of history so remarkable. . . . These periods [the Reformation, the French Revolution, and die Aufklärung] differed widely in the particular opinions which they developed; but they were alike in this, that during all three the yoke of authority was broken. In each an old mental despotism had been thrown off, and no new one had yet taken its place. . . . Appearances have for some time indicated that all three impulses are well-nigh spent; and we can expect no fresh start until we again assert our mental freedom." Mill's whole life, devoted as it was to the furtherance of political freedom and to the amelioration of the oppressed lower classes, is in itself the greatest monument to his belief in intellectual freedom and a conscious social progress, a belief in the practicability of Bacon's vision that in the application of scientific knowledge lies the great hope for the betterment of man's estate.

The significance of the work of John Stuart Mill is seen not so much in the actual contribution which he made to scientific or to philosophic thought, but rather in the impulse which he gave to this idea that all humanitarian thought should be based upon scientific knowledge. His work is the culmination of one phase of that great movement toward industrial democracy, which began when English genius first turned science to account in the invention of machinery. Out of that movement there has come a new respect for the common man, a new appreciation of his individual worth, which in turn have led to a new solicitude for his welfare. It is this recognition of the rights of the common man that has recast our constitutions and remade our institutions. It is that same social sentiment, so vividly set forth by English utilitarians, from Locke to Adam Smith and Bentham, so amplified and vitalized by Mill, whose finer idealism and more spiritual humanitarianism gave to the world a new conception of the common dignity of man,—it is that same social sentiment which has found expression in the rapid formulation of all the social sciences; the same social sentiment which has brought with it a new "vision of all the wonder that would be," when science should be harnessed to the chariot of a conscious social progress. But before that mighty movement could come to full fruition in twentieth-century advance, it had to wait upon another great achievement in English scientific thought, another great step in the liberation of man's spirit from the chains of authority, ignorance and blind superstition. That new step, that great achievement, was to be the establishment of the evolutionary or dynamic view of human life and of the universe.

In the meantime English thinkers were preparing the way for such a view through that long series of brilliant generalizations and discoveries in pure science which characterizes the third great period in the history of English thought. This new period did not begin until the close of the Napoleonic wars. During that protracted struggle the whole strength of the nation had been expended on the work of self-preservation; and even after the war itself was over, England had to fight her way through the desperately straitened financial conditions, which the long conflict had involved. Practically the whole first quarter of the nineteenth century had passed before England entered upon the new and extraordinary career of scientific development extending through the last hundred years, which has so vastly extended man's powers of observation and research, and so immensely broadened his intellectual horizon.

Any attempt to enumerate all the achievements which make up this new series of discoveries and generalizations would require not merely pages, but many volumes. The briefest mention is sufficient to recall to us some of the greatest. Through the work of Priestley, Cavendish and Dalton, the science of chemistry experienced a rebirth in the promulgation of the atomic theory of multiple proportions. At the same time, a new field was added to experimental chemistry through a series of brilliant electro-chemical researches begun by Sir Humphry Davy in the early years of the nineteenth century,—a series which prepared the way for the triumphs of Michael Faraday in the investigation of electrical phenomena, a series, too, which went far toward the establishment of the mechanical theory of heat. It was Davy's emphasis, moreover, upon the vital relation of science to industry which inspired some of his finest work; it was this practical application of science which made his lectures on agricultural chemistry the basis of England's leadership in the science of agriculture; and his invention of the safety lamp, another instance of his Baconian practicality which made possible another great advance in mining industries. On the foundations laid by Priestley, Dalton and Davy, later generations were to build the chemistry which we know to-day. Meanwhile, Sir Charles Bell had announced his discovery of the specialization of functions in the brain, an event in the realm of physiology which had not been matched in its importance since the days of Harvey's discovery of the circulation of the blood. In astronomy, too, the English mind was by no means idle; Herschel had already, in 1781, made his memorable discovery of Uranus, the first new planet to be added to the ancient list of seven, the calculation of whose orbit was found to conform completely to those laws of planetary motion which Kepler and Newton one hundred years before had formulated. During the first third of the nineteenth century, the expansion of the British Empire in the southern hemisphere was accompanied by the English conquest of the southern heavens through the building of observatories at the Cape of Good Hope and elsewhere. But of far more significance was the computation by John Couch Adams in 1841, simultaneously with Leverrier in France, of the exact location of another new planet, Neptune, hitherto unobserved. In 1837, that year so memorable in English history, the year of the accession of Queen Victoria, the year of the invention of the electric telegraph by the American, Samuel F. B. Morse, there had occurred another great discovery in science,—the law of the "Conservation of Energy," a law which by the importance of its revelation that energy is in the same degree indestructible and uncreatable as matter has entitled its discoverer, James Prescott Joule, to be ranked side by side with Newton in the history of physical science. Greater still, however, was the work of Michael Faraday, whose name stands among the most illustrious of the century; for it was his discoveries in the field of electricity and magnetism which did more than anything else to place at man's disposal all those practical applications of electrical power which are so rapidly transforming human industry, communication and transportation. Faraday's discovery of electro-magnetic induction made possible the dynamo which runs so much of our machinery; and his investigation of the laws which govern electrolytic action provided us with the most accurate of methods for measuring the strength of an electric current. The great significance of these events, however, is not merely in the added power which these new achievements placed at man's disposal; their ultimate value can be fully appreciated only when we realize that each of these discoveries means a new extension of the frontier line of scientific knowledge over that vast wilderness of ignorance and prejudice, superstition and "infallible authority," the conquest of which was necessary before the human mind could think its way clear to that greatest of all achievements of nineteenth-century science, the formulation of the theory of evolution as a scientific hypothesis capable of demonstration on a basis of observed facts.

An event so great in the history of science, so vital to the philosophy of social progress, could not occur unheralded. The way had been prepared through centuries of thought, groping slowly but surely through the maze of phenomena, receiving new light with each discovery of science, and new opportunity for observation with each advance of civilization. Some vague conception of the theory of evolution, or the gradual unfolding of the universe of matter and of the forms of life which it contains, had been held by the ancient Greeks. But upon a subject so vast in its sweep, so endless in its ramifications, so bewildering in the variety of phenomena involved,—upon such a subject it is inconceivable that any scientific hypothesis could be formed and demonstrated until all the other great branches of science had been sufficiently developed to be able to contribute, each its due share, to the great body of observed facts which alone could form a sound basis for so sweeping an hypothesis. That stage in the advance of scientific thought was not reached until the middle of the nineteenth century.

The *idea* of evolution, however, as suggested by the Greeks first reappeared upon the scene of modern scientific thought about the middle of the eighteenth century. Up to that time not only the great mass of the people, but scientists and philosophers as well, had accepted the ancient Hebrew account of a special and divine creation. The date of this event which had been variously estimated by the great church fathers, had, in the days of Cromwell, been fixed "with laudable precision," by Archbishop Usher, who assigned it to Friday, October 28, 4004, B. C. The matter was accordingly regarded—by the theologians at least—as finally settled; it is only within the last half century that coercion of belief on this point, from ecclesiastical authority, has been rendered fruitless by the advance of scientific knowledge.

The first serious attempt to establish a new conception of the formation of the earth had been made by a Frenchman, Buffon, in 1749; but he had been most summarily compelled to retract his hypothesis and affirm that he believed implicitly in the Biblical account. Later, at the beginning of the nineteenth century, another Frenchman, Laplace, as we have seen, put forth his Nebular hypothesis, which in its turn was also denounced by theologians; nevertheless by the profound impression which it made upon scientific thought in emphasizing the idea of a gradual evolution or development of the physical universe, it prepared the way for a similar conception of evolution in the realm of living forms.

Meanwhile the attack upon the Scriptural account of creation developed from another quite unexpected quarter. In consequence of the deeper mining made possible by the use of steam pumps in the latter part of the eighteenth century there had been much speculation as to the origin of the various types of rock observed. The earliest theory—that of the Frenchman, Cuvier—attempted to explain stratification and fossil remains by imagining a series of catastrophes of fire or water, each of which had been fatal to all living creatures and had been followed by a new exercise of creative force, the last of which supposedly was the one described in Genesis. This theory served for a time to save the belief in divine intervention through a series of special creations, a series of processes alien, however, to those of every-day experience. It was but natural that such an explanation would not appeal to the English mind, the doubting Thomas of science, which demanded some theory which could be explained on the basis of the ordinary processes which could still be seen in operation. Such an explanation, now known as the "uniformitarian theory," was put forth by James Hutton in the late eighteenth century; but it was not until the publication in 1815 of William Smith's "Map of the Strata of England and Wales," that there was established a basis of observed fact sufficiently broad and sound to justify acceptance of the Huttonian theory. This theory, expounded by Sir Charles Lyell in his "Principles of Geology" (1830), attributed stratification to the deposition of material by the action of seas and rivers and other natural agencies acting through long periods of time. By comparison of the fossil remains of plants and animals found in different layers of rock, geologists were then able to classify the rocks and determine their chronological sequence. From these facts in turn it became evident that the gradual formation of the rocks had been accompanied by an ascending series of plant and animal types; and furthermore, that the period of time required for these transformations was infinitely greater than had ever been conjectured. In consequence of Lyell's exposition of this "uniformitarian" theory of Hutton's, the whole science of geology, with its amazing revelations of the great age of the earth, was brought into being. Thus had been established by the English mind, during the first third of the nineteenth century, that science which, apart from biology, was to do more than any other toward overturning false conceptions of chronology and opening up new vistas in the history of the formation of the earth and of the development of living forms upon that earth.

But before an adequate working hypothesis could be formulated in explanation of that development of life, another step was necessary,—the transformation of the "natural history" hobby of the seventeenth and eighteenth centuries into the biological sciences of the nineteenth. We have already noted the work done by Nehemiah Grew and by John Ray, late in the seventeenth century, in laying the foundation of botany and zoölogy. The greatest of the naturalists, however, the man whose work marks the transition from mere accumulated information to the beginnings of a systematic and organized knowledge of the phenomena of life, was the Swedish scientist, Carl Linnaeus, whom Huxley characterized as "the supreme law-giver of living nature." But though Linnaeus was not an Englishman, his work, nevertheless, was based upon that of the Englishman, Ray. About the middle of the eighteenth century, Linnaeus had announced his famous classification of plants and animals, in which he assigned man to the highest place in an ascending series of plant and animal species,—to the natural order, class mammalia, order of primates, genus homo. The work of Linnaeus was followed half a century later by that of Baron Cuvier of France, whose "Animal Kingdom" (1818), basing classification upon internal as well as external resemblances, formed the point of departure for all subsequent zoölogical speculation. Both Linnaeus and Cuvier had noted the close resemblances between various species, and their classifications reveal an ascending series, but neither of them had any theory to offer, other than that of innumerable special creations, which would account for the origin of species. That work remained for Charles Darwin.

By the middle of the nineteenth century, the

time was ripe for the appearance of such a theory. The idea of evolution, as has been said before, was not a new one. But in the form suggested by the Greeks, and reappearing occasionally down through the Middle Ages it signified merely a *gradual* process in the formation of the universe and in the development of the forms of life. In this same sense the word "evolution" first appeared in the scientific world during the eighteenth century, as a term to denote the *gradual* unfoldment of an organism from a miniature embryo, complete from the beginning in all its parts. This application of the idea of evolution had been made by the opponents of William Harvey's theory of "epigenesis,"—the theory that the growth of the organism takes place by the successive addition of parts. In the resulting controversy, "epigenesis" won out over "evolution"; but the word "evolution" was still retained in its more general sense to signify as before the *gradual* unfolding of the universe rather than a six-day act of special creation. By the middle of the nineteenth century, the idea of evolution had already become practically established in all the physical sciences, partly as a result of Laplace's Nebular hypothesis, partly through the work of Stokes in spectrum analysis, but more conclusively through the work of James Hutton, William Smith and Charles Lyell, in the development of the "uniformitarian" theory of the structure of the earth. In the field of biological thought, too, the Frenchman Lamarck had in 1809 advanced his theory of evolution as based upon the adaptation of the organism to its environment, and of the transmission of acquired characteristics. But it remained for Charles Darwin to fix the meaning of the word "evolution" as we understand it today, "the transmutation of species," as opposed to a series of innumerable "special creations" for each and every organism.

Darwin's great achievement, therefore, was not the mere suggestion of the idea of evolution. His work, rather, was the formulation of the theory as a scientific hypothesis capable of demonstration on a basis of observed fact. For some twenty years he wrestled with the problem, summoning for its solution an amazing range of facts, drawn from every conceivable source, from a comparison of fossil remains to a study of the whole range of living forms; from the simplest rules of deliberate selection followed by the farmer in breeding domestic animals, to the unconscious natural selection which was suggested to him by a chance reading of Malthus' observations upon the tendency of population to increase at a rate much more rapid than that of the means of subsistence. Throughout all this immense accumulation of observed fact, Darwin was the first to see a single principle continuously acting. Having observed that throughout all nature the number of young born was far in excess of the number which could subsist upon the available food supply, he accounted for the origin of species by assuming that, through a slow process of natural selection, there would survive in the struggle for existence only those individuals of a species which were best adapted to their environment through some favorable variation of structure or of function. Through the advantage gained by the occurrence of a useful variation a series of organisms would then, through the course of ages, develop permanent modifications, and thus exhibit the variety of characteristics which distinguish the surviving species. This is Darwin's theory of evolution as substantiated by the principle of natural selection upon which he placed so strong an emphasis. By his establishment of this principle, he laid the foundation for a new and vastly broader study of organic structure, making it possible to account for more complex organisms as the result of a series of useful variations, and of simpler organisms as survivals of those earlier forms which constitute the common ancestry of both. But not only did he set forth an explanation of that continuous process of evolution through which the highest forms of life have been developed from formless protoplasm, the simplest living matter,—that in itself was an achievement great enough to win for him a willing recognition as the greatest scientific thinker of the nineteenth century,—not only did his work place the science of biology upon a new and permanent foundation, but it also wrought a revolution in the whole course of scientific thought, the effects of which are altogether beyond our calculation. The application of his theory has raised innumerable questions and problems; the nature and causes of variation, the question of heredity and of educability, of transmission of instincts and acquired characteristics, the question of hybridization and mendelism, of pangenesis and eugenics,—these are but a few of the many problems, storm-centers of controversy still, growing out of one phase or another of the theory advanced by Darwin. Some of these investigations are even tending, in themselves, to be classed as separate sciences within the general field of biological research. But apart from any discussion of these problems, which would lead too far afield, there can be no question of Darwin's supreme position as leader of the ever-increasing host of earnest investigators who are extending the realm of biology as a science over regions which before had been shrouded in the fogs of superstition and of mysticism.

That such a theory of the development of life, with all its implications, would result in nothing less than a complete revolution in modern thought is inevitable. That it would meet with fierce objection was a matter of course. But as John Tyndall has pointed out, Darwin's "vast resources enable him to cope with objections started by himself and others, so as to leave the final impression upon the reader's mind that, if they be not completely answered, they certainly are not fatal. Their negative force being thus destroyed, you are free to be influenced by the vast positive mass of evidence he is able to bring before you. This largeness of knowledge and readiness of resource render Mr. Darwin the most terrible of antagonists. Accomplished naturalists have leveled heavy and sustained criticism against him—not always with the view of fairly weighing his theory, but with the express intention of exposing its weak points only. This does not irritate him. He treats every objection with a soberness and thoroughness which even Bishop Butler might be proud to imitate, surrounding each fact with its appropriate detail, placing it in its proper relations, and usually giving it a significance which, as long as it was kept isolated, failed to appear. This is done without a trace of ill-temper. He moves over the subject with the passionless strength of a glacier; and the grinding of the rocks is not always without a counterpart in the logical pulverization of the objector. But though in handling this mighty theme all passion has been stilled, there is an emotion of the intellect incident to the discernment of new truth which often colors and warms the pages of Mr. Darwin. His success has been great; and this implies not only the solidity of his work, but the preparedness of the public mind for such a revelation."

The most immediate effect of Darwin's thought is seen in his influence upon the philosophy of his contemporary, Herbert Spencer, who was already formulating his evolutionary theory of knowledge, when Darwin's work came to his attention. What Darwin had done for the physical world, Spencer had set himself to do for the world of mental phenomena. What, he asked himself, is the principle of growth of that power which has culminated in Reason? How may the various orders of mind be accounted for? Accepting the work of the physicist and of the physiologist, Spencer sought to build, upon these as a foundation, a system of psychology. He recognized two obvious factors in the problem, the organism and its environment; between these he saw going on a continuous interaction which led him to define life as "a continuous adjustment of internal relations to external relations." From a vaguely diffused sensitiveness of tissue in the lowest organism there has been a gradual development of the five senses, which in turn modify the conduct of the organism in its adjustment to its environment, both through extent in space and through extent in time. There is also a corresponding increase in complexity of sensation and of conduct as development is traced through the orders of brute life up to the human mind. In the life of the individual, sense impressions constituting its experience of the external world are stamped upon the brain, thus forming states of consciousness and determining all the mental processes of perception, memory, and so on. Repeated sensations producing the same repeated reaction, combined with hereditary transmission, lead to the formation of instincts. Two or more phenomena occurring invariably together are stamped to equal depths and result in ideas indissolubly connected, thus determining the "law of inseparable association." Just here Spencer departs from the view of John Stuart Mill, who would recognize only the registered experiences of the individual. Spencer's view maintains that there exists in the human brain at birth a power of organizing race experience previous to its individual experience; in other words the human brain, he says, is the "organized register of infinitely numerous experiences received during the evolution of life, or rather during the evolution of that series of organisms through which the human organism has been reached. The effects of the most uniform and frequent of these experiences have been successfully bequeathed, principal and interest, and have slowly mounted to that high intelligence which lies latent in the brain of the infant. Thus it happens that the European inherits from twenty to thirty cubic inches more of brain than the Papuan. Thus it happens that faculties, as of music, which scarcely exist in some inferior races, become congenital in superior ones. Thus it happens that out of savages unable to count up to the number of their fingers, and speaking a language containing only nouns and verbs, arise at length our Newtons and our Shakespeares."

Neither Darwin nor Spencer had any theory to offer as to the origination of life. Nor did they attempt to explain the nature of the external world, from which all our sensations are received; that, in the words of J. S. Mill, is "the great battleground of metaphysics." Spencer does not, as Berkeley would, deny its existence, but maintains rather that it is an outside entity, the real nature of which we can never know. "In fact," as Tyndall says, "the whole process of evolution is the manifestation of a Power absolutely inscrutable to the intellect of man. As little in our day as in the days of Job can man, by searching, find this Power out. Considered fundamentally, it is by the operation of an insoluble mystery that life is evolved, species differentiated, and mind unfolded from their prepotent elements in the immeasurable past."

It was inevitable that such a theory of life would turn the whole course of modern science, philosophy and religion into entirely new channels. While the discoveries of Davy and of Faraday, of Morse and Stephenson and Bell, were working a complete transformation in the outward aspect of the world, Darwin's theory and philosophy were working a similar transformation in the inner life of man. Every phase of modern thought,

—from biology, psychology, and anthropology, through all the present array of nascent sciences on the one hand, to history and literature, philosophy and religion on the other,—every phase of modern thought has felt the impulse given by the "Origin of Species"; for it supplied that dynamic element in our modern evolutionary theory which has made possible for us to-day a new and vastly greater conception of the possibility of human progress than that inherent in the old idea of the "perfectibility of man." As Professor Dewey in his "Influence of Darwin on Philosophy" has pointed out, the very title, "Origin of Species," is a declaration of the modern intellectual revolt against traditional assumptions of an age already long past,—"the assumption of the superiority of the fixed and final." The whole superstructure of all classical philosophy based upon the idea of fixity, and of the old theological dogma based upon a series of "special creations,"—all this has gone down in the general demolition wrought by the introduction of the evolutionary view of life.

Shorn of the old philosophies and dogmas, feeling the old foundations crumbling, doubting the efficacy of the new philosophy, the Pragmatism of William James, or the Creative Evolution of Henri Bergson, humanity is asking over and over again the old, old question, "Is there a God? What is God?" The question is being asked not only by the "intellectuals," but also and far more poignantly by the great masses of the people, who, untrained in philosophical subtleties, feel the need of some practical working faith to replace their broken images. And many and varied are the answers given to that insistent cry of a bewildered, struggle-torn humanity. From one extreme comes the grim reply of Friedrich Nietzsche, with his supreme contempt for the Christian conception of an atoning, self-sacrificing God; with his violent assertion of an uncompromising naturalism, his doctrine of self-realization and of a brutal individualism gone mad; but Nietzschism is a symptom rather than a solution. From the opposite direction comes the answer to Leo Tolstoy with his visionary theory, his almost pathetic reliance upon a God of passive non-resistance. From another quarter still are heard the assurances of theosophists, offering to a haste-driven world the calm and peace of an Oriental faith.

But one of the most characteristic of modern religious reactions "against the despotism of fact" imposed by natural science, perhaps the most significant in its emphasis on the idea of universal brotherhood, and in its power to stem the tide of pessimism by galvanizing flagging human energy into positive action, is the rise of Christian Science, which its founder, Mary Baker Eddy, defined as "the law of God, the law of Good, interpreting and demonstrating the divine Principle and rule of universal harmony." God, according to the Christian Science doctrine, is "incorporeal, divine, supreme, infinite, Mind, Spirit, Soul, Principle, Life, Truth, Love. All causation is Mind, and every effect a mental phenomenon." "It results from this definition," says one of its expounders, William Denison McCrackan, "that the basis of Christian Science, the Principle of its healing is wholly metaphysical, *i.e.,* beyond the realm of physical sense perception; that this Principle has no material form or body, is the highest possible authority, and is boundless in power and existence. Truth defines God as an established fixed reality; Love sums up within itself every quality of good, such as tenderness, purity and justice, and this final synonym proclaims that God attracts and rules on the basis of the immutable law of mercy. It teaches first of all the absolute goodness of God and as a consequence the essential goodness of man made in God's image and likeness. . . . The immediate consequences, therefore, of the acceptance of the teachings of

Christian Science, is to establish a hopeful outlook upon life, to found the expectation of good upon definite facts capable of proof by all mankind. A further effect is to lessen fear, apprehension of the future, and worry, to dissipate the mystery and mysticism generally associated with spiritual matters and to bring them into every-day affairs as available and regenerative; to transform religion from a matter principally of preaching or ceremonial into a matter principally of practice and regeneration with its proof and rewards made apparent now instead of in a future state of existence only. It is the supreme merit of Christian Science," its expounder continues, "that it clarifies the true position of God in human consciousness and dignifies the essential nature of man with the glory of his sonship with God. The necessary consequence of this scientific understanding is to produce healing in its fullest and broadest sense, both mental, moral and physical; to bring about the transformation of the body through the renewing of the mind."

There can be no doubt that the Christian Science movement has in one generation enormously increased the number of followers of Christian teachings. Its power has been especially marked in English-speaking countries and is as rapidly spreading throughout the world. Whatever may be the judgment passed upon it by human experience in generations yet to come, the movement is nevertheless most significant as an illustration of the growing social consciousness of universal brotherhood, and of the essential unity of man on the plane of his higher life.

This conception, expressed by "the brotherhood of man," has already played a great rôle in the cultural advancement of man. Hitherto the force it has had, as Professor Ritter points out, "has been almost wholly in its appeal to the emotional side of man's nature and very little in its appeal to the rational side. Hitherto 'the golden rule' has had little or no positive unqualified support from the side of reason and science. It has indeed been too widely assumed both by men of science and men of religion and ethics, that these great conceptions are the exclusive province of religion. Such a view seems to be the chief ground on which Tolstoy, Brunetière, and other intense lovers of mankind have based their indictment of modern science as having proved its inability to contribute anything essential to human welfare and happiness. The province of human biology is to take the very widely observed phenomenon of fellow-feeling as it takes any other fact pertaining to man, and see what can be made of it. Such a study discovers, for one thing, that fellow-feeling is the extreme term of the integrative series of human evolution. We must recognize that to the affectional elements in human brotherhood, mighty in power but often fitful in action, there is added a rational element which, though less applicable to the rank and file of men and less intense in action, is more solid and trustworthy and enduring. . . . On its integrative side, progress in human culture consists in preserving a balance between the affective and rational elements of the brotherhood of man. From the standpoint of biological evolution, progress in civilization may be characterized as the differentiation and intensification of love and intellect, and of the intellectualizing of love and the affectionizing of intellect. What we need is less a city of Brotherly Love than a Land of Brotherly Wisdom, a Sophodelphia. The world's prayer at this time should be for an understanding of head and heart. Therethrough alone runs the road to any sort of human brotherhood and love, for which strong, active men can care. Such a course would fill millions of persons with an enthusiasm that would be irresistible and permanent because sustained by reason as well as by emotion.

It is this same idealism, this same consciousness of social ends, which has been so marked a characteristic of the course of English scientific thought. It is in order to achieve those ends that it has struggled so determinedly to be free. It was that same idealism that Huxley had in mind when he declared that "science prospers exactly in proportion as it is religious." It is that same passion for serving social ends through intellectual freedom which inspired Tyndall's memorable address at Belfast; his words on that occasion are peculiarly characteristic of the high seriousness of English scientific thought: "Mr. Buckle sought to detach intellectual achievement from moral force. He gravely erred; for without moral force to whip it into action, the achievements of the intellect would be poor indeed. . . . I would set forth equally the inexorable advance of man's understanding in the path of knowledge, and the unquenchable claims of his emotional nature which the understanding can never satisfy. The world embraces not only a Newton, but a Shakespeare; not only a Boyle, but a Raphael; not only a Kant, but a Beethoven; not only a Darwin, but a Carlyle. Not in each of these, but in all, is human nature whole. They are not opposed, but supplementary; not mutually exclusive, but reconcilable. And if, still unsatisfied, the human mind, with the yearning of a pilgrim for his distant home, will turn to the mystery from which it has emerged, seeking so to fashion it as to give unity to thought and faith—so long as this is done, not only without intolerance or bigotry of any kind, but with the enlightened recognition that ultimate fixity of conception is here unattainable, and that each succeeding age must be held free to fashion the mystery in accordance with its own needs, then, in opposition to all the restrictions of Materialism, I would affirm this to be a field for the noblest exercise of what, in contrast with the *knowing* faculties, may be called the *creative* faculties of man. Here, however, I must quit a theme too great for me to handle, but which will be handled by the loftiest minds ages after you and I, like streaks of morning cloud, shall have melted into the infinite azure of the past."

Such then is the ideal of a conscious social progress set before the world by men of science among English-speaking peoples. Never before in the history of civilization has there been so marked a tendency to synthetize the knowledge gained from all fields of scientific thought into one grand science of human welfare, whose supreme object will be not merely the joy derived from discovery of yet greater fields of knowledge but also, and far more potently, the satisfaction of man's highest aspirations through the application of scientific knowledge to the perplexing problems of social readjustment. Such was the vision of that first of English men of science, Roger Bacon. Such was the ideal set by his greater namesake, Francis Bacon. Such is the possibility latent in the evolutionary view of a continuous advance toward ever greater heights of human achievement. Such, too, is the hope held out by men of science in all lines of earnest research,—a hope the promise of whose fulfilment may be seen in the work of organizations like the Smithsonian Institute, founded on American soil by a man of English birth for the enlightenment of all mankind. In order that we may attain that intellectual liberty upon which all social progress ultimately depends, science must be free to burst the bonds of prejudice and ignorance and set new standards for the race. Not only must science be unfettered. If she would accomplish for mankind that social readjustment which her men of vision promise, she must find coöperation and support from the emotional impulses of man. There must be no further warfare between science and religion. Both must work together toward a common social end—the betterment of man's estate.

THE ENGLISH GIFT TO WORLD LITERATURE

GRACE F. CALDWELL

THE ENGLISH GIFT TO WORLD LITERATURE

ON the Fourth of July, 1918, there was held in London a meeting most significant in the course of human freedom,—a meeting similar in import to that of the Barons at Runnymede, or the Continental Congress in Independence Hall, the signing of the Federal Constitution, or the taking of the Tennis Court Oath. It was the meeting of the Anglo-Saxon Fellowship, called to celebrate, for the first time on English soil, the 142nd anniversary of the Declaration of American Independence. On that day all the English-speaking peoples of the earth joined hearts and hopes in commemoration of an event which no longer savored of hostility and defiance on the one side, nor of grief and regret on the other, but rather had come to symbolize a common heritage of freedom, a mutual pledge of affection and coöperation toward a common ideal.

The world will longer remember the words spoken on that occasion by Mr. Winston Churchill: "The Declaration of Independence is not only an American document. It follows on the Magna Carta and the Bill of Rights as the third great title-deed on which the liberties of the English-speaking peoples are founded. By it we lost an empire, but by it we also preserved an Empire. By applying its principles and learning its lesson we have maintained our communion with the powerful Commonwealths which our children have established beyond the seas. . . . Deep in the hearts of the people of these islands lay the desire to be truly reconciled before all men and all history with their kindred across the Atlantic Ocean, to blot out the reproaches and redeem the blunders of a bygone age, to dwell once more in spirit with them, to stand once more in battle at their side, to create once more a union of hearts, to write once more a history in common. That was our heart's desire. It seemed utterly unattainable, but it has come to pass. . . . So let us celebrate to-day not only the Declaration of Independence; let us proclaim the true comradeship of Britain and America, to stand together till the work is done, in all perils, in all difficulties, and at all costs. . . . That is the Declaration of July, 1918; and, to quote words that are on all American lips to-day, 'for the support of this declaration, with a firm reliance on the protection of Divine Providence, we mutually pledge to each other our lives, our fortunes and our sacred honor.' "

These were the words of a world-rcnowned Englishman, spoken on time-honored English soil. Almost at the same hour President Wilson was voicing the same sentiments from the sacred slopes of Mount Vernon: "What we seek is the reign of law, based upon the consent of the governed and sustained by the organized opinion of mankind. These great ends cannot be achieved by debating and seeking to reconcile and accommodate what statesmen may wish with their projects for balance of power and national opportunity. They can be realized only by the determination of what the thinking people of the world desire, with their longing hope for social freedom and opportunity. I can fancy that the air of this place carries the accents of such principles with a peculiar kindness. Here were started forces which the great nation against which they were primarily directed at first regarded as a revolt against its rightful authority, but which it has long since seen to have been a step in the liberation of its own people as well as of the people of the United States; and I stand here now to speak—

speak proudly and with confident hope—of the spread of this revolt, this liberation, to the great stage of the world itself!"

This revolt, this liberation,—an aim which is nothing other than the spreading of the spirit of democracy,—this is the mission for whose fulfilment the English-speaking peoples of the world, on July 4, 1918, mutually pledged in enduring brotherhood their lives, their fortunes, and their sacred honor. But what is this spirit of democracy, and how may it be fostered? What ends may it be made to serve? That is a problem to the solution of which the English people set themselves many centuries ago. How far they have succeeded in the fulfilment of their self-imposed task can be judged only by their national experience. And that national experience is recorded nowhere more adequately and forcefully than in their literature. We see in English science, law and government its rationalized and abstract record. But in English literature we find a far more vital, because emotionalized and personal, expression of the spirit of the nation,—that great complex of elemental feelings which have played so large a part in determining its career. "Let me make the ballads of a nation and who will may make its laws." If we would know the spirit of the English people, we must search its literature; and English literature from "Beowulf" to Walt Whitman is nothing at all if not a magnificent chorus whose voices echo, through the halls of time, the strains of a national anthem whose theme is the spirit of democracy. That anthem is the English gift to world literature.

The first strains of that anthem were heard, long before the Magna Carta, far back in those grim dark years when the Anglo-Saxon first set foot on British shores. Deep-chested and huge-limbed, with dauntless courage and fierce resolution, these ancestors of the modern English had braved the fierce storms of the Baltic and of the North Sea in order to find a new home more attractive than the old. They had come from the dismal wastes of Northern Europe with its dull gray blanket of chilling fog, and its tangled forests dripping with rain,—a land swept by fierce storms which lashed the neighboring sea into mountainous waves and drove them in pitiless fury over the marshy and sunken coasts. In such a land there was no place for the weakling or the coward; life was one continuous struggle against overwhelming odds; only those could live at all who lived nobly and masterfully. Coarse, cruel and pitiless though men living under such circumstances must inevitably have been, they were nevertheless fit men to found a new nation; for under their brutality lay immense stores of unwasted energy, and an altogether undeveloped capacity for thought, feeling and action, which was to make them not merely warriors, but heroes and conquerors, founders of nations and builders of empire. It was men such as these, farmers and sailors, who, settling in Britain, laid the foundation of the England that we know to-day. It was men such as these whose life and ideals we see reflected in that first great English epic, "Beowulf," brought by our Anglo-Saxon forefathers from their continental home.

The spirit of the whole poem is that of war,—not the clash of armies nor yet the struggle of man against man, but far more significantly the single-handed combat between a great hero, Beowulf, and three successive incarnations of the monstrous powers of evil. The first of these conflicts takes place in Jutland. Hrothgar, king of the Danes, had built a magnificent mead-hall, Heorot, where he and his warriors feasted and slept. One night, however, the sounds of minstrelsy reach the ears of a fiendish monster, Grendel, who lurks in the marsh near by. In jealous rage he enters the hall and devours thirty of the sleeping warriors. Night after night the fiend continues his raids, till finally the splendid hall is abandoned. This story comes to the attention of the young Swedish prince, Beowulf, already renowned for his wisdom and his many deeds of valor. Coming with his followers to Hrothgar, he offers his services to free the land of this hideous monster. His offer is accepted, and that night they occupy the hall. Beowulf alone is keeping watch when Grendel enters. In the deadly struggle which ensues the champion, using no weapon but trusting solely in his own great strength, inflicts on the monster a mortal wound. Finally Grendel, with the loss of an arm, wrenches himself free and escapes to the marshes to die. Great are the sounds of rejoicing next day when the Danes are gathered to celebrate Beowulf's victory,—a victory, it must be remembered, of sheer human strength over supernatural forces of evil.

But the next night joy is turned into panic by the appearance of Grendel's mother, a hideous water-fiend, who, breaking into the hall to avenge the death of her son, carries off one of the Danish warriors. Again Beowulf offers his services. Tracking the fiend through foul marshes and moors, he comes to a stagnant pool livid with flame. Plunging into its filthy waters, he fights the fiend in her den, trusting again in his own mighty strength. "So it behooves a man to act when he thinks to attain enduring praise,—he will not be caring for his life." But the fiend is too strong, and Beowulf falls. Close to his hand, however, he sees a pile of weapons. Snatching a giant-forged sword, he slays the monster, thus winning his second great victory over the forces of evil.

After these exploits, Beowulf, laden with gifts from the grateful Danes, returns to Sweden, his native land, where he ultimately becomes king. After he has ruled the land in all wisdom for some fifty years, his kingdom is threatened with devastation by a terrible fire-breathing dragon, who hoards up treasure in a dark cave near the sea. The old king, once more "trusting in the strength of his single manhood," goes out to do battle with this new incarnation of evil. He wins in the combat, but is himself mortally wounded. About to die, he calls his warriors about him, and feasting his eyes on the treasure speaks his last words: "I have held this people fifty years; there was not any king of my neighbors who dared to greet me with warriors, to oppress me with terror . . . I held mine own well; I sought not treacherous malice, nor swore unjustly many oaths; on account of all this, I, sick with mortal wounds, may have joy. . . . Now, I have purchased with my death a hoard of treasures; it will be yet of advantage at the need of my people. . . . I give thanks that I might before my dying day obtain such for my people . . . longer may I not here be." So the great hero dies. His followers erect in his honor, on a cliff near the sea, a great mound which sailors can see from far out on the deep, and so keep in mind the memory of their King. The poem ends in a simple requiem:

"Lamented thus
The loyal Goths
Their chieftain's fall,
Hearth-fellows true;
They said he was,
Of all kings in the world,
Mildest to his men
And most friendly,
To his lieges benignest,
And most bent upon glory."

Such in barest outline is the framework of the poem,—crude and weird, trivial and almost absurd, if we think only of the incidents told. Such tales of combats with monster and dragons are, of course, by no means peculiar to the English. In that they are like all other primitive peoples.

But that which distinguishes this poem from other hero tales is its high seriousness, its profound earnestness, and its simple intensity. In its uncompromising honesty, in its quiet but determined facing of what were to those early English the grim realities of life, it strikes the keynote of that tragic mood which characterizes so much of what is best in English literature. Its significance for the spirit of democracy, too, lies not in the events related but in the character of its hero. Primitive peoples, in the absence of an organized government, turn instinctively to men of superior worth to deliver them from crime and oppression, from natural and social evils with which on every side they see themselves beset. Beowulf, the embodiment of all those qualities which the English most admired, stands before us in heroic proportions,—a man of unfailing courtesy and kindness, of unflinching courage and of calm self-reliance, not dependent as were the Greek heroes, upon the aid or intervention of some supernatural agency, but relying solely upon "the strength of his single manhood," ready to employ all his energies, even to give his life if need be, for the welfare of others. Pagan though he is, this Anglo-Saxon hero typifies, none the less, one of the most vital elements in our modern spirit of democracy; for he has gathered from his experience of life a deep realization of the moral truth that the highest satisfaction for the individual life can be found only in the voluntary dedication of whatever strength and wisdom he possesses to the deliverance of his fellowman from evil and oppression. "He who has the chance should work mighty deeds before he die; that is for a mighty man the best memorial." Nothing could be more significant for democracy than this vivid sense of the *obligation* of leadership, the necessity laid upon the man of superior merit to employ his talent in the cause of human freedom, in the furtherance of social progress. That is the spirit which dominated Pitt and Franklin, Gladstone and Lincoln. That is the spirit, too, which has guided English men of science like Francis Bacon and Sir Isaac Newton, Samuel F. B. Morse and Thomas Edison. Such, too, is the spirit which inspired Wycliffe and Milton, Wordsworth, Lowell and Rudyard Kipling. That high conception of the obligation of leadership is the very breath of that which is most distinctively English in literature.

But along with that conception, English literature has given to the world another vital aspect of the ideal of leadership, without which even the highest sense of obligation would be rendered ineffectual. That other aspect is the *recognition* of leadership. Though the feats of Beowulf, in characteristically English fashion, were accomplished by relying solely upon his own magnificent strength, that strength was in turn made doubly powerful through the loyal support of his devoted followers. If there is among these early English any trait more remarkable than their indomitable individualism it is their matchless loyalty to leadership. It is that spirit which prompts the cry of one of Beowulf's men, when they see their chief in mortal peril: "Well do I mind when we drank mead in the hall, how we promised our lord who gave us these rings that we would repay him his war-gifts, if ever the need should arise. Us he picked from the host for this venture, and heartened with hope of glory; he gave us these gifts because he thought us good fighters, gallant wearers of helmets; though all the while our lord meant to do this deed alone and unaided, shepherd of his people, who of all men is foremost in glorious deeds of daring. Now is the day come that our chief needs the strength of good spearmen. Up! let us go to him now, help our hero while the heat sore tries him. As for me I would rather that the ruthless flame should wrap my body together with his: 'tis not meet, methinks, for us to bring home our shields before we have felled the foe, saved the life of the lord of the Weder-people."

This was the spirit that made Beowulf's chieftainship possible—voluntary submission to acknowledged superiority, unflinching loyalty to leadership. What could be more inspiring than that same devotion to a leader which thrills through every strain of the old English war chant, the "Song of the Fight at Maldon"? In that furious battle against Danish invaders, not only does English honor scorn to take vantage ground of the foe, but man after man rushes forward, keeping the sacred pledge of loyalty to avenge the death of his leader, crying that not one inch of English earth must be yielded to the foot of a foreign invader. That was the spirit of English devotion, of English recognition of leadership which at the battle of Hastings, piled high the mound of bodies about the fallen Harold. That is the clarion call that echoes through English verse from the "Fight at Maldon" to "The Charge of the Light Brigade," from old English and Scottish ballads, through Campbell and Scott to Lowell and Kipling. It is this exaltation of the ideal of leadership which in Elizabethan times finds expression in English historical drama with its apotheosis of patriotism.

But perhaps its most significant development is seen in the literature of Puritan democracy. Beowulf, in the struggle for the liberation of his people from the dragon of oppression, had given up his life. In a similar struggle a thousand years later, John Milton, devoted champion of Puritan idealism, suffered the lost of his sight. The spirit of "Beowulf" and the "Battle of Maldon," of English balladry and Elizabethan drama, speaks once more in the lines of Milton in reference to his blindness:

> "Yet I argue not
> Against Heaven's hand or will, nor bate a jot
> Of heart or hope, but still bear up and steer
> Right onward. What supports me, dost thou ask?
> The conscience, friend, to have lost them overplied
> In liberty's defense, my noble task,
> Of which all Europe rings from side to side."

In that premature struggle of English democracy against the forces of absolute monarchy and irresponsible authority, Milton saw no hope for England save in the triumph of its stern and unyielding leader, Oliver Cromwell. In him Milton recognized

> "Our chief of men, who through a cloud
> Not of war only, but detractions rude,
> Guided by faith and matchless fortitude,
> To peace and truth thy glorious way hast ploughed."

But Milton saw, too, and none more clearly than he, that much remained

> "To conquer still; Peace hath her victories
> No less renowned than War: new foes arise,
> Threatening to bind our souls with secular chains,
> Help us to save free conscience from the paw
> Of hireling wolves, whose Gospel is their maw."

But the day of a free republicanism was not yet come. With a despair that grew ever deeper and sterner, the blind poet and statesman watched the ideal he had cherished, the cause he had so unflinchingly supported, go down to defeat in the hands of a leader whose narrowing and hardening policy tended farther and farther from the liberal ideal of the earlier Puritanism. In the failure of Puritan democracy, the forces of reaction triumphed. Disillusioned and blind, almost solitary in his grim resolution to hold fast the old faith, Milton took refuge in poetry.

The old Anglo-Saxon consciousness of the sacred obligation of leadership had inspired the first great epic in English literature. It is no mere coincidence but rather the inevitable outworking of the English spirit which made the violation of that sacred obligation the theme of the other great epic which the English spirit has contributed to the literature of the world. Great works of art are in one sense created in those upper regions of human thought and feeling which are independent of time and place. But magnificent as "Paradise Lost" unquestionably is as an expression of universal emotions, it is inconceivable that it could have been produced at any other period of English history, even at any earlier period of Milton's own life. For into its fabric are wrought not only those tremendous ethical forces which had produced the England of Milton's day, but also all those experiences of Milton's own life which had made possible for him such sublime reaches of thought and emotion. One of the deepest of his convictions was that of the sacred responsibility of leadership. It was against the abuse of ecclesiastical power that Milton had flung out his protest in "Lycidas,"—against pretending shepherds

> "that scarce themselves know how to hold
> A sheep-hook, or have learned aught else the least
> That to the faithful herdsman's art belongs! . . .
> The hungry sheep look up and are not fed."

He had watched the irresponsible exercise of authority by Charles I plunging the nation into Civil War. And he had watched that same nation,—saved as he had thought by Puritan democracy,—subjected again to servile dependence upon the will of a dissolute sovereign,—a nation betrayed, as Milton despairingly realized, by the tragic misdirection of energy, the fatal misconception of power on the part of those very same Puritan leaders in whom Milton had anchored his hopes for the nation. Small wonder, then, that these experiences should color all his later work, that all through "Paradise Lost," "Paradise Regained," and "Samson Agonistes" should run an uncompromising rebuke of the misuse of power and a stern condemnation of all human weakness.

> ". . . If weakness may excuse,
> What murderer, what traitor, parricide,
> Incestuous, sacrilegious, but may plead it?
> All wickedness is weakness; that plea, therefore,
> With God or man will gain thee no remission."

In "Paradise Lost" it was not so much the story

> "Of Man's first disobedience and the fruit
> Of that forbidden tree, whose mortal taste
> Brought death into the world, and all our woe,"—

nor was it so much the desire to "justify the ways of God to men," that inspired Milton to such incomparable majesty of verse; his real purpose was rather to set forth, in all its unspeakable baseness and in all its tragic consequence, Satan the Arch Fiend's abuse of that most sacred of trusts, the capacity for leadership.

> "He it was, whose guile,
> Stirred up with envy and revenge, deceived
> The mother of mankind; what time his pride
> Had cast him out from heaven, with all his host
> Of rebel angels; by whose aid, aspiring
> To set himself in glory above his peers,
> He trusted to have equaled the Most High,
> If he opposed; and, with ambitious aim
> Against the throne and monarchy of God,
> Raised impious war in heaven, and battle proud,
> With vain attempt. Him the Almighty Power
> Hurled headlong flaming from the ethereal sky,
> With hideous ruin and combustion, down
> To bottomless perdition; there to dwell
> In adamantine chains and penal fire,
> Who durst defy the Omnipotent to arms."

But Satan was too determined a foe to be thus easily disposed of. Rising from the fiery lake, he gathered his followers together for counsel.

"After short silence then,
And summons read, the great consult began.
High on a throne of royal state, which far
Outshone the wealth of Ormus and of Ind, . . .
Satan exalted sat, by merit raised
To that bad eminence."

After discussing various plans for revenging themselves against the Almighty, they at last decide to frustrate the whole plan of creation by causing the fall of Adam and Eve. But each of his followers fears to undertake so hazardous a task and Satan decides himself to carry out the project.

"But I should ill become this throne, O peers,
And this imperial sovereignty, adorned
With splendor armed with power, if aught proposed
And judged of public moment, in the shape
Of difficulty or danger, could deter
Me from attempting. Wherefore do I assume
These royalties, and not refuse to reign,
Refusing to accept as great a share
Of hazard as of honor, due alike
To him who reigns, and so much to him due
Of hazard more, as he above the rest
High honored sits?"

His followers humbly accept his proffered service;

"toward him they bow
With awful reverence prone; and as a God
Extol him equal to the Highest in heaven,
Nor failed they to express how much they praised
That for the general safety he despised
His own; for neither do the spirits damned
Lose all their virtue."

The remainder of the poem describes the forging, link by link, of the chain of tragic consequence that ultimately bound Satan and his host and all mankind in slavery to sin.

Whatever may be our point of view with regard to Milton's theology, Satan stands before us here, as heroic in proportion as Beowulf; but it is borne in upon us that while the one did all in his power to debase mankind, the other gave of his strength toward its upbuilding and ennoblement. At times Milton seems to be overpowered by his own creation. Here and there we catch glimpses of Satan almost, as it were, the personification of that spirit of republicanism which had for so long been Milton's ideal. But the more attractive the attributes that Satan displays, the more tragic the figure becomes. The Arch-Fiend has all the great qualities of leadership, except that one most essential of all, the high ethical purpose that keeps man true to the Eternal Verities. It was Satan's rebellion against universal law, his setting up of his own will, his own aims, in opposition to those of the whole moral order, which plunged not only himself but all of his followers with him "down to bottomless perdition." "Paradise Lost" is the tragedy of power misdirected, of leadership misconceived. English literature has given to the world many such tragic figures, but none so colossal as this of Satan, "the arch-enemy of all mankind."

Both Beowulf and Satan, however, were of stature too heroic to be humanly possible. They typify perfectly the English conception of leadership, one in its positive, the other in its negative aspect, but on an enormously exaggerated scale. For a more truly human ideal of the English hero, we must pass over the hundred years that intervened between the Restoration and the dawn of the Age of Revolutions. The eighteenth century was a period of cynicism and artificiality, of "freezing reason" and "common sense," a period when the English spirit was cramped into foreign molds and forced to find expression under narrowly aristocratic and classical disguises. But that spirit was too strongly ethical and emotional to remain long buried under the ashes of a burnt-out formalism. The democratic ideal was too vitally inherent in the English mind to be altogether quenched. To stir the smoldering embers into flame, however, England needed some new and poignant national experience, some new national crisis to fire once more into fresh and vigorous expression the old Anglo-Saxon ideals of leadership. That crisis came when the American Revolution broke out across the seas, when Napoleonism loomed across the Channel, threatening the very life of the English nation. Only then were England's dormant energies roused to protect the empire she had founded; only then did her patriotism rise to save the civilization she had builded; only then did she call forth a Burke, a Nelson and a Wellington to battle once more, like Beowulf of old, in the cause of human freedom But how different the spirit now, and yet how like. In "Beowulf" the conflict had been one of sheer physical strength, and the loyalty he inspired had been personal devotion to a chosen personal leader. In Milton's poem, the struggle was a moral one, based largely on religious principles, while the recognition that Satan won was merely the awed worship felt for a leader of manifestly superior qualities. But in the days of Burke, of Nelson and of Wellington, the English conception of leadership was lifted to a higher plane. The issue now was not merely that of Burke against George III, or of Nelson against Napoleon, but of the English spirit of free government against the tyranny that would overthrow it. Every American minute-man fought not *for* Washington, but *with* him. Every English sailor on board the "Victory" fought, not for Nelson but with Nelson, for England and all that England stood for. The ideal of leadership, with its obligations on the one side and its recognition on the other, had become a bond of mutual coöperation toward a common end. To this voluntary recognition of an innately superior leader had been added another element in the modern spirit of democracy,—that of a mutual coöperation on the part of the whole community toward a common social welfare, in other words a new sense of social equality. This new conception once attained, the foundations of a truly democratic government at last were laid.

This new experience in the history of the English-speaking peoples, this new ideal of leadership, found expression in their literature in the two characteristically differing reactions it produced, on the one hand the individually conservative, on the other the socially democratic. In Wordsworth, the spiritual conception of the dedication of the individual life to a great ideal finds expression in his "Character of the Happy Warrior":

"Who doomed to go in company with Pain,
And Fear, and Bloodshed, miserable train!
Turns his necessity to glorious gain;
In face of those doth exercise a power
Which is our human nature's highest dower;
Controls them and subdues, transmutes, bereaves,
Of their bad influence, and their good receives;
. . 'Tis he whose law is reason; . . .
Who, if he rise to station of command,
Rises by open means; . . .
Who comprehends his trust, and to the same
Keeps faithful with a singleness of aim; . . .
Whose powers shed round him in the common strife,
Or mild concerns of ordinary life,
A constant influence, a peculiar grace;
But who, if he be called upon to face
Some awful moment to which Heaven has joined
Great issues, good or bad for human kind, . . .
Through the heat of conflict keeps the law
In calmness made, and sees what he foresaw; . . .
Who, whether praise of him must walk the earth
For ever, and to noble deeds give birth,
Or he must fall to sleep without his fame,
And leave a dead unprofitable name,
Finds comfort in himself and in his cause."

In this portrait of the ideal leader, we see the features of all that line of noble Anglo-Saxon ancestors, who yielded up their lives in answer to the call of Duty, "stern Daughter of the Voice of God." But this is the ideal of the Wordsworth of later years, the "lost leader" who deserted the ranks of the fiery revolutionists, Shelley, Keats and Byron, to view the human struggle from apart, to take refuge in that traditional English conservatism which saw in Duty as dictated by Reason the power that "calm'st the weary strife of frail humanity." Steadfast in the assurance of the eternal rightness of this inner voice, Wordsworth would have his ideal hero draw his last breath "in confidence of Heaven's applause." Whether he was accepted of men or not, was of no essential consequence.

Carlyle's "Heroes and Hero Worship" carries this idea to its culmination in the very apotheosis of solitary individualism. In his opinion, it is solely the consecrated work of heroes "sent by God," which makes a nation's history. The few, the best and strongest, should command; to these the many, ignorant and weak, must yield obedience, forced if necessary. "Liberty? The true liberty of a man," Carlyle says, "consists in his finding out, or being forced to find out, the right path, and to walk thereon. Whatsoever forwards him in that, let it come to him even in the shape of blows and spurnings, is liberty." "Democracy, the chase of Liberty in that direction shall go its full course. The Toiling Millions of Mankind, in most vital need and passionate instinctive desire of Guidance, shall cast away False-Guidance; and hope, for an hour, that No-Guidance will suffice them. But oppression by your Mock-Superiors well shaken off, the grand problem yet remains to solve: That of finding government by your Real-Superiors!" "Democracy, which means despair of finding any Heroes to govern you, and contented putting-up with the want of them,—he who discovers no God whatever, how shall he discover Heroes, the visible Temples of God?"

How strange such doctrine sounds to modern ears! Can it be in any sense a voicing of the English spirit? In its sublime protest against a growing materialism and in its clarion call to high spiritual endeavor on the part of the wise, the strong and the fit to bear the burdens of the weak, yes. In its setting up of an aristocracy of individual worth, yes. In its emphasis upon the supreme importance of ethical principles in the shaping of human conduct, he is even more distinctly English. In his stern unbending Puritanism, he is nothing less than a direct lineal descendant of the Oliver Cromwell whose biography he so sympathetically set forth. But in his blind worship of the hero, Carlyle is anything but English. The Englishman doesn't worship his heroes. He willingly entrusts them with authority and then sternly holds them to account,—the English hero is not above the law. He must be, too, a hero *per se,* neither by divine right nor by heredity, nor yet by his ability to lead—Satan could lead. In English eyes the hero is a hero only by his own innate ability to prove himself a benefactor to the race. Carlyle's hero is a "divine right" being, whose strength to achieve is his own justification for being. That conception fastened itself upon Carlyle in consequence of his over-fond devotion to German philosophy. Such a conception of a hero above the law leads inevitably to that paternalism, that autocracy which to-day is wasting the land of its birth. The English hero is not a Bismarck but a Gladstone, not a Kaiser but a Lincoln. Carlyle, with his hero worship gone mad, stands in solitary negation of that vital principle of democracy that is so essentially English, so preeminently American, that intense democratic idealism that glows through Emerson's "Representative Men." To English-speaking peoples, heroes are not beings to be worshiped, but, as Emerson so aptly quotes from Sterling,

"Our nobler brothers, though one in blood."

This is the very quintessence of the English ideal of leadership,—a universal brotherhood of men in which the wiser, the more experienced lends a hand to cheer and guide his fellows along the path where each and all, together, must

"Strive upward, working out the beast."

It is this, the democratic, ideal of leadership which is revealed in Emerson and in Tom Paine, in Whittier and in Curtis, in Walt Whitman's "Pioneers," and, most emphatically of all, in Lowell's portrait of Lincoln:

"Nature, they say, doth dote,
And cannot make a man
Save on some worn-out plan,
Repeating us by rote:
For him her Old World moulds aside she threw,
And choosing sweet clay from the breast
Of the unexhausted West,
With stuff untainted shaped a hero new,
Wise, steadfast in the strength of God, and true.
How beautiful to see
Once more a shepherd of mankind indeed,
Who loved his charge, but never loved to lead;
One whose meek flock the people joyed to be,
Not lured by any cheat of birth,
But by his clear-grained human worth,

And brave old wisdom of sincerity!
They knew that outward grace is dust;
They could not choose but trust
In that sure-footed mind's unfaltering skill,
And supple-tempered will
That bent like perfect steel to spring again and thrust.

. . . .

Great captains, with their guns and drums,
Disturb our judgment for the hour,
But at last silence comes;
These all are gone and standing like a tower,
Our children shall behold his fame,
The kindly-earnest, brave, foreseeing man,
Sagacious, patient, dreading praise, not blame,
New birth of our new soil, the first American."

It is this Anglo-American democratic ideal which has sounded the note of social progress through all our modern literature during the last one hundred years. But that high-souled conception would never have been possible had it not been for the firm establishment, by the beginning of the nineteenth century, of that other great element which the English spirit has contributed to our modern democracy. That element is the idea of social equality. It was, indeed, a plant of slow growth, but a very sturdy one, withal.

In primitive Anglo-Saxon days, there had been

but little social inequality. There was a rude nobility, but one based for the most part upon the idea of individual worth, a genuine aristocracy, the rule of the best and most worthy. Such is the social world portrayed in "Beowulf." These early English had their ceremony of royalty, "their dignities an' a' that," but there is nowhere any hint of social condescension, nowhere any suggestion of hard and fixed class distinctions. The old Anglo-Saxon society was a free field for the demonstration of individual worth.

With the coming of the Normans, however, all was changed. Upon the ground work of early English institutions a new régime was built. A new nobility was created, based upon distinction of birth. The Anglo-Saxon thegn was made vassal to a Norman overlord; the English freeman became a serf. Class distinction between Lords and Commons never grew hard and fast as on the Continent, but this did not apply to the lowest class, the great substratum of toilers upon whom rested the burden of production. For these the Magna Carta made no provision; for these there was no redress of grievance through representation in parliament. For more than three centuries they labored on,—patient, mute, but not unfeeling, accepting the appointed order as fixed and inevitable. Then in the fourteenth century came the wars with France and the resulting Black Death. Half the population died of the plague, fields were left untilled, crops ungarnered and granaries empty. Many that had escaped the pestilence died of famine. The cry of the poor went up in vain over the land. But at last their sufferings found effective utterance in the words of John Ball, the "mad priest of Kent." It was in his preaching that English men first listened to a declaration of social equality and the natural rights of man. "Things will never be well in England," the historian Green represents him as saying, "so long as goods be not in common, and so long as there be villeins and gentlemen. By what right are they whom we call lords greater folk than we? On what grounds have they deserved it? Why do they hold us in serfage? If we all came of the same father and mother, of Adam and Eve, how can they say or prove that they are better than we, if it be not that they make us gain for them by our toil what they spend in their pride? They are clothed in velvet and warm in their furs and their ermines, while we are covered with rags. They have wine and spices and fair bread; and we oat-cake and straw, and water to drink. They have leisure and fine houses; we have pain and labor, the rain and the wind in the fields. And yet it is of us and of our toil that these men hold their states." Ball's leveling doctrine epitomized in the popular rhyme,

> "When Adam delved and Eve span,
> Who was then the gentleman?"

became the watchword of that great mass of restless, starving toilers in whose behalf Wycliffe labored with such devotion.

In literature their grievances found expression through a poem of William Langland's, the "Complaint of Piers the Ploughman," which reveals to us with terrible fidelity the life of that great substratum,—its misery, its moral and religious questioning, its social revolt against the selfishness and corruption of the rich with which it contrasts so strongly. Nothing could be greater than the gulf between this world of the struggling masses and that other world of wealth and beauty, ease and luxury which we see reflected in the work of Chaucer. Langland's world is the world of toil and hunger, of narrowness, misery and dull monotony, whose grim earnestness is made only the more intense by the coarse laughter and rude revelry of the unlettered peasant.

"I was very forwandered," says the poet, "and went me to rest under a broad bank by a burn side, and as I lay and leaned and looked in the water I slumbered in a sleeping, it sweyved (sounded) so merry." Sleeping thus, the poet sees in a dream the world of his every-day life going on pilgrimage, not to Canterbury but to Truth. In the crowd are traders and chafferers, hermits and beggars, minstrels and jinglers, ploughmen, weavers and laborers, lawyers who plead only for large sums of gold, bishops given to overmuch haunting of courts, pardoners from Rome driving good bargains with conscience-smitten peasants and "parting the silver" with the village priest. As a guide on their pilgrimage in search of Truth, they desire neither clerk nor priest, but Piers the Ploughman whom they find at work in his field. He bids them to wait till he's finished his half-acre. Piers' philosophy is of the simplest and most practical sort. He bids the knight to cease cheating the poor man: "Though he be thine underling here, well mayhap in heaven that he be worthier set and with more bliss than thou." Two doctrines he preaches with homeliest wisdom,—the gospel of quality and the gospel of labor. Piers' chief aim in life is to work; his chief duty, he believes, is to make the rest of the world work with him. Hunger, he says, is God's whip in driving the idler to toil. On the eve of the struggle between capital and labor, Langland thus strives to be fair to both; but pervading the whole poem is a sense of pathos, loneliness and terrible despair, for it is only in a dream that the world will repent at the preaching of Reason. The poem closes with the prophecy of a religious revolution, when man's inherent right to think and judge for himself would be established. Thus two centuries before the Reformation there was foreshadowed, in the "Vision of Piers Ploughman," that spirit of free inquiry, that right of "the masses" to decide for themselves, which was later to result not only in a religious reformation, but far more significantly in a great social revolution in which all artificial distinctions of rank and class would be gradually swept away and the principle of social equality be established on a firm and enduring basis. But that time was yet five centuries and more away. In the meantime the cry of the people was heard in their literature, voiced sometimes by plowman or tinker, sometimes by priest or noble, but more often by members of the great middle class, a noble band of poets, dramatists and novelists, essayists and orators, self-consecrated champions of the down-trodden and the oppressed, the "nobler brothers" of the poor, who reach out the helping hand of understanding sympathy to cheer and guide their lowlier fellows on to ultimate attainment of their own long-fought-for freedom. That element in English literature, as contrasted with the courtly verse and prose of the Renaissance and of the classical age, that element which voiced the thoughts and feelings of the lower classes, the humanitarian element, is a distinctly English contribution to world literature.

Of the presence in the ranks of the people themselves of the power to achieve that freedom, there can be no doubt. All through the pages of literature are pictured in ever-increasing numbers scenes which portray the spirit of the masses,—their native roughness and energy, their traditional Anglo-Saxon courage, assertiveness and dignity, their unfailing Celtic optimism, resourcefulness and versatility, their characteristically English delight in fair play which scorned all treachery, cowardice and baseness. The combination of all these qualities gave them that essential sanity of outlook which expressed itself on the one hand in a quick response to sincere and intelligent leadership, on the other to a prompt repudiation of all artificial restraints, conventions and distinctions. They felt, too, a profound reverence for law,— not the man-made laws of the statute books, but those fundamental principles of moral law and order which had been wrought out through centuries of human experience in living.

These traits that make for democracy are reflected nowhere more vividly and forcefully than in the ballads of Robin Hood, that popular hero of the Middle Ages, beloved from end to end of Merrie England. Bold and dauntless yeoman, he embodies the spirit of the free out-of-doors in all its vivid objectiveness, its fresh adventure and constant activity. If we would seek his counterpart in modern life, we should find it, more than anywhere else, in the fast vanishing cowboy life of the American West.

"I'm a rowdy cowboy just off the stormy plains,
My trade is girting saddles and pulling bridle reins,
Oh, I can tip the lasso, it is with graceful ease;
I rope a streak of lightning, and ride it where I please."

But Robin as a mediæval hero was more significant than the cowboy of to-day; for he was, as Professor Lawrence says, the very "incarnation of democratic revolt; born not of human parents, but of the imagination of the English peasantry; a bold outlaw, created to typify resistance to abuses of the law, he typifies above all else the protest of the English people against social injustice." The popular songs and ballads that have gathered about his name are many and varied; but the central theme of them all is that of Robin as a champion of the rights of the common people against the oppression of nobles and clergy. Perhaps the most typical ballad is the "Gest," which opens with a description of Robin, clad in Lincoln green with his trusty bow at his side, telling his men that he cannot feel any appetite for dinner till he has brought in some wealthy evil-doer to share the meal and pay right roundly for it afterwards. But Robin is no ordinary outlaw—he has his code which he is careful to impress upon his doughty follower, Little John.

"Maistar," than sayde Lytil Johnn,
"And we our borde shal sprede,
Tel us wheder that we shal go,
And what life that we shal lede."

"Thereof no force," than sayde Robyn;
"We shall do well inowe;
But loke ye do no husbonde harme,
That tilleth with his ploughe.

"No more ye shall no gode yeman
That walketh by grene-wode shawe;
Ne no knyght ne no squyer
That wol be a gode felawe.

"These bisshopes and these arche-bisshopes,
Ye shall them bete and bynde;
The hye sherif of Notyingham,
Hym holde ye in your mynde."

"This worde shal be holde," sayde Lytell Johnn,
"And this lesson we shall lere;
It is fer dayes; God send us a gest,
That we were at oure dynere!"

Soon a knight comes riding by; after treating him to a hearty meal, they find that he has but ten shillings in his purse. He tells them that his estate is mortgaged to a wealthy abbot, who threatens to take it from him. Robin lends him money to pay his debts, and goes out to make good his own loss by robbing the abbot's treasurer of the required amount; when the knight finally returns to repay the borrowed money, Robin not only refuses to accept it, but gives the knight enough to start life over again. When the knight attempts to express his gratitude Robin assures him there is no need,—he has already been paid, as is fit, from the abbot's treasury.

Such, then, was the English popular hero, Robin

Hood, champion of the needy and the oppressed, enemy of the rich and unprincipled, dispenser of justice among the people in a day when courts were the tools of personal power rather than the instruments of an impartial justice. A people whose imagination could produce a hero so bluff and wholesome, so fair in fight, so generous of heart, could well be trusted to attain its rightful place in the social order; and having achieved that aim, it could be trusted, also, to embody its ideal in a democracy whose fundamental principles would be safe and sane leadership, true social equality and generous humanitarianism. It was the people visioned forth in "Piers Ploughman" and in the Robin Hood ballads, people with a strongly ethical bent and with a hearty appreciation of a good story truthfully told, who laid the foundation for the development of the English drama; it was these people who made up the larger part of Shakespeare's audience, these people for whom he wrote, these people from whom he drew such unforgettable figures as Falstaff. It was the experiences of a virtuous serving maid from the lowly walks of life, which form the plot of that earliest of English novels, Richardson's "Pamela."

It was the homely life of a village parson with all his guilelessness, his charity and unworldliness "more skilled to raise the wretched than to rise," which appeals to us still in "The Vicar of Wakefield." It is that same village life with all its host of characters from the common walks of life, its Silas Marner and its Tess of the d'Urbervilles, its chastened Hester of the Scarlet Letter no less than its irrepressible Tom Sawyer and Huckleberry Finn; it is that same village life described by Goldsmith which forms the setting of so much of English poetry and fiction:

> "Sweet Auburn! loveliest village of the plain;
> Where health and plenty cheered the laboring swain,
> Where smiling spring its earliest visit paid,
> And parting summer's lingering blooms delayed:
> Dear lovely bowers of innocence and ease,
> Seats of my youth, when every sport could please,
> How often have I lingered o'er thy green,
> Where humble happiness endeared each scene!"

It was these same people of the great lower classes whose cause at the close of the eighteenth century was pleaded by Gray and Burns, as well as by Goldsmith:

> "And thou, sweet Poetry, loveliest maid, . . .
> Still let thy voice, prevailing over time, . . .
> Aid slighted truth with thy persuasive strain;
> Teach erring man to spurn the rage of gain;

> Teach him that states of native strength possest,
> Though very poor, may still be very blest;
> That trade's proud empire hastes to swift decay,
> As ocean sweeps the labored mole away;
> While self-dependent power can time defy,
> As rocks resist the billows and the sky."

It was these people of the village and the countryside whose interests were so vitally at stake in the great Industrial Revolution which so transformed the whole face of English life in the closing years of the eighteenth century. It was these people whose insistent demands accomplished the establishment of social equality, and the consequent up-building of the greatest democracy which the world has yet seen, a democracy based upon a combination, for the first time in history, of those two vital elements, leadership and social equality, both of which had been wrought out of English experience through centuries of struggle.

The spirit of this new democracy found expression in literature in the spread of the Romantic movement, the "Renaissance of Wonder." "If I were to make one characteristic of this movement the essential or most prominent one," Curtis Hidden Page has said, "I should choose an aspect which I think has not even been mentioned before, namely, that it is the beginning of democracy in literature, of the expression in literature of the life of every man and of all the people; that it at last transformed the Aristocracy of Letters, which had been made even more aristocratic than ever by the Renaissance and by the Classical Rule, into a true Republic of Letters; and prepared the way for the democratic, the all-inclusively realistic, and even the social, literature of the future." Gradually that popular revolt "against rationalism, convention, artifice, dullness, narrowness, formality, and rules of all kinds" had become "revolution, emancipation, and the complete creation of a new society. Freedom is its war-cry, individual feeling its basis of citizenship in the new Republic of Letters. The liberty of the individual, and the right to expression in Literature of each individual's inmost and most peculiar feelings, whether typical or not, whether rational or not, whether social or anti-social,—in short, the rights of the individual ego to complete independence and self-expression,—that is what the Romantic movement first of all stands for."

The literature of the "classes" in England had all too often been molded and almost disguised by foreign moods and forms; but the spirit of the people themselves, the truly English spirit, with its love of freedom and its reverence for law, its insistence upon social equality and its willing submission to worthy leadership, was making itself heard down through the centuries; it was that spirit which, in the last hundred years, has come into its own. That intense English individualism, almost anti-social, led Shelley and Keats and Byron to fling to the world their magnificent challenge,—the right to think and act as their inmost highest impulse prompted. But that same English love of social justice which had forced a world to recognize the rights of the individual was the power that sooner or later was bound to force the individual to recognize the rights of the world, the rights of humanity. And so the Romantic movement found its corrective in the Realism which dominates our modern novel and our social drama. English individualism, given social opportunity, is the trait which prompts to consecrated leadership. Love of justice, reverence for law, this is the trait which inevitably finds expression in social equality. These two ideals, leadership and social equality, have been wrought out for us to-day through centuries of English experience. Those strains are heard again and again, throbbing through all that is truly English in literature. Harmonized by English genius, we hear them to-day blended into that great anthem whose theme is the spirit of democracy.

What end may that spirit of democracy serve? The world has already, we hope, been made safe for democracy; it remains now to make democracy safe for the world. It was the English-speaking peoples who gave to a world oppressed that ideal of individual freedom under social law which we call democracy. It is that ideal for the preservation of which they have mutually pledged in enduring brotherhood their lives, their fortunes and their sacred honor. If that ideal is to be preserved, it must be on the basis of those two great elements which English experience has wrought out through the centuries. On the one hand there must be a broad social equality which levels all those artificial restraints and distinctions which classes have erected in the past; all men must be equal before the law; there must be equality of opportunity for all; each man must have his fair chance to make the most of whatever ability he has; humanity has need of it every whit. If we would make democracy safe for the world, we must see to it that "government of the people, by the people, for the people shall not perish from the earth." But on the other hand, if there is to be any progress at all, the good must always give way to the best; humanity must be ready, in truly English spirit, to submit itself willingly, loyally, to the leadership of its best. The great hope for democracy is that it is founded on that biologic law that leadership *is* instinctively recognized. If we would, then, attain the heights of a new world freedom, we must not disregard the helping hand of "our nobler brothers, one in blood," with whom we are struggling upward along that steep and rock-strewn path of a conscious social progress, the story of which

"Continues yet the old, old legend of our race,
The loftiest of life upheld by death."

If we would make our democracy safe for the world, we must heed the warning of that most earnest of earnest Englishmen, Rudyard Kipling:

"Keep ye the Law—be swift in all obedience.
Clear the land of evil, drive the road and bridge the ford.
Make ye sure to each his own
That he reap what he hath sown;
By the peace among Our peoples let men know we serve the Lord."

And if we would keep our course true to the star of the new democracy, we must not forget that we sail for the port of Universal Social Welfare, bearing with us, as Walt Whitman, that venerable prophet of the New Democracy, reminds us, the precious freight of all the past experience of the race:

"Sail, sail thy best, ship of Democracy;
Of value is thy freight; 'tis not the Present only,
The Past is also stored in thee.
Thou holdest not the venture of thyself alone, not of the Western continent alone;
Earth's résumé entire floats on thy keel, O ship, is steadied by thy spars.
With thee Time voyages in trust, the antecedent nations sink or swim with thee;
With all their ancient struggles, martyrs, heroes, epics, wars, thou bear'st the other continents;
Theirs, theirs, as much as thine, the destination-port triumphant.
Steer then with good strong hand and wary eye, O helmsman, thou carriest great companions;
Venerable priestly Asia sails this day with thee,
And royal feudal Europe sails with thee."

INDEX